MAPPING AND MEASURING THE INFORMATION ECONOMY

British Library Cataloguing in Publication Data

Miles, Ian
Mapping and measuring the information economy. - (Library and information research report, ISSN 0263-1709; 77)
1. Great Britain, Information systems. Technological development. Statistical information
I. Title II. British Library *Research and Development Department*
III. Series 001.5

ISBN 0-7123-3212-X

Ian Miles is a Senior Fellow at the Science Policy Research Unit, University of Sussex, where he has worked since 1972. His original training was in psychology at the University of Manchester. His research interests cover a wide range: social forecasting and social indicators; the service economy; and, increasingly, information-technology-related issues.

Library and Information Research Reports are published by The British Library Research and Development Department and distributed by The British Library Publications Sales Unit, Boston Spa, Wetherby, West Yorkshire LS23 7BQ, UK. In the USA they are distributed by the American Library Association, 50 East Huron Street, Chicago, Illinois 60611; in Canada by the Candian Library Association, 200 Elgin Street, Suite 602, Ottawa, Ontario K2P 1L5; in Japan by Kinokuniya Co Ltd, PO Box 55, Chitose, Tokyo 156; and in India, Burma, Pakistan, Nepal, Bangladesh and Sri Lanka they are distributed by Arnold Publishers (India) Private Ltd, AB/9 First Floor, Safdarjung Enclave, New Delhi 110029.

ISBN 0 7123 3212 X
ISSN 0263-1709
R & DD/04/35

Typeset by Laser Images (0270 760531) and printed in Great Britain at the University Press, Cambridge.

MAPPING AND MEASURING THE INFORMATION ECONOMY

A Report Produced for the Economic and Social Research Council's **Programme on Information and Communication Technologies**

Ian Miles

with contributions from
Tim Brady, Andy Davies, Leslie Haddon, Nick Jagger, Mark Matthews, Howard Rush and Sally Wyatt

Library and Information Research Report 77

Abstract

Mapping and measuring the information economy is a detailed critical guide to data and data sources which depict the development, in the UK, of activities involving new information technology (IT). The study has a number of original features, which should make it an invaluable work of reference for those interested in this fast-moving area:

- It provides a critical discussion of various approaches to defining the much-vaunted "information economy", and stakes a claim for an approach based on the development of new IT-based activities.

- It discusses the main sources and methods of production of statistical data, identifying the features that restrict their utility for capturing structural change, and discussing the prospects for making the most use of the data even under such constraints.

For a number of key areas of IT-based activity - the production of IT, its diffusion and application, its implications for employment and for broader social issues - major statistical sources are reviewed, and the issues arising from their data are outlined.

Proposals are made concerning both the better utilisation of existing statistical material, and the sorts of changes that are required if we are to get a better grasp of patterns of social and economic change around the information economy.

The report draws upon studies undertaken by a group of researchers at the Science Policy Research Unit, University of Sussex. It is the first attempt to provide an overview and route-map to the empirical material on this broad set of topics, and provides a marked contrast to the provocative but speculative visions, and rich but restricted case studies, which constitute so much of the literature on the "information economy".

Contents

List of Tables

Introduction

There has been much commentary concerning the inadequacy and inaccessibility of data concerning the growth (or otherwise) of the UK "information economy". For instance, *Computer Weekly* of March 10 1988 commented sardonically:

> "The Government does not know how many computer discs, tapes and cartridges were sold in the UK and how many exported, according to written answers from the Department of Trade and Industry. However the DTI does know how many ballpoint pens, pencils and parts have been sold..." (p6)

The National Economic Development Office (NEDO) (1984) is less sardonic, and more sensitive to the reasons for statistics being limited, but nevertheless its table of "Statistics for the UK IT Industry" carries, like a health warning, the note that:

> "Because of the changing nature of the industry, its statistical base is poor, partial and misleading. These figures should be regarded as a general indication of trends and relative magnitudes" (p6)

An earlier NEDO report (1982b) was equally forthright about data it presented:

> "(m)any of the technologies and products of information technology are comparatively recent and constantly changing such that it would be unrealistic to expect accurate and comprehensive information to be readily available. In addition, imports of software are by the very nature of the 'product' difficult to attach monetary value to...Lack of disaggregation, and inconsistency in collection and presentation of production and trade data, combine to make analysis of the performance of this sector less than fully authoritative." (p59)

Giving evidence to the House of Commons Trade and Industry Committee (1988, volume 2) Alastair Macdonald of the Department of Trade and Industry (DTI) was challenged on the quality of information technology (IT) statistics: he noted that we may have problems now:

> "the classification system used for statistical purposes is made more difficult by the rapid changes in technology and in industrial

> sectors which are taking place in this fast-changing sector. Electrical equipment, one sees each year, is becoming more electronics based, but it is at present being recorded under its original industry classification...our colleagues on the statistical side are displaying constant vigilance, but one could almost reach the point where some classifications would need to be changed every year..."(p23)

And he went on to warn that:

> "The price of convergence of telecommunications, computing and broadcasting is going to make that tracing of what is actually happening increasingly difficult."(p24)

What is more, such concerns are not confined to the computer and telecommunications fields. They are also expressed with respect to consumer goods, as the British Radio and Electronic Equipment Manufacturers' Association (BREMA) points out:

> "One major problem giving increasing cause for concern is the product coverage and interpretation of Customs and Excise imports data [for consumer electronics]. Problems of definition and coverage, as new products continue to be introduced and as manufacturers and assemblers move into and out of various activities, means it is becoming increasingly difficult to establish the true level of finished goods imports and the true level of UK production. This affects not only the historically difficult audio markets, but also new areas such as CTV and VCR [colour TV and video cassette recorders]." (BREMA, 1988, p28)

Such examples could be multiplied many times over. But it is not our intention to launch or join a bandwagon of carping about the shortcomings of official (and unofficial) statistics. There are often good reasons for statistical systems not to be *too* responsive to changing conditions; for example, rapid accommodation to what may be temporary trends can lead to data that may be topical, but that allow for few comparisons to be made over time. It is important to be able to "map" data from one time - or one country - to others. There are also more and richer data available than is often believed, although there are substantial lacunae and problems in interpretation.

Nevertheless, the issue is not just an absence of data. There are often substantial contradictions - or apparent contradictions - in data coming from different sources. The Director of the Computing Services Association (CSA), Douglas Eyeions, for instance, dismissed official estimates of the size of the computing services sector in a speech made at the

Association's 1986 conference. He argued that CSA data, which showed a sector with 39,000 employees and £1.4 billion turnover, were substantially more accurate than government estimates of 70,000 employees and £2.8 billion turnover (reported in *Computer Weekly*, March 20 1986). Given such disagreements, it is clearly necessary to examine the assumptions and methods that are being used to produce the contested data.

While we cannot go into great depth on every single statistical issue that emerges, it is the purpose of this study to review and provide an overview of data and data sources which can provide us with information about Britain's information economy. This will be a critical review, and one guided by analysis of what the term "information economy" means. We hope to contribute to debates about the latter as well as to provide a guide to data and data sources, and to suggest fruitful revisions that might be made in statistical systems. As such, we hope that this report will help further the recommendations of the House of Commons Trade and Industry Committee (1988, volume 1) for improvement of IT statistics.

At this point, we should briefly note certain areas which this study will *not* seek to cover. First, the case will be made in Chapter 1 for a view of the "information economy" based on the IT revolution. Accordingly, we shall not set out to deal with the "information industries", or with patterns of information use in the UK - except insofar as these are sectors and activities where statistical issues related to IT are raised. Within the Programme on Information and Communication Technologies (PICT) - the network of which this study is a product - the information industries are being studied intensively by the Centre for Communication and Information Studies (CCIS) at the Polytechnic of Central London, which also has a project entitled "Mapping and Measuring the Information Economy". A second group in the programme, the Centre for Research into Innovation, Culture and Technology at Brunel University, is also carrying out studies in broadcasting and related areas.

Second, we shall not be attempting to deal with the military uses of IT, or with the role of defence and the defence sector in the information economy, in this study. The subject is an exceedingly important and complex one, and in recognition of this it has been assigned its own research project, which is being carried out by William Walker at the Science Policy Research Unit (SPRU), University of Sussex. An early output of this work, dealing with the statistical issues raised by defence electronics, is Walker (1988).

Third, there are some types of data with which we shall not deal. Probably the most important one to specify here, given readers' likely expectations, is consultancy data. This study is not a review of consultancy reports on the information economy, nor is it a guide to the data contained in them. Reasons for the comparative lack of attention to these sources, and the focus on official, academic, and trade sources are spelled out in Chapter 2. In addition, we should note that the data that concern us here are very largely *quantitative* statistics, and that we shall focus on material that gives us extensive coverage (rather than, say, data that contrast the experience of different experimental groups). This is not to suggest that other forms of data are not valuable; simply that they are relevant to purposes other than the "mapping and measuring" objectives of this study.

The structure of this book is very straightforward. The two opening chapters review, first, issues in the definition of the "information economy", and, then, the production and availability of statistics. Subsequent chapters follow through with analyses of the availability of data, and guides to data sources, in each of a number of key areas: research and development; the IT-producing sectors; the diffusion of new technology across the economy; specific technologies and economic sectors; employment issues; consumer goods and services; and broad social implications. A final chapter gathers together the conclusions derived from this set of reviews.

Acknowledgements

This report has been prepared at SPRU, University of Sussex, as part of our contribution to the Economic and Social Research Council's (ESRC's) PICT project on "Mapping and Measuring the Information Economy". I would like to express my gratitude to the PICT for supporting this work, both financially and intellectually. I would also like to thank the ESRC and the DTI for their support of the PICT research.

The research represented in this study is clearly beyond the scope of any single individual - at least, if the reviews of different areas of statistics are to remain topical. Several colleagues have contributed substantially to the chapters of this study with the support of PICT funds, and I would like to thank them for their important and timely contributions to this study. Their contributions typically extend beyond one chapter or section of the study, but I have drawn on written material prepared for particular parts of the study as follows:

Tim Brady:	Chapter 7, Sections 1 and 2
Andy Davies:	Chapter 3, Sections 2 and 4
Leslie Haddon:	Chapter 8, Section 1
Nick Jagger:	Chapter 4, Section 2.5
Mark Matthews:	Chapter 4, Sections 1 and 2.1
	Chapter 5, Sections 1 and 2
Howard Rush:	Chapter 6, Sections 3.1 and 3.2
Sally Wyatt:	Chapter 6, Section 3.1.

This study has already benefited from much input of information from numerous trade bodies, researchers and editors who responded to circulars I sent out in summer 1987, and from a smaller number of academic, civil service and industrial interviewees with whom I and my colleagues subsequently had discussion. Among these I would like to thank especially John Bessant, Dominic Cornford, Frank Land, Ananad Mehta, Gordon Pask, and John Riley. Responses to my circulars were very uneven, with some magazine editors, for instance, providing voluminous material, others maintaining strict silence. This may be reflected in some unevenness of coverage in this text, perhaps especially in Chapter 6. Rather than thank each person with whom I corresponded, I would like to express my gratitude to them all here, and also express my hopes that the references to their work and materials are found to be constructive.

A first draft of this study was subjected to searching criticism from a large number of colleagues, among whom I would particularly like to thank L J Caffery, David Collie, Rod Coombs, Leslie Haddon, Diana Hicks, Stuart Macdonald, Robin Mansell, Nick von Tunzelmann, Jeffery J Wheatley, Dominic Wilson, and Sally Wyatt. But, as usual, any attribution of responsibility for the shortcomings of this study has to be made to me as the prime author.

Little did I realise when I set out on this task just how immense a labour it was to prove; so much is happening in this area that it is impossible for anything less than a team of experts completely devoted to the task to keep fully informed and up-to-date on every detail. While the general themes and arguments of this study will, one hopes, remain cogent for some time, some of the specific empirical material and sources that I cite will rapidly date. Further elaborations of this study may be required - see Chapter 10 for a discussion of this point. But at the very least I hope I have cleared a path for others to follow and improve upon.

1 Issues in Information Technology and Society

1.1 "The Information Economy"

What is the "information economy"? Why is it important? Why should we be interested in "mapping and measuring" it?

To some extent, the answers to the last two questions depend on that given to the first. But let us begin with them nevertheless, as a way of casting some initial light on the more profound first question. Many commentators argue that Western industrial societies are being (or have been) transformed into "information economies", and that this marks a more or less substantial change in how they operate. If this is correct, then clearly it is important to know what this transformation entails, how rapidly and evenly it is taking place, and how far our existing statistical apparatus - forged to cope with the problems of industrial societies - is able to cope with it.

But it has to be admitted at the outset that very different concepts of the information economy exist. Indeed, this report is an output of one of three projects, each of which uses a different analytic framework, supported by the PICT programme of the ESRC. The other centres where parallel studies are under way are led by Professor Nicholas Garnham at the CCIS, Polytechnic of Central London, and Professor John Goddard, Centre for Urban and Regional Development Studies (CURDS), University of Newcastle. The former is mainly concerned with the "information industries", the latter with regional issues. A joint publication drawing on the three centres' work on "Mapping and Measuring the Information Economy" is in preparation.

The terms "information economy" and "information society" were being used in Japan in the early 1970s, but really became popular in the 1980s. We have elsewhere argued (Miles and Gershuny, 1986) that in many respects these popular accounts were taking on the mantle of the previously dominant, but increasingly discredited, theories of "post-industrial society". Just as post-industrial theories asserted that a service sector and service occupations were inexorably growing in importance owing to shifts in final demand toward services, and that this would mean a weakening of economic power based on the ownership of material capital, so information economy theorists were talking of the rise of an *information sector*, of the growth of *information occupations,* of *information products* as "superior goods" (in the economists' sense), and of knowledge displacing wealth as the basis of power.

This approach identifies the information economy with the economic role of information. Now, of course, information has always been important for economic affairs, so that an information component might be said to have been a feature of all societies. But, the argument goes on, there is an important change under way, which has brought the information economy notion to the fore. This is the expansion of so-called information sectors and information occupations, so that these are now numerically important, and in some cases dominant, parts of industrial economies.

These "information" categories are not ones familiar in official statistics, and considerable effort has gone into reclassifying national data so as to chart their development. Studies such as those of the Organization for Economic Co-operation and Development (OECD) (1981, 1986b) show the expected increase in employment and economic output in these categories. These analyses thus build on and partly address the weaknesses of the post-industrial approach. One of its problems was its treatment of "services" as effectively homogeneous, whereas in fact different branches of the service sector displayed very different trends. By distinguishing an "information sector", the information economy approach was able to make more subtle differentiations - and, what is more, its information sector grew in the way that all services had previously been claimed to do, while other services showed a more faltering development path. But there are several reasons to be wary of taking this approach to the information economy:

- The definition of what constitutes information employment and information products is a problematic one. After all, all human labour involves information-processing; and as we shall argue at more length below, all commodities produced by the economy embody and provide information. One consequence of all jobs having information-processing components is that "information occupations" are not necessarily the jobs that are most affected by new information technologies: robots displace production-line workers, for example, rather than scientists!

- In practice, problematic classifications do often have to be made in marginal cases in economic affairs. But in the instances involved here, the margins begin to invade the centre, since for large swathes of the labour force, for example, we are asked to attribute one-half of their activities to information labour, one-half to services (or whatever). (In his pioneering analysis, Porat (1977) was proud to report that the classification of half of doctors' work as information work appeared to be borne out by time-use studies.)

- While some of the studies distinguish within the information sector - for instance the OECD studies refer to primary and secondary information sectors - they still lump very heterogeneous activities together. Thus the OECD information occupations range from "information machine workers" (e.g. bookbinders!) to "process control and supervisory workers" (e.g. sales supervisors), from "communication workers" (e.g. stage directors) to "scientific and technical workers" (e.g. metallurgists).

- The explanation for the growth in these diverse activities is hardly likely to be a unitary one. The implication that growing demand for information (or for information products *and* communication services) is driving the process along - even if this demand is disaggregated into final and intermediate components - is not very helpful. Theoretical arguments can be made concerning the rather uneven pattern of expansion of demand for these goods and services, of course. But such arguments demand more sophistication than this approach to the information economy thesis.

- In part the expansion of "information work" is the result of a division of labour in which some (but never all) of the informational components of other jobs have been stripped away from them and transferred to specialised staff. This may result in improved efficiency and new capabilities in their information-processing, features stressed by some commentators. But whether or not there are these gains, the information work has become more visible through being in part identifiable with a particular set of workers, while it was invisible before.

- In any case, the development of a quantitative trend (perhaps a reversible one, at that, if IT is applied to rationalise the efforts of information workers) is hardly an adequate basis for distinguishing the information economy as a new stage of development.

- The information economy argument often appears in a more millenarian version. This account goes beyond portraying the information economy as merely a new stage of industrial society. Rather, it is seen as marking a threshold in the development of civilisation. Accounts abound in which the "information revolution" is compared with the agricultural or industrial revolutions. Thus information society is identified as being as distinct and epochal a formation in human history as agricultural and industrial civilisations are commonly viewed as having been. These accounts are usually associated with an emphasis on the revolutionary nature of IT. We would make an alternative case, however: whatever the long-term challenges posed by IT, its current development and applications resemble earlier technological revolutions *within*, more than a break with the social formations of, industrial capitalism. (For a detailed contrast of perspectives on this issue, see Miles et al. (1988), Miles (1988b).)

The approach which underpins the present study takes off from the "alternative case" mentioned above. It is our contention that in large part, the reason that the term "information economy" is so prominent now is not because of a steady growth of information workers or sectors. Rather, it is prominent because of the emergence of new IT, and the widespread recognition of the revolutionary role of the technologies involved. Our approach to the information economy takes off from this. We see the term as being a useful one for indicating the distinctions between economic affairs before and after the development and diffusion of new IT.

The information economy, then, hinges upon the application of new IT. "Information economy" is thus a term that really does describe the whole economy; we are not simply referring to "information sectors" alone, nor to an economy that is dominated by these sectors. Nor are we referring to IT-producing sectors alone. All sectors are potentially IT-using sectors - and in advanced industrial societies devices such as personal computers have already been used to effect in every branch of extractive, construction, manufacturing and service industries.

We shall need to consider what we mean by "IT" below, but first let us set out the approach to information economy that our approach implies. IT is at the heart of a technological revolution. Tremendous changes are taking place in the power and price of "heartland technologies" - i.e. technologies that can be applied across an extremely wide range of production processes and embodied in an extremely wide range of products.

When such revolutionary technological change occurs, the calculus of economic decision-making is affected: new opportunities appear, the structure of costs and markets appears in a new light as the practicability of applying the new heartland technology is recognised. If the calculus is perceived as being favourable (which may involve non-economic considerations, such as, for instance, whether the technology is socially acceptable), then innovators will seize these opportunities to effect change in production processes and in products and markets. New ideas of what constitutes best-practice production, in the light of the changes wrought in the availability and capability of factors of production, are established. (See Freeman and Perez (1986), Perez (1983, 1985) for lucid versions of this argument.)

Relating the information economy to IT in this way is bound to be seen as crass technological determinism. We reject this charge. It is by no means our claim that new technology is causing the emergence of an information economy. New technology does not drop out of the sky; it is produced by social agents acting under various influences, and since it depends upon the properties of the natural world it does not just reflect our unfettered desires. But once it has been created, it remains decidedly material: it does not cause social behaviour, but those aware of its potential are liable to act upon it. Our forecast is that some of the many opportunities presented by new IT will be seized upon so as to transform substantially many social and economic activities. This we extrapolate from our understanding of entrepreneurial behaviour, our observation of the diffusion and application of IT to date, and our estimations of how far current developments will lead to changes in entrepreneurial behaviour (rather little) and in IT diffusion and application (somewhat more).

It is common for social researchers to describe distinct phases in the development of industrial societies. Most recently, the establishment of systems of mass production and consumption, with associated organisations of working practices and remuneration systems, is referred to as the "Fordist" system. Many commentators would now argue that we are moving now toward a "post-Fordist" system, resulting both from the stresses and strains accumulated in the earlier system and from recognition of the potentials of IT. Such analyses make the important point that major shifts in structures of production and consumption are liable to be associated with the diffusion of new technologies. Authors variously refer to these as "changes in technoeconomic paradigms", "transformations of the mode of accumulation", or "shifts in sociotechnical systems". (Cf. Freeman and Perez (1986), Petit (1986), Gershuny and Miles (1983); for a discussion of some of the differences in emphasis here see Miles (1985a).)

It is our contention that the information economy is best conceptualised as involving a particular stage in the development of industrial society. "Information economy" is a shorthand description for this complex of changes associated with - *not* caused by in a simple deterministic sense - IT and its diffusion through the formal economy and society at large. Mapping and measuring the information economy then becomes, in part, an empirical analysis that can help us ascertain the features of this new "sociotechnical system". Furthermore, by sensitising us to cross-sectoral, cross-national and other differences in forms of organisation emerging around the application of IT, it can help explain the particular form taken by this system, the variations in the detail of technoeconomic paradigms across firms or regions, for example. It may thus contribute to our understanding of how far it is possible to shape and direct these new patterns of organisation. (This would contrast with much of the IT literature, whose flavour suggests that these new patterns flow relatively unproblematically from the characteristics of the new technology - except insofar as misguided individuals oppose the "new common sense".)

Now certainly these new patterns of organisation are liable to be associated with different patterns of information use. But we would still want to insist upon the importance of IT in understanding the information economy, as opposed to the focus on a rather undifferentiated "information as such". Indeed, much of this change in patterns of information use goes well beyond the activities of the "information sector" as understood in the first approach outlined above. The data processed on the factory floor and, indeed, in the household kitchen, *may* be turned into part of a marketed data-base commodity, in which case they would enter the information sector. But whether this is the case or not, we can forecast that much more of the information that is generated in social and economic activities will be processed using IT. This will lead to the data being used in new ways, adding new capabilities to production and consumption.

Of course, IT developments have substantial implications for the "information sector". This is already visible in the development of electronic publishing, online data bases, management information systems, and the like. These can be seen as early manifestations of a transformation of all sorts of traditional information and intelligence functions in firms and public agencies, and to involve considerable development of new activities and actors. The information economy means a changed information sector, then. But in the present study we treat this sector only insofar as it is part - an important part and an interesting case study - of the more general complex of changes that constitute the information economy.

We are thus relating the information economy directly to IT. But what do we mean by IT? Although the answer may seem self-evident, what turns out to be self-evident for different readers may prove to be distinctly variable. Thus we need to explicate the approach taken in this study.

1.2 The Definition of IT

1.2.1 Approaches to IT

What constitutes IT? As with the "information economy", there are several ways of answering this question, and we shall need to argue for the orientation to be taken in this study. A first approach is to say that any technology that handles information is IT. There are two major problems with this:

- (1) It is arguable that all technologies deal with information. Apart from operating instructions, alarm signals, and verbal or other types of overt message that are often embodied in (or on) devices, all technological products can be said to carry information that can be decoded by users with the appropriate tacit or formal knowledge. Thus the definition would need to be more specific about what is meant by "handling information" - the approach usually adopted involves specifying that the technology is yielding an information product. (Again, since all products could be said to have informational components, the argument would go that the product has to involve a text, video, broadcast, etc. as its *main* feature.)

- (2) This definition would include all sorts of traditional information-handling product as IT: books and printing presses, LP records and record players, typewriters and even erasers! On the other hand, it would exclude some devices whose critical role is that of handling information on the grounds that the product which this contributes to is not itself centrally an information product: for example, a computer that controls the production process of some material artefacts such as potato crisps or motor cars. (In principle, this could be handled by defining some part of the technology to be IT, some part a production technology. Presumably one could similarly assign varying proportions of all artefacts to an IT or information product category - the labels on a yogurt pot, the brand name on a stapler, the dashboard on a car, and so on.)

This first approach, then, may have its virtues when one is seeking an analysis of the "information sector", of those components of the economy producing information or communications services as final or intermediate products. But it is not very helpful in assessing developments associated with the emergence of new IT.

A second approach to defining IT involves specification of novel features of information-processing associated with new ITs. Thus Monk (1987, p 165) defines IT as:

> "That machine-based technology which *actively* processes information rather than merely storing or transmitting it...'machine' in this sense may be physical or abstract: the term is meant to include software systems...technology must also include non-machine information resources such as relevant theoretical and practical knowledge..."

This distinguishes IT from traditional and non-electronic information-handling, and from basic communications and storage devices, and identifies a large set of technological characteristics. Monk further goes on to describe IT as an abstract technology consisting of five types of information resource: hardware, software, theoretical, blueprint and tacit knowledge. (He then argues that innovation occurs when any of these is developed or extended.)

This is a useful but rather complicated approach. It draws our attention to the role of software and similar products which may not directly embody electronics but whose application is dependent on data processing equipment - and vice versa. By not being tied to a particular technology it remains open to the possibility of including as IT future developments based on principles very different to those of electronics: for instance, optronics or biochips. It also takes on board the point that is actually implicit in the linguistic roots of the word "technology", that more than just artefacts are referred to, that human knowledge is crucially involved. But "active information-processing" remains poorly defined: and it may be a highly contentious issue as to whether a new medium - say, CD-ROM - is merely involved in data storage or is rather actively processing information.

A third definitional approach has actually been taken up in many popular discussions of IT, where the terms "information technology" or less often "informatics", "telematics", etc. have largely displaced the focus on, say "the computer and society", "automation", and "the chip and employment" which dominated prior to 1980. (It is instructive to note the evolution of the titles of Tom Forester's two popular readers in the field: from *The Microelectronics Revolution* (1980) to *The Information Technology Revolution* (1985).) In the current discussions, IT is often described as involving "the convergence of computing and communications". In some Japanese work in particular, this development is also referred to as "C&C" (see Kobayashi, 1986). But as a definition of IT, this too is rather imprecise:

- Does it refer only to devices, systems and applications that combine these two areas of activity? If so, stand-alone microcomputers, or telephone systems which do not interconnect with computers would seem not to be IT.

- If not, does it encompass all computer and communications systems? If so the abacus and the smoke signal will need to be included as IT - raising the same sorts of problems as noted with the first approach.

Nevertheless, this third approach does point in a more fruitful direction than the first two. We could construct an argument along the following lines: (a) some process is leading to the convergence of computers and telecommunications, (b) this process is at the heart of new IT, and thus (c) to the extent that computers and telecommunications have been transformed by this process they are at the core of IT. We can go on to argue that this process is facilitating transformations in the whole economy that are leading to an "information economy". And since it is a matter of *change* in products and activities, the issue may be posed as to how far they are, or are becoming, "IT-intensive", rather than whether they are all themselves wholly IT or IT activities.

What is the process (a) involved in the argument above? The factor that has promoted computer-telecommunications convergence - together with the reduction in costs and increase in power of computers and telecommunications - is popularly referred to as "the microelectronics revolution". Crucially, it is the radical, rapid, and continuing development of microelectronics power that has provided the basis for the development of new IT: for the proliferation of new products and processes throughout the economy. In order to make sense of this development microelectronics needs to be understood in terms of its own history and trajectory of change.

1.2.2 The Coming of Microelectronics

Microelectronic "chips" are often described as VLSI - Very Large Scale Integration - products. This refers to their being an advanced form of integrated circuit (IC). ICs operate on the basis of the physical properties of semiconductor materials, and are generally supposed to date from 1959; a little more than a decade after the development of transistors, which are also based on semiconductors.

Transistors, among their other numerous advantages as compared to earlier valve technologies, enabled considerable miniaturisation of electronic components. This also suggested that further miniaturisation was possible, and various means of achieving this were explored. Individual transistors had to be connected physically to provide desired configurations of information-processing system, and ICs achieved further miniaturisation by reducing the need to connect individually manufactured devices together.

In the IC, electrical rather than physical separation of transistors was achieved; effectively, whole circuits were put on a "chip" of silicon. With Small Scale Integration (SSI) the equivalent to 10 transistors/chip was achieved. The evolution of IC power is indicated by the terms that have come to identify subsequent developments: Medium Scale Integration (MSI) with the equivalent of around 100 transistors/chip, Large Scale Integration (LSI) thousands, VLSI tens of thousands, and now (with rather less consensus over terms) Ultra Large Scale Integration (ULSI) over 100,000, and Super Large Scale Integration (SLSI) in the hundreds of thousands of transistors per chip.

Many studies display data on the trends over several decades in the core technologies of microelectronics - trends so dramatic that "Moore's Law" has been used to describe them. (This "Law", coined in 1964 to describe trends then apparent, suggests that the number of IC elements that could be placed on a chip would double every year. The forecast has been fairly well fulfilled subsequently.) As well as increases in computing power and decreases in size, there have been marked IC cost reductions, of the order of c28% per annum, with a reduction of 35% per annum in the cost of each bit processed being estimated. Output of ICs has grown elevenfold in 17 years; vastly above the growth rates of GNP or population. (For a good popular account see Forester (1988). Braun and Macdonald (1982) provide a readable discussion of the development of ICs and microelectronics.)

In consequence, it has been possible to incorporate ICs economically into an ever-widening range of products and processes. Tasks that would have taken a roomful of valves can now be carried out by ICs carried on a calculator in one's pocket. They can be used in practically any mechanical device, and are even found in some goods such as running shoes and birthday greetings cards! But more serious applications led the way when the first chips were relatively expensive, of course.

Solid-state devices (beginning with transistors, of course) were rapidly incorporated into computers, from about 1960 on. The first microprocessor (a central processing unit - CPU - on a single chip) was an effort to simplify the construction of calculators: it replaced an 11-chip design which had been equivalent to 2,250 transistors. Microprocessors have subsequently emerged from the arena of Data Processing (DP) - understood as large-scale number-crunching or scientific calculations - into industrial control (e.g. regulating process operations, allowing for programmable machine tools), into new types of computer application (such as word processing) and communications, and more and more widely, so that they now play roles in the control and information-processing functions of a great many intermediate and final goods.

The development of microelectronics, as described above, is central to the information economy, in our view. This development is the trajectory of a heartland technology, which, beginning with the integrated circuit and its subsequent miniaturisation, is providing unprecedented information-processing capability to a wide range of economic activities. This trajectory is at the core of the majority of IT developments. Electronic data-processing devices - computers, telecommunications equipment, scientific instruments, and many more devices - become based on microelectronics. The "convergence" of computing and communications reflects these trends: networks become "intelligent" and computers communicate, increasing the functionality of communications (by adding error-trapping and other data-processing features to systems) and of computers (by allowing them to communicate with each other and with devices like sensors and robots). Data of all kinds are handled in digital ways: this makes it easier to transport information from one device and/or process to another. Microelectronics brings Monk's (1987) "active information processing" to all sorts of information and information-using products.

1.2.3 Towards a Classification of IT Activities

At the heart of IT, then, are ICs and microelectronics. Does this mean that only products based on this heartland technology are IT? Does it mean that all products using this heartland technology are IT? This would seem a logical demarcation criterion, but perhaps we do not need to draw such all-or-nothing boundaries.

After all, if we do follow this approach we would be confronted with the situation where increasing swathes of the economy, simply because they are incorporating microelectronics into their products, are regarded as IT sectors producing IT products. The computerised running shoes mentioned earlier, or the washing machine with microelectronic controls, would automatically become IT. Meanwhile, a valve-based electronic computer or telephone exchange would not fall within the classification, and the status of non-hardware components of technology (inputs such as software, outputs such as VANS) would be doubtful.

Another approach is in keeping with our view of the information economy. Recall that we use this term to refer to the transformation of all types of economic activity as IT is applied within sectors and production processes. This suggests that the information economy develops by a process of diffusion of new technologies and associated practices, and that it makes sense to think of degrees of informatisation of different sectors or national economies. Likewise, we can think of individual products of all sorts being informatised - rather than their becoming IT themselves, products from all sectors may become more IT-intensive (in terms of their incorporation of microelectronics and related technologies as a proportion of their total make-up). And sectors can be similarly treated: we do not have to see them as all becoming IT sectors simply because they incorporate IT in their products or have high levels of IT investment in their processes.

This approach, then, will treat most sectors of the economy as IT-using sectors. The degree to which they are high or low users - more or less IT-intensive - is then a matter for empirical analysis: Chapter 5 considers statistics from which we may compare the uptake of IT across sectors. There remain problems, of course, in operationally defining IT-intensity. Value measures (expenditure on IT as compared to other products) are liable to be distorted by the rapid decreases in IT costs, while physical measures (microcomputers per employee, for example) may run aground owing to the substantial quantitative and qualitative differences between distinct generations of IT (to be taken up in the next section). But these are practical difficulties, on which more light will be cast in our review of statistics; the basic approach proposed is not challenged.

But what are to count as IT-producing sectors? Are these merely to be those branches responsible for the manufacture of ICs and microelectronics? Again this seems hard to justify, since it would exclude many firms, sectors, and products that are generally recognised as new IT, such as microcomputers, whose manufacturers generally buy in the chips around which their models are built. And what about "complementary technologies", such as optical fibres for telecommunications, which effectively depend upon microelectronics for their utility and which are vital components of one of the sectors which converge in the popular definition of IT?

Chapter 4 will focus on the IT-producing sectors, but we can anticipate its argument a little here. Our approach will be to continue to see the production of chips and related semiconductor based materials as the "IT heart". But around this heart there lies an "IT core", a set of related industries which are also producing IT products. In large part this core is producing multipurpose IT products rather than IT-using products for specific applications; thus we would consider the telecommunications and computer industries to be parts of the core whose overall product ranges are not targeted to a narrow spectrum of consumers, while the machine tool industries or the household appliances industries are not producing core IT products and furthermore are more focused in terms of markets.

One source of data that impinges upon this definitional issue is the *Purchases Inquiry* published by the Business Statistics Office (BSO) as a special edition of *Business Monitor* (see Chapters 2 and 4). This details the purchases for current consumption made by different manufacturing sectors. From this we can see which of these sectors purchase ICs or other active components (including microelectronics) for incorporation into their products. It turns out that very few sectors are recorded as so doing. What is more, when considered as a proportion of all purchases, telecommunications equipment and EDP (electronic data processing - i.e. computers) manufacturing stand out dramatically, with more than twice the proportion of expenditure on ICs and related products than any other sector, both having more than 20% of their expenditure going to these items. Thus, in addition to the argument from "convergence", these industries would seem to form part of the IT core in terms of being heavily dependent on IT heartland technology in a relatively "unpackaged" form.

Only four other sectors are recorded as making IC and related purchases. Of these the highest is the electronic consumer goods sector, although it should be noted that this sector is even more outstanding as a consumer of "active components". The others are radio and electronic capital goods; electronic instruments and controls; and alarms and signalling. On a wider definition of IT-producing sectors, these industries might well be included.

The *Purchases Inquiry* will have been recognised to omit services from its purview. Yet at least two groups of services are virtually *sine qua non* for EDP and telecommunications equipment. These are computer and telecommunications services, respectively. The former covers software production and maintenance but also hardware maintenance and (in British official statistics at any rate) VANS and professional services such as training and consultancy for computer use. The latter covers basic telephony, cellular and related communications systems, and some data communication services; it might be thought appropriate for VANS to be included within this service group, and presumably the reason for this not being the case at present is that some VANS historically originated in online computer services associated with the leasing of time on remote mainframes for company data processing.

These two groups of services are not themselves direct consumers of ICs to any extent, but their activities are almost completely centred around the microelectronics-based hardware supplied by their associated manufacturing sectors. They are services that do more than add value to the hardware: they enable the value of the hardware to be realised. If we understand technology in its proper meaning - i.e. not merely as material artefacts, but also as involving knowledge and skills - then we can see such services as intrinsic components of new IT. Thus we should treat them as part of the IT-producing sector rather than as IT-users. In principle, the realisation of IT capabilities could be achieved without the two service sectors actually existing as separate sectors, if the service work was internalised within companies in other sectors, which indeed is to some extent the case. Many firms prepare their own software, and while telecommunications workers are relatively few - other than switchboard operators - there is a growing demand for IT-experienced communications managers. Other services are also important here: especially, services associated with IC and microelectronic production, such as independent chip design facilities. Our discussion here and in Chapter 4 reflects our being constrained by the emphasis on manufacturing and hardware in statistical sources.

Now this clearly means that the IT-producing sector is not homogeneous; it contains several distinct industries which have their own dynamics, whatever broad "convergence" tendencies exist. Simply contrasting the fortunes of national computer and telecommunications firms across a few European countries makes this clear. A corollary of this is that we could conceive of numerous indicators of IT-intensity related to different classes of IT product. For sectors these might involve, for instance, consumption of computers, of software, of telecommunications equipment, of communications services; for products we could similarly consider the embodiment of IT hardware, of lines of software code, etc. In practice, the selection of IT-intensity indicators that will be available is generally limited, and we are lucky to be able to experiment with more than one! Even if this were not the case, we would be inclined to view this heterogeneity of the IT-producing sector as indicative of issues to explore in research, rather than as a regrettable obstacle to analysis. For instance, we can imagine examining patterns of emphasis in the consumption of different classes of IT product across sectors of the economy, which should be a fruitful way of examining both the actuality of "convergence" in practice and the factors leading to distinctive applications of IT.

We have achieved at least a provisional definition of the IT-producing sector, then: it contains a "heart" producing ICs and related active components, and a "core" of computer and telecommunications equipment and service sectors. This definition may not stand the test of time - what if we develop non-electronic optical chips? - but it represents a starting-point for analysis of the information economy. It is a starting-point that we shall not always be able to use in practice - as Chapter 2 notes, many existing statistical classifications run at 90 degrees to this approach - but it does provide us with an orientation from which to assess the merits of existing statistics.

It should be emphasised that the approach outlined here, and developed in subsequent chapters, proposes a "fuzzy", rather than a sharply demarcated, view of IT. Whereas some products may be clearly labelled IT, many other products are acquiring IT components. We are proposing restricting the IT label to those products whose function is centrally a matter of programmable information-processing (computers, calculators, telecommunications systems, etc.). But we recognise that other products (including some, such as robots, that many commentators would term IT, and others, such as motor cars, that they would not) are increasingly acquiring microcomputer controls and even communications facilities so as to enhance their core functionality (e.g. handling materials, transporting people).

Likewise for economic sectors - many sectors beyond the "core" IT sectors are acquiring microelectronics to build into their products as well as merely to control their processes. And likewise for jobs: there are "core" IT jobs such as electronics engineering, software writing, and network management, but many other occupations are acquiring an IT component. This fuzziness reflects the diffusion of IT-related activities throughout the economy, and poses a considerable statistical challenge - not only are new categories of activity being forged, but existing ones are being transformed.

1.3 Generations in IT

One further issue needs to be addressed before we move on to considering statistics. The fact of rapid change in IT heartland technologies (integration on a successively larger scale) and associated change in the core computing and communications technologies has already been emphasised. But this has implications which we have not so far taken up. They can be summed up in the phrase: a computer is not a computer is not a computer.

What this means when unpackaged is that the pace of change in IT products is such that products are often rapidly obsolescent. Counting up the number of computers in an establishment, for example, may mean enumerating devices that have been produced over a span of perhaps a decade. In the building in which this draft is being prepared, for example, we have desktop microcomputers with internal RAM ranging from 32k to four megabytes - a hundredfold difference. It is not that the more powerful machine is worth a hundred of the less powerful machines; in price terms its cost is only about double - without taking inflation into account! Concerning its utility, the difference would need to be accounted for in terms of the ease and speed of carrying out common tasks, where the improvement might be one order of magnitude, but is unlikely to be two orders of magnitude.

Within the IT research community, a common convention used in tackling these problems is to talk of successive "generations" of IT equipment. Since some empirical data are expressed in terms of these generations, and since they suggest a useful approach for future data production efforts, we shall briefly outline one instance of this approach.

Kahn (1985) follows common practice in distinguishing five generations in IT (with the fifth being more of a forecast than a reality). They span 1946-56 (1st), 1957-63 (2nd), 1964-81 (3rd) and 1982-89 (4th). He provides illustrations of computer hardware, software and performance, and telecommunication technology for the five generations: these are summarised below.

First Generation
computer hardware: vacuum tubes; magnetic drum; cathode ray tube
performance: 2k memory, 10k instructions/sec
software: stored programs; machine code; autocode
telecommunications technology: telephone; teletype

Second Generation
computer hardware: transistors; magnetic core memories
performance: 32k memory; 200kps
software: high-level languages
telecommunications technology: digital transmission; pulse code modulation

Third Generation
computer hardware: ICs; semiconductor memories; magnetic discs; minicomputers; microprocessors
performance: 2m memory; 5mips

software: very high-level languages; structured programming; timesharing; computer graphics
telecommunications technology: satellite communications; microwaves; networking; optical fibres; packet switching

Fourth Generation
computer hardware: distributed computing systems; VLSI; bubble memories; optical discs; microcomputers
performance: 8m memory; 30mips
software: fourth-generation languages (4GLs); widespread packaged programs; expert systems; object-oriented languages
telecommunications technology: Integrated Services Digital Network (ISDN)

Fifth Generation
computer hardware: advanced packaging and interconnection techniques; ULSI; parallel architecture; 3D IC design; Gallium Arsenide technology; Josephson junction technology; optical components
performance: 1 giga instruction - 1 terainstruction per sec
software: concurrent languages; functional programming; symbolic processing (natural languages, vision, speech recognition, etc.)
telecommunications technology: extensive development of distributed computing, and of modularity; merging of computing and telecommunications technology

Efforts to distinguish among generations, such as the one set out above, are both helpful and frustrating. They are helpful in that they act as powerful reminders that IT and IT-based activities themselves undergo "little revolutions", that the apparently smooth trends of increasing IT power are associated with discontinuities in IT use. While in many respects the five generations can be related to steps in the capability of the heartland technology, from valves through transistors and then successively more powerful ICs, there are clusters of related IT innovations whose incorporation into a new technology system reflects other simultaneous innovations. The sort of periodisation that is suggested here could form a basis for classification of specific products and modes of activity.

Such efforts are frustrating, too, for several reasons. There is limited consensus as to the specificities of the distinct generations, both in terms of timing and in terms of content. Why are some items included and not others? Are there not profound developments within many of these periods (for example, current microcomputers are sometimes themselves described as being generationally distinct from earlier microcomputers)? Especially when more recent or future generations are concerned, is there not an element of wishful thinking (e.g. is ISDN really characteristic of the 1982-89 period)? More generally, are the generations defined by state-of-the-art products, technologies under development, commercially available devices, or dominant and well-diffused products?

Despite these problems, this discussion underlines the point that simply totalling up items of equipment of different vintages may in effect be like adding up apples and oranges (especially given the emergence of new applications using more powerful equipment). In many surveys of IT equipment, distinctions are made between different classes of equipment: microcomputer, minicomputer, mainframe computer, etc. In some surveys items are graded in terms of current price bands. Very few researchers have sought to document trends in IT power - e.g. amount of RAM available, level of information flow in bits/second, etc. - although there are some efforts in this direction (notably Pool et al., 1984, who sought to prepare compatible estimates of the bits of information circulating in different media in Japan and the USA). Efforts to address the distinct generations of IT systems are rare indeed, although there are specialised surveys of specific generations of equipment or services (for example, studies of the diffusion of 4GLs).

The increased performance and decreased cost of IT are factors that will need to be borne in mind when evaluating data on diffusion or IT-intensity. Equally important are qualitative changes, those associated with "convergence" in particular. As computer and communications systems become linked, a computer is not a computer is not a computer - because it is part of a network! While commentators have drawn attention to the growing role of systems integration in IT products, and a number of surveys document that this trend does indeed exist (as we shall see in later chapters), most statistics seem blithely unaware of it. In the words of our colleagues at CURDS (see Section 1.1 above), we are left with "data on amputees" when using statistics that treat personal computers, for example, alike whether they are stand-alone units or acting as terminals.

1.4 Conclusions

This chapter has sketched out an approach to the information economy. The approach is based upon the revolutionary nature of IT, which is facilitating a wide spectrum of changes in the economic organisation of industrial societies. While the dynamic nature of IT means that the approach raises as many questions for statistical analysis as it answers, we argue that this approach is self-consistent and, because it attempts to address significant change processes, it should prove more fruitful than received studies of the "information sector". In the chapters that follow, we shall see how far we can follow up the approach with available data, how useful such data analyses are liable to be, and what changes in statistical practices are feasible and desirable.

2 Data and Data Sources

2.1 Introduction: Statistics Count

Data are social products, not facts that have appeared out of thin air. However reliable, or however inadequate, they may be, they have been constructed:

- *by* social actors (theorists, statisticians, interviewees, data entry staff);
- *for* (narrower or wider) purposes;
- *using* resources both financial and intellectual - which include research instruments, conceptual structures, amounts of time of skilled and unskilled labour, etc.

The process of constructing data can be a complex one, including large numbers of individuals, operating in many different organisational environments, each making judgements about how to classify and enumerate events (Miles, 1985b). It is indeed so convoluted, when examined in detail, that many social scientists have more or less abandoned the use of statistical sources. Under various guises ("phenomenology", "ethnomethodology", "deconstructionism", etc.) they have shifted away from the use of data to the examination of data, to what often seems to be an endless interrogation of the assumptions that underpin particular sets of data, and the processes whereby consensus about meanings is reached or (more often in their studies) is not reached. To such commentators, data on the "information economy" tell us much more about how ideas about the latter are changing than about the latter itself - if indeed they accept that there is any social reality outside of concepts!

But it is not necessary to choose between adopting this complete and seemingly permanent suspension of belief about statistical data, and uncritically accepting data at their face value. Statistics may be more or less useful for analysis depending upon four factors:

- (1) **Degree of Conceptual Adequacy**
  How far the concepts which structure the data are ones which correspond to those guiding the analysis, or can be roughly translated into them so that the statistics can be treated as more or less adequate *indicators* of the phenomena conceptualised.

- (2) **Appropriateness of Instruments**
  How far the instruments used are ones which do not do violence to

these concepts, and meet the various criteria of *validity* which statisticians have enumerated.

- (3) **Technical Rigour**
  How far the data production has been carried out in a systematic and responsible way, with the instruments being applied correctly to an appropriate population (and with due efforts subsequently to ensure that mistakes have not crept into the encoding or computer processing stages).

- (4) **Suitable Presentation**
  How far the data are presented with accompanying information that allows the potential users to establish how far the above conditions have been met.

We can briefly indicate what each of these points entails. Thus, for (1), the degree of adequacy, the issue is whether the concepts that structure the data are ones that correspond to the desired analysis.

For instance, if we are interested in the diffusion of computer technology across an economy, a simple count of computers installed in different firms, different sectors, etc., would provide a starting point - but given that computers are themselves very diverse, and that there is a considerable danger of not comparing like with like, it makes more sense to disaggregate the concept "computer". (See Chapter 1.) And in fact, many surveys do exactly this. Often they provide data classified into mainframes, minis and micros (though even this classification is somewhat embarrassed by new descriptions in the trade such as "super-mini" and "supermicro", and by the wide range of different types of device that fall into each category - micros, for instance, covering anything from home computers to Sun workstations). Other studies draw distinctions in terms of different price bands, or (especially in market research) of specific models. But if we are interested in the utilisation of these computers, it would be relevant also to seek data about the applications they are put to, even the amount of time which goes into specific activities; a simple count of machines tells us nothing about whether they are being used for word processing or process control - or, indeed, being used to do contract work for other firms or not being used at all.

As for (2), the appropriateness of instruments, the key concept of "validity" has several components, and social scientists have put in much effort seeking to develop criteria for assessing the validity of their measures.

Perhaps the most elementary is "*face validity*" - which essentially asks, does this survey question look as if it is addressing the question we want answered? If we are enquiring into the use of VANS, for instance, do we need to define what we mean by the term, so that we can be sure that respondents will have the same thing in mind when they provide answers (and aren't referring to commercial vehicles!) In practice, we are often using data that were originally created for a different purpose, a purpose whose underlying concepts may be slightly different to those we are seeking to develop. In such cases, it is necessary to judge how far the existing measures are re-usable as indicators for present purposes. Sometimes this judgement may be made as face validation, but researchers have proposed further criteria.

"*Convergent validation*", for instance, involves attempting to use more than one indicator of each construct - for example, the computer-intensity of a sector might be assessed by both the expenditure on hardware and the number of computer staff employed. We are said to have convergent validity to the extent that the two measures intercorrelate highly - in which instance, they may even be combined in some fashion to give a (hopefully more accurate) composite indicator. "*Construct validation*" involves comparisons of trends and patterns displayed by the data against the criterion of what results would be expected on the basis of some theory (or even "common sense"). Thus, an indicator of computer-intensity should be expected to show certain sectors more intensive than others, to show a general increase over the last few decades, and so on: to the extent that it does not, its validity will be suspect.

Validity extends to the composition of the population chosen for analysis. Is it the appropriate population for the study in question? Trade associations typically present their own statistics based on surveys of their members only; in the UK one has to take care as to whether official statistics concern the United Kingdom, Great Britain, England and Wales, or other units - failure to check on this may mean putting the wrong numerator and denominator together, or making inappropriate time series comparisons.

Point (3), technical rigour, concerns the implementation of the data-production exercise. How far has the study been carried out in an appropriate fashion? If it involves interviews, have the interviewers really interviewed the people they were supposed to (and what have they done in the event of their non-availability)? Have the questions been posed accurately, or has there been slippage - which quite often happens when interviewers fail to understand the meaning of enquiries, or when they are poorly motivated?

These points are often difficult to establish, and there are reasons to believe that some market research bodies and some interviewers do not meet the highest professional standards in their survey work. This is most likely to be a problem when one is seeking to analyse results for small subsamples of the population in question: serious dereliction such as to undermine the major results is fairly rare (but not unknown, as we have found to our cost when using survey firm data in the past!). Nevertheless, there have been persistent criticisms of the quality of studies of computer markets; for instance, some researchers have based their results on suppliers' claims (and suppliers may have self-interests in apparently boosting their product's sales), and double-counting is believed to occur when different data sources are combined.

Point (4) involves the suitability of the presentation. Thorough explication of the sources and methods of data production evidently can help the user establish how far any given data source meets the criteria discussed above. Unfortunately, there is a wide spectrum of explication in practice, with official statistics and academic surveys generally providing ample details, but market research and, especially, consultancy studies, often leave the reader quite in the dark as to what sort of sample was asked what sort of questions.

Data about the "information economy" may be particularly prone to the problems mentioned above. Recalling the quotations reproduced in the Introduction concerning the limitations of statistics for addressing this area, at least three factors seem to be operative:

- IT is itself a fairly recent phenomenon, and our accounting systems have yet to accommodate it fully.
- IT is rapidly evolving, and it is hard to establish enduring classificatory schemata in many areas.
- Many IT-related products and activities pose problems for quantification: software products were mentioned by NEDO (1982b), as particularly tricky, but to these should certainly be added network activities and telecommunications services.

These are factors that are liable to reduce clarity. It is hard to develop (or to be confident in) valid questions and sampling frameworks when things are in such flux, and when even experts disagree as to what the important elements of change are. Many figures that are flung around are being used as propaganda and hyperbole in competitive markets - which are also markets in which it is often difficult to justify investments by conventional criteria. Nevertheless, we argue that a large number of potential data sources can be used to gain some insights into the "information economy". It is our firm belief that these have only been exploited to a very limited extent.

2.2 Official Data Sources

2.2.1 Features of Official Statistics

Official statistics are usually the starting point for any effort at mapping and measuring social, economic or technological affairs. They have a number of features that position them advantageously:

- The state, as producer of official statistics, has requirements for large volumes of information in order to engage in its management activities; it thus has developed considerable resources to this end - e.g. the BSO, the Central Statistical Office (CSO), the Office of Population Censuses and Surveys (OPCS), and various departmental statistical offices. It has relatively large numbers of trained personnel and access to considerable computing power.

- The state is able to command political as well as financial and technical resources, and to order individuals and firms to respond to enquiries. Those surveyed are more likely to treat requests for information seriously if they come from official sources.

- Many official studies are comprehensive: they survey the entire population of individuals or firms, rather than samples, and thus allow for more precise documentation.

- Official statisticians are naturally prone to human error like everyone else; but they usually take their professional standards especially seriously: they are concerned about data quality, take care to check the correctness of publications, and make clear the assumptions and methods that are in use (though their political masters and mistresses may be more cavalier in using official data).

- The state is generally perceived as more "neutral" than other sources of data - such as, for instance, trade associations. Although concern may be expressed about the "massaging" of politically sensitive data - such as unemployment figures - such a fear tends to be localised to very few statistics.

On the other hand, there are several factors that limit the usefulness of official statistics, especially where it comes to depicting issues subject to rapid technological change:

- Official statisticians are reluctant to change statistical definitions without going through an extensive consultation process. They are more interested in establishing widely useful and robust data systems than in capturing what may be transient phenomena. One of the main reasons for this is their obligation to produce information in such a way that trends and comparisons over time can be made. Increasingly, too, there are efforts to enhance international comparability, and to move in step with other industrial countries.

- Many official statistics are *by-product data*; unlike *direct data*, which result from deliberate enquiries, these by-product data represent information produced in the course of the routine administrative or other activities of government agencies. Substantial changes in these data are unlikely in the absence of substantial procedural change, and even then it is the practical needs that take precedence over the data requirements.

- In the climate of deregulation and restricted public expenditure which prevails at the time of writing, strong constraints are placed on official statisticians. As some activities move away from state control and into the market, the entry of by-product statistics into the public domain may be reduced. And direct statistics, requiring public expenditure and often requiring time-consuming cooperation from businesses, may be less attractive to produce.

The *Guide to Official Statistics* does not feature the term "Information Technology" in its index (!). It should be admitted that the 1986 edition does feature "computers" and "telecommunications" in its index, though many other IT-related terms are absent. The *Guide* is an invaluable directory of official data sources, and will usually be the first port of call in a study of official data.

2.2.2 Production and Employment

Several regular sources of data on the main sectors of the UK economy are good starting points for statistical examinations. In general, these sources of official data are better for orienting us to developments in what we have termed the IT-producing sector, than they are for examination of patterns of use of IT in the IT-using sectors.

The annual Census of Production produces data in terms of the Standard Industrial Classification (SIC) at the three-digit level. These appear as issues of *Business Monitor*, titled *PA* followed by the SIC(80) code for the industry. However, these only cover manufacturing sectors. *Business Monitors* also provide material drawn from more frequent sectoral surveys, with *PQ* and *PM* series reporting quarterly and monthly data respectively. *(Business Monitors* coded PA contain results from the

Census of Production; quarterly series are preceded by PQ, monthly series by PM.) Other *Business Monitors* include material on some service industries (the Business Statistics Office does not concern itself, for example, with public services).

As noted, the issues of *Business Monitor* are given code numbers corresponding to the SIC (80) codes for the industries. In general each report of the Census of Production provides for the relevant industry information on output and costs; capital expenditure; stocks and work in progress; size analysis of establishments; percentage analysis of real returns, and percentage of employment accounted for by these; operating ratios (gross and net output per head, gross value-added per head). (Prior to 1980 - when an earlier industrial classification system was used, making some comparisons difficult - further data on employment were presented: its regional distribution, and breakdown into full- and part-time jobs and by sex.) It should be noted that the Census of Production is only compulsory for firms with more than 20 employees; and estimates provided for smaller firms are liable to be flawed. (All enterprises with more than 100 employees are surveyed, and one in two of those with 50-99 employees, one in four of those with 20-49 employees.)

Quarterly series typically present data covering the last five quarters and annual totals for the last two years. Based on Quarterly Sales Inquiries, they not surprisingly focus on sales, broken down into main product classes, and usually accompanied by data on trade, employment, etc. As will be apparent, these are largely what we have termed direct, rather than by-product, statistics.

Among other issues of *Business Monitor* that also provide materials on IT-producing (and more generally on IT-using) sectors of the economy, or that explicate the data sources used in these studies, we should mention:

PA 1001: introductory notes to the Annual Census of Production.

PA 1002: summary tables from the Annual Census of Production, issued after all of the sectoral volumes have been published. Sectors are compared at both the establishment and enterprise levels, and trends over five years provided.

PA 1003: statistics of the size distribution of UK businesses, presenting sectoral breakdowns (four-digit level) of the number of businesses in different turnover and employment size bands; VAT data are used to give material on service industries as well as manufacturing.

PO 1006: statistics of the product concentration of UK manufacturers, giving sectoral data for manufacturing industries on the value and proportion of sales accounted for by (usually) the five largest enterprises in each sector, classified into both industry sectors and major product groups. (These data show high levels of industry concentration in most IT sectors and products.) The most recent volume of these tables was published in 1980, giving data only up until 1977.

PO 1008: this contains data from the 1984 Purchases Inquiry (earlier studies concerned 1974 and 1979). With very few exceptions, for each four-digit level activity headings of the SIC(80) - but not including services - data are provided on the purchases of these branches of industry. While the data categories are not completely compatible from branch to branch, these statistics can be used to gain an idea of purchases by and from IT sectors of the economy. Indeed, these data are used heavily in the construction of input-output tables. We shall discuss the use of these data to develop indicators of an ''IT sector'' in Chapter 4; meanwhile it may be interesting to note that among the statistics provided are each sector's purchases of paper and stationery, which might be used as an indicator of the volume of communications which they undertake.

MQ 12: data on import penetration and export sales ratios for over 200 sectors of manufacturing.

Other statistical sources bring together many of these sectoral data. *British Business* and a special *Business Monitor* (PA 1002) provide summary tabulations from the Census of Production. *Employment Gazette* and *Economic Trends* report major data of interest with sectoral disaggregation. *Employment Gazette*, published monthly by the Department of Employment, in particular is a good up-to-date source of information on employment trends in different sectors. Other data that it provides regularly (on vacancies, hours worked, etc.) tend to be highly aggregated, but the magazine often contains articles relevant to mapping and measuring the information economy. For example, it has carried several studies reviewing relations between technological change and employment and working patterns.

Employment data of various kinds are produced as a result of by-product and direct enquiries. The most comprehensive source of the latter is the decennial Census of Population, which provides data cross-classified by both industry and occupation. Similar cross-classifications are carried out in the New Earnings Survey, based on a 1% sample of employees covered by PAYE schemes in Great Britain. This cross-classification makes it possible to assess the occupational composition of each sector of the economy - which can be used to develop measures of the "information workforce" (e.g. clerical or library workers).

Unfortunately occupational categories, like many others, have not really accommodated the development of IT to date: rather few data on "IT occupations" are provided. *Employment Gazette* annually carries occupation by industry data, and the *Annual Abstract of Statistics* carries summary tables of this sort. The Census data can be analysed at many levels of disaggregation and with further cross-classifications (by region, sex, etc); they are available from the Census Office of the OPCS and various depositories. The *Guide to Official Statistics* lists a large number of bound reports and microfiches published by HMSO or available from the OPCS.

2.2.3 Trade Statistics

HM Customs & Excise is the source of data on overseas trade. The annual *Guide to the Classification of Overseas Trade Statistics* outlines the product categories in which goods are treated. These categories very largely follow the international Standard Industrial Trade Classification (SITC) system for trade classification, based on the type of product rather than the class of industry involved. The *Guide* draws some distinctions between different classes of product that are quite interesting when viewed in terms of mapping and measuring the information economy. For instance, among digital computers there are distinctions based on the RAM capacity, different types of data storage system are distinguished, and among TV sets those with teletext and videotex facilities are distinguished.

Trade data are, as noted, typically produced on a commodity basis - although the classification of some products may be influenced by their industry of origin (this is usually held to lead to an undercounting of services trade, when some services are supplied, for instance, by computer manufacturers). *Business Monitor MQ10* provides data processed so as to indicate imports and exports classified by sectors (on the basis of attributing products to the sectors of which they are the main products).

British Business carries import and export data disaggregated into broad commodity groups on a monthly basis. The April 1988 edition, to take the most recent example at the time of writing, also provides data, on a quarterly basis from the fourth quarter of 1985 to that of 1987, on the import penetration and export performance of the UK. Data are provided on a two-digit level for manufacturing industries, allowing us to examine, for example, "office machinery and data processing equipment" and "electrical and electronic engineering".

The annual *Overseas Trade Statistics of the United Kingdom* provides data for products disaggregated to c1,800 commodity headings, and in many instances distinguishes trade with the European Community, and with other significant trading partners for that product, from the rest of the world. There may be some limitations on the detail of data owing to commercial confidentiality - i.e. one company may constitute a major portion of the trade in a product.

Trade data are also worked into the Input-Output Tables at the appropriate level of aggregation for the latter. This offers some scope for assessing the consumption of imports by different sectors of the economy - and computers and telecommunications equipment feature here.

Finally, Eurostat produces (in numerous volumes) *Eurostat External Trade Statistics* which includes trade data for the UK and the EC; in some respects these data are more detailed than in the UK's own publications. The most recent volumes available (in summer 1988) cover 1986.

2.2.4 Data on Consumption

Final consumption is not treated in anything like the same detail as is production. The main official source, the annual *Family Expenditure Survey,* does provide details of the expenditure and ownership patterns of various classes of household, based on survey and diary studies. This provides information on the ownership of various electrical and electronic products, and expenditure on media and communications services. The *General Household Survey* is a continuous multi-purpose sample survey, which provides data on households' ownership of various durables and occasionally includes material on activity patterns (thus questions about leisure and the use of time give some picture of media usage). These are large data sets which extend back over decades, and are available to some extent for re-analysis; however, for detailed direct statistics on final consumption it is necessary in general to turn to market research and scholarly studies. (See Chapter 8.)

2.2.5 Other Official and Semi-official Sources

Several agencies and semi-official bodies produce data relevant to IT activities, or present existing data in new ways. NEDO, for example, has sector groups (previously Economic Development Committees (EDCs)) in such areas as electronics, and these have in the past been the source of many specialised studies and reports; its *List of Publications* cites these. (Until the 1987 reorganisation NEDO featured as well as an electronics EDC a consumer electronics and an IT EDC.)

By-product data are also often provided by agencies, where statistics dealing with their own activities, or needed in order to fulfil their responsibilities, cast light on IT activities more generally. An example is the Cable Authority, which publishes data on cable communication systems in the UK; Oftel similarly publishes some data supplied by British Telecom (BT) on the quality of the telephone service.

2.3 Trade Sources

2.3.1 Trade and Professional Associations

Many trade associations supply statistical data on the production and markets for their IT-related products. We include a wider range of bodies here than strictly necessary, since this will be useful for readers with ideas of the "information economy" divergent from our own:

- **AMDEA,** the Association of Manufacturers of Domestic Electrical Appliances
- **BEITA,** the Business Equipment and Information Technology Association
- **BPI,** the British Phonographic Industry
- **BRA,** the British Robots Association
- **BREMA,** the British Radio and Electronic Equipment Manufacturers Association
- **BVA,** the British Videogram Association
- **CSA,** the Computing Services Association
- **ECIF,** the Electrical Components Industry Federation
- **EEA,** the Electrical Engineering Association
- **GAMBICA,** the Association of the Instrumentation, Control and Automation Industry in the UK
- **TEMA,** the Telecommunications Equipment Manufacturing Association

We have not included in the above list all of the trade and professional associations whose members may be using rather than producing IT products. In our experience it is rare for these bodies to produce statistics on IT trends, except in the form of special reports. (In these instances the appropriate trade press is often a good guide.) The associations of retailers (e.g. the Computers and Peripherals Trade Association, the Computer Retailers Association) sometimes produce information on deliveries and sales. A fairly up-to-date guide to trade and professional associations is published by CBD Research as its *Directory of British Associations*. A guide to non-official data sources that captures the output of some such bodies is Mort and Siddal (1985); unfortunately it provides rather few IT-related references.

The data produced by such bodies are often enlightening, and even where they overlap with official data on the activity of a sector they may be presented in original ways. But there are, as usual, limitations. First, the data are scattered: each association has to be contacted to gain access to the material, and very often these bodies are only willing to circulate heavily processed material such as is published in their annual reports and hand-outs (on the grounds of commercial confidentiality). Second. the quality of the data is at issue: these bodies have rarely embarked upon comprehensive surveys, rather they are reporting results that are typically confined to their member organisations. The degree to which the bodies are representative of the sectors in question thus has to be addressed. Do they capture only the large companies? Only the British-owned companies?

In practice, many trade associations can claim to achieve good coverage of their sectors, although this may be more prevalent in ''mature'' or heavily concentrated sectors. Haddon (1988) notes that:

> ''In the case of VCR production, Brema members account for a clear majority of all sales...there are a limited number of larger producers of VCRs, 12 of whom are in Brema. Where there are many small producers, as with the home computer peripherals market, organising a representative trade association can be more difficult...reliable software figures are generally more difficult to obtain than hardware ones because of the different industry structures. Having said that, since the BVA represents 24 distributors, it actually covers virtually all sales data on pre-recorded videograms.''

Many trade associations do attempt to justify the accuracy of their own statistics. Typically this takes the form of statements that the data cover a certain high percentage of industry sales or output. Thus the ECIF notes in its annual report that its members (on whom statistics are presented) account for over 70% of UK component manufacture. The absence of such statements may indicate either poor coverage, or a drop in coverage which is not statistically so important but which the association is seeking to downplay.

2.3.2 User Associations

User associations of various sorts exist in the IT field, especially to cater for owners of particular brands of computers. The independence of such associations from the manufacturers varies considerably, as does their level of professionalism. It is rare to find systematic data production among such associations, although sometimes surveys of their members are organised; however, they can be playing valuable roles in terms of abstracting and circulating data from other sources. Among noteworthy user associations (we have excluded those involved with particular systems) are:

- **ITUSA**, the IT Users' Association, which mainly involves large users and organises study groups on a variety of topics.
- **SOCITM**, the Society of IT Managers, which covers local authority IT users and which, unusually, has carried out its own original surveys.
- **TMA**, the Telecommunication Managers' Association, which mainly covers large users.
- **TUA**, the Telecommunication Users' Association; its quarterly *Journal* often reproduces statistics on topics such as the growth of telecommunications markets and the attitudes of users to BT.

2.3.3 Companies

Companies depict their own affairs in their annual reports, press releases, etc. Rarely do they essay broader overviews - but in the few cases where a company is as dominant in its field as, say, BT, these may be very informative about the whole branch concerned. Too many companies produce magazines to attempt to list them all; it should be sufficient to note that while some of these are glossy public relations exercises, many are highly informative, and that they form invaluable sources for those interested in the activities of the corporate actors in the IT industries.

Occasionally companies support wider-ranging or more scholarly publications. ICL provides convenient examples of both. It has recently published a report (ICL, 1988) on the use of IT in local government, for instance, while the *ICL Technical Journal* is running a series of historical studies discussing research and development (R&D) in the companies that formed ICL's predecessors.

2.3.4 Trade Press

Of course, many sectors receive extensive coverage in a flourishing trade press, and in some sectors the application of IT is so advanced (and so profitable for the suppliers whose advertisements largely sustain the press) that magazines are dedicated to this topic - e.g. *Retail Automation*, *Engineering Computers*, *Government Computing*. While these magazines seem to be firmly planted, it must be admitted that many more spring up and wither overnight. Fortunately lists of UK magazines, arranged by topic area, are provided for purposes of marketing and public relations; for example Metra's *PR Planner UK* has a section on the "computers and automation" press which is divided into five subsections (automation and instrumentation, computers and DP, professional personal computers, personal computing, and related journals), and also refers readers to application areas such as computer-aided design (CAD) and office equipment, and to components such as electronics. Inspection of such sources suggests that several hundred UK magazines and journals have an IT focus although only a small proportion of these regularly carry statistics.

Weekly trade newspapers that frequently carry reports of interest include *Computer Weekly*, *Computing*, *Datalink*, and *Electronic Times*. These papers sometimes commission surveys of their own (using their mailing lists as a sample, for instance), and even more frequently report on consultancy and other studies. Newspapers also cater to the media and advertising industries which may carry relevant data, and of course the science, computer, and financial columns of the daily press - especially the *Financial Times* - not infrequently report statistical news. *Information World Review* and *I'M* (Information Market) are newspapers covering the online industry in particular.

2.4 Market Research and Consultancies

Many firms are active in providing data on IT-related activities. We have deliberately chosen not to cover these sources exhaustively in the present study for several reasons:

- much of the data produced is confidential or restricted-circulation;
- published reports tend to be excessively expensive, although they

may often be acquired from The British Library Science Reference and Information Service and a few other privileged sites;
- very few of these studies are at all explicit about the means whereby they have arrived at their figures, and data are often reported in a form that strongly suggests spurious precision;
- there have been strong qualms expressed about the quality of some of these data, for example figures on microcomputer sales, where it has been suggested that conflicts between different market research studies' results indicate an uncritical attitude to manufacturers' claims on the part of the researchers (see Chapter 6).

This being said, such studies are often the *only* source of quantitative data on some key topics, and thus prove of inestimable value to corporate planners and marketing directors. The quality of the best consultancy and market research studies is very high indeed, but this is, predictably, usually correlated with their price.

Guides to market surveys for 1986 were produced by Aptus Marketing Services (1987); they cover computing and telecommunications, and claim to cover all surveys on such IT topics as sales of different types of computers and peripherals, different types of telecommunications equipment, software, online services. Many surveys are reported in the trade press. For a brief and rather uncritical discussion of leading consultants, see Cottee (1987).

While it would not be possible to summarise the activities of all the consultant and market research firms providing data here, a number of major sources of regular data may be indicated. No endorsement of these firms or their products is intended:

- Fintech, which runs a number of proficient newsletters covering telecommunications, media and computer markets.
- IDC, which produces much sales data on markets for computers of different types (including second-hand equipment), and also covers telecommunications issues.
- Keynote, which specialises in secondary documentation, putting together convenient summaries of the main points arising from surveys of markets such as home computers and videotex.
- Logica, which operates "Telematica", a multi-client information service on IT in Western European countries, and "Tarifica", which reviews postal, telephone and telegraphy operators (PTTs) and telecommunications services and tariffs, also in Western Europe.
- Price Waterhouse, whose annual *Information Technology Review* reports surveys of computer users (mainly DP managers).

- Romtec, which provides information (mainly for suppliers) on micro and minicomputer markets.

2.5 Academic Sources

Academic research about IT (as opposed to research in establishments of higher education aimed at actively developing IT) is rather diffuse and uncoordinated. The various social science disciplines typically have their own social networks and publication outlets, so that it is difficult to gain a satisfactory overview of what, given the "awakening" to IT issues of many social scientists in recent years, would seem to be a rapidly growing field.

Mansell and Richards (1986) have provided something of a guide to this confusing field by preparing a directory which lists, *inter alia*, researchers working on IT topics (these are specified, together with main publications and other data) by the institutional base. An index provides a guide to research topics by keywords. While not providing a guide to statistics, this source does suggest academics who might be in a position to provide data - and in the preparation of the current study some 300 of those cited in the book were asked whether they could help identify data sources. There is, incidentally, little information provided by the authors on the breakdown of research (except by institution), perhaps because they were aware that the questionnaire used to compile the directory was prone to errors of omission and commission.

In a companion volume (Melody and Mansell, 1986) some data on the ESRC's support for IT research are provided, and there is a helpful overview of research institutions active in social scientific study of IT. A report of *Research Supported by the ESRC* is available from the ESRC in London, and its *Newsletter* carries notes of recent publications. Postgraduate research can be scrutinised by consulting Aslib's quarterly *Index to Theses*. These are rather all-purpose compilations; some educational bodies offering social science training on IT-related issues do make available their own lists of student studies - for example, SPRU's *Annual Report*. Lists of topics studied by students at Master's level are provided by the Department of Information Science at City University and the Department of Information Studies at the University of Sheffield.

Few academic researchers have the financial resources required to engage in large-scale data production exercises, and the main activities of most social scientists are engaging in smaller-scale studies (often case studies) or re-analysing larger (usually official) data sets. There are notable exceptions, of course. To cite merely a few highlights, including purely research institutions alongside educational establishments:

- the Centre for Urban and Regional Development Studies, University of Newcastle, is involved in developing several data bases of regional statistics, and has recently turned its attention to regional innovation, telecommunications facilities, and occupational trends;
- the Employment Research Institute, University of Warwick, is responsible for much analysis of occupational and employment data in the UK;
- the Policy Studies Institute (PSI) has been responsible for several large-scale surveys of the diffusion of microelectronics in manufacturing industry and on relations between technical change and industrial relations;
- the Programme of Policy Research on Engineering, Science and Technology (PREST), University of Manchester, has been working on, among other topics, cable communication systems and the Alvey Programme;
- SPRU, University of Sussex, works with a number of technology-related data bases, including information on patent statistics, on innovations in the UK, on bibliometrics (scientific publications and citations), and on the Alvey Programme - as well as with other data sources cited in this volume;
- Social and Community Planning Research publishes an annual *British Social Attitudes Yearbook* which contains accounts of major areas of attitude change and stability in the British population.

Many data sets created by academic researchers (especially those funded by the ESRC, which requires its researchers to deposit their data), are available from the Data Archive, at the University of Essex. Its *Data Archive Bulletin* provides an update of new acquisitions and news about statistical research; data tapes and disks may be obtained from the Archive for a handling fee. A full Data Catalogue is in existence, within which are categories such as "science and technology", "management and organisation studies", "consumer behaviour" and "labour and employment studies". Several major official series, and some studies carried out by private researchers, are also held by the Archive.

2.6 Other Sources

Few other original data sources exist, although international governmental organisations such as, in particular, the OECD, may sometimes request new data of their member countries (for example, on telecommunications regimes). More often international organisations simply collate and reconcile national statistics - and sometimes play a valuable role in so doing. The OECD's ICCP (Information, Computers & Communications Policy) Division has published several studies of national "information economies" (defined in terms criticised in Chapter 1), and of issues in the telecommunications field (videotex, cable and satellite, etc.); elsewhere in the OECD the Statistical Division of the Directorate for Science, Technology and Industry is currently active on developing statistics in the information and IT area; the United Nations Industrial Development Organization (UNIDO) and the United Nations Commission on Science and Technology for Development (UNCSTD) are prominent among UN organisations in providing information on IT; the International Telecommunications Union publishes a large (but limited) data set on national and international telecommunications; the FAST programme of the European Community publishes a great many studies of social and technological change, while the Commission of the European Communities' (CEC's) Eurostat is responsible for numerous economic data bases and is also developing new statistical series that may be relevant to IT.

Overseas consultancies should also be mentioned: on occasion these may provide data on the UK scene in comparative context, although it is common to find Western Europe or the EC being lumped together.

US government agencies have been known to provide good "intelligence" on British and European IT activities - and, sometimes, of the activities of US firms in other countries. Among studies that provide "snapshots" of various countries to contrast with the USA, the Office of Technology Assessment (OTA) (1985) considers R&D activities, and the Department of Commerce (1984) covers data-processing services industries, while the Department of Commerce (1988) provides valuable analyses of the state of various sectors in the USA, together with details of trade and international market issues. These sectors include computer equipment and software, radio communication and detection equipment, telephone and telegraph equipment, and telecommunications services, among others, with useful discussion and presentation of trends and forecasts.

3 Research and Development

This chapter deals with data focusing on R&D activities bearing on IT innovation. R&D covers a variety of activities, from "pure research" (usually carried out in higher education and government laboratories) to "experimental development" or "design and development" (usually carried out by supplier firms but sometimes taking place within user organisations). With a technological revolution in IT, and the emergence of major new technologies (possible future revolutions?) round biotechnology and new materials, however, there has been much discussion of the blurring boundaries between pure and applied research, with categories like "strategic research" being introduced to address this.

R&D statistics have been developed remarkably over the last few decades. But they have also been subject to considerable criticism. For instance, it is argued that much innovative activity may be omitted from such statistics. This is because much experimentation and innovation takes place not in the laboratories (which are easy for statisticians to identify and study), but in such locations as production lines where, for instance, production engineers modify equipment to operate better in its actual environment and with the materials and staff to hand. This sort of argument may be particularly relevant to some IT R&D - especially the development of software within user organisations. And IT itself, as a new category which has yet to be captured fully in most statistical series, also poses problems.

Additionally, it is generally recognised that R&D data are much better developed as sources dealing with the *inputs* to R&D activities (levels of expenditure, or of scientific and technical employment) than with their *outputs* (which might be for pure science scientific papers, while for applied research it might be patents, actual inventions, etc.).

We shall discuss data sources as they roughly deal with the continuum ranging from pure research - i.e. scientific activities - to innovative activities within firms. Diffusion of IT will be dealt with in more detail in Chapter 5.

3.1 General Sources

A number of official publications attempt to assess the overall levels of R&D in the UK; some of their data are useful in bearing upon IT activities.

The CSO's *Annual Abstract of Statistics* is a convenient regular source of R&D data. Tables cover the expenditure and financing of R&D by sectors; these sectors are central government (disaggregated into defence, research councils and other), local government, universities and further education establishments, public corporations, research associations, private industry and other. Other tables, to be noted later, give more detail on government and industrial financing of research.

The Cabinet Office's *Annual Review of Government Funded Research and Development* mainly features those issues signified in the title, but provides tables comparing, for example, government and private financing for industrial R&D.

A valuable source of material on R&D in general is the Proceedings of the House of Lords Select Committee on Science and Technology, although these are organised in the form of statements of evidence (oral or written) and are thus not well structured as data sources. A report produced in the 1986-87 session deals with civil R&D in the UK, and is notable in several respects. The volume devoted to oral evidence (House of Lords, 1986a) contains several interesting discussions, though few carry statistical data that are not available elsewhere: the DTI provides information on its R&D policy and its pattern of support for "high-tech" R&D; the ESRC presents information on international differences in government funding of R&D and in trends in the share of citations in different areas of research (including "engineering and technology"); there are presentations of their activities by the Department of Education and Science and the Science and Engineering Research Council (SERC); and statements of position from GEC and Plessey.

The volume of written evidence (House of Lords, 1986b) contains descriptions of their own R&D activities by BT, IBM, ICL and Ferranti - these differ in detail but some (e.g. BT) are informative overviews of activity. A number of bodies interested in the IT field - e.g. the ECIF and the Institute of Electrical Engineers (IEE) - provide evidence, and some other material is included on IT R&D activities (e.g. Lighthill on supercomputer research, Gummett and Watson on civil/military relations and electronics R&D). The volume also contains succinct statements of the R&D activities of the Northern Ireland and Scottish Offices.

Another Parliamentary Committee which has obtained and published evidence on IT topics is the House of Commons Trade and Industry Committee (1988, volume 2), whose specific data are considered later. For now, it should be noted that a broad overview of the UK IT industry provided by the DTI is here complemented by some searching questioning by Committee members.

The OECD has been a major spur to the development of internationally comparable R&D statistics, and has published a number of reports and studies that are useful in terms of situating UK R&D in a wider context. IT is not the focus of these studies, but relevant data are included in volumes falling into the *OECD Science and Technology Indicators* series. Thus volume 2 (OECD, 1986a) provides information on researchers in the electrical/electronics industry group for OECD countries, and breaks down expenditure into "electric" and "electronic" components, and into public and private finance, and provides growth data for the periods 1975-79 and 1979-81. It also provides data on R&D in higher education.

Finally, Martin (1987) provides a concise introduction to statistics on UK R&D.

3.2 Pure Research and Scientific Activity

Pure (or basic) research is generally described as being oriented toward producing understanding and scientific knowledge rather than inventions or innovations. Its inputs will tend to be academic research staff and expenditures; its outputs are liable to be rather diffuse, but considerable effort has been devoted in recent years to "bibliometrics", the measurement of outputs such as publications and the citations that are made to publications (which can be interpreted as a measure of the "impact" of research on the scientific community). Output measures of the latter kind have become increasingly central to discussions of national performance in various scientific fields, and even brought to bear in assessing individuals' career potentials.

3.2.1 Staff and Finance

Data on R&D staff in higher education institutions - such as those provided on a comparative basis by the OECD - are of limited value in documenting IT R&D. The categories they use are often unsuitable for addressing a new interdisciplinary field of research, and the data are not presented in sufficiently disaggregated form to allow for specification of IT activities. Categories such as "physics" and engineering" no doubt contain many IT researchers, but so probably does "psychology" (work on artificial intelligence and human-machine interfaces, for example). Problems in assessing staff and expenditure on academic R&D

are intensified by the variety of sources from which funds are obtained, and the need to impute portions of the time of University Grants Committee funded staff to research (as opposed to teaching in particular).

A detailed discussion of problems in determining levels of academic research is provided by Martin, Irvine, and Minchin (1986). They note four problems with OECD's international data on R&D expenditure in higher education, which also suggest qualifications that need to be borne in mind in interpreting UK data:

- lack of comparability in what institutions to include in the higher education sector (does it include only university-level establishments or also technical colleges? does it include research council establishments, government department R&D centres, university hospital health care components, international facilities?).
- research expenditure itself is calculated from various sources, with estimation procedures used to attribute the proportion of general university funding going into research being very variable (in form and in quality) across countries).
- lack of disaggregation by topic, except in very broad categories.
- lack of distinction between different types of support (e.g. for infrastructure or for specifically budgeted research).

These authors went on to attempt to develop superior statistics for the UK and five other countries, and their report describes these in great detail. Data are presented on academic research funded by general university funds, separately budgeted research, and a category of "academically related research". For IT-related activities, trend and comparative data are presented on academic and related R&D on electrical and electronic engineering, and on computer science. There may be some problems even yet in interpreting such data, since the criteria for assigning research to particular categories may differ across countries. (This may be a particular problem for computer-related research, since this often crosses disciplinary boundaries and involves elements of ergonomics, psychology, etc.) But it seems from these data that the UK and France are below West Germany, Japan and the USA in expenditure on electrical and electronic engineering (although the totals may not be so different on a per capita basis), and below the others (figures for Japan not available) for computing. Martin (1987) comments of the two closest European competitors that:

> "the lead that France and Germany now have is largest and growing most rapidly in those fields of basic research which would seem to have the greatest technological potential, such as physics, computer science, and biology." (p35)

The annual reports of the Research Councils provide some information on academic R&D, though use of these data is limited by their different reporting conventions and the change in their programme support and organisation year by year. The *Science and Engineering Research Council Annual Report* is evidently the most likely source of data, and this provides statistics on levels of support (applications considered, grants recommended, and numbers of fellowships of various types) for Information Engineering. Data are also provided on Alvey funds administered through SERC, and on studentships supported by the IT Directorate. Eggington (1987) discusses SERC's role in academic/industry links, from which we see that as well as the IT Directorate, SERC runs Application of Computers to Mechanical Engineering (ACME), and Teaching Company Programmes, Cooperative Research Grants, and cooperative awards in science and engineering. (He provides data on the distribution of these by industrial sector, with the "electrical" sector taking 30% of teaching programmes, being involved in 24% of cooperative grants, and being 22% of studentship award partners. The report provides data on ACME grants and studentships.) There is in the text of the report also a discussion of central computing arrangements (mainly supercomputers and support for the Joint Academic Network); and from other SERC sources (e.g. their 1985 *Corporate Plan*) it is clear that some SERC research areas (e.g. transport) are heavy IT users.

Other Research Councils do not bear so heavily on IT, though the ESRC's Programme on Information and Communication Technologies (which produced its own *Annual Report* for 1987-88) is featured in the *Economic and Social Research Council Annual Report*, and in the ESRC's 1988-93 *Corporate Plan* (1988), where PICT is estimated to account for 16.9% of directed research (itself constituting some 65% of all ESRC research funds) over the period 1988-93; other directed research covers "data issues and methodology" which includes the Data Archive and a Centre for Economic Computing among other activities. (We have already cited Melody and Mansell's study (1986) of ESRC IT research in Chapter 2.)

The Agricultural and Food Research Council (AFRC) provides no IT-relevant statistics in its report, although the 1986-87 report carries an extensive discussion on research into sensors in agriculture and food processing; the AFRC's Institute for Engineering Research, which carries out many projects with a high IT content, provides financial data in its 1986-87 report, and within the categories it uses (distinguishing between Department of Education and Science (DES) and Ministry of Agriculture, Fisheries and Food (MAFF) funds) are "control engineering and data communication" and "instrumentation and control in food processing, storage and distribution''. The Natural Environment Research Council's 1986-87 report provides information on expenditure on various fields of research: in ''The Solid Earth'' there are data for information and for computing, in ''The Seas'' for information services, and in ''Inland Waters'' and ''The Terrestrial Environment'' for scientific services, methods and information. The report also provides a detailed discussion of the various scientific services involved, which include scientific computing, administrative computing, image analysis, office systems, and network communications; and under the heading of ''planning and services'' are included remote sensing and thematic information systems (e.g. digital cartography).

3.2.2 Bibliometrics

The Research Council reports do try to give a flavour of the achievements of their work, typically by citing successful publications or applications based on their research. Furthermore, as noted above, efforts in recent years have intensified into establishing methods for quantifying research outputs, with bibliometrics proving a particularly popular approach. Bibliometrics mainly involves such methods as (1) counting the number of publications produced by named researchers, by particular research groups, by specific institutions, or even by the research communities of whole countries, in various fields of endeavour, and (2) mapping the citations that papers receive in other scientific papers. The key assumptions here are (1) that publications are a valid measure of scientific output, i.e. that the results of basic research are published (and, in some analyses, that thc volume of publications - perhaps qualified by the prestige of the publishing journal - corresponds to the research achievements), and, (2), that citations form a basis for estimating the impact of research (in terms of its addition of knowledge to the scientific community; again efforts may be made to elaborate on such assumptions, for example, by grading citations as to the importance of the journals in which they are located).

The data bases that contain such bibliometric information mainly deal, incidentally, with refereed journals, i.e. those that follow the main scientific quality-control procedures. Some data bases do cover also conference proceedings (which may well be particularly important in ''leading edge'' areas of IT R&D - artificial intelligence is one such field) and books. Most analyses are restricted to journal articles, however. There have been some suggestions that the main data bases are lagging somewhat behind the scientists, too, in that new journals (which may also incorporate a significant proportion of IT research) are not immediately incorporated into them. (Other challenges to validity are discussed in the bibliometric literature, such as biases in the selection of journals towards First World and English-language sources, and the neglect of research impacts in engineering and other applied fields.)

While some studies undertake original data production, most recent research has made use of the Institute for Scientific Information's *Science Citation Index*. Research conducted at SPRU has made use of data bases created from this source for the US National Science Foundation (by CHI Research), the *Science Literature Indicators Data-Base*. The SPRU researchers argue (Irvine et al., 1985, Martin et al., 1987) that these data bases form the most comprehensive and readily accessible sources of information on national research outputs. In these studies, they have set out to describe trends in British scientific outputs. The earlier paper covers the period 1973-82, the later 1976-84. The general picture they provide is one of relative decline in the UK's share of publications (as against large increases by Japan and smaller increases by several other countries - but decreases by West Germany and the USSR). Likewise, there is a decline in the UK share of citations.

These researchers discuss bibliometric trends in national performance in various fields of basic research as well as in aggregate data, and while the eight fields they give most of their attention to are too aggregated for us to identify an IT component, they also discuss subfields of research that are more useful for our purposes. A general conclusion was that British science is in general weak in areas of strategic technological significance, although electrical and electronic engineering features as one of the stronger subfields (with Britain gaining about 10% of world publications and citations in 1984), though apparently one whose global contribution is declining. An earlier study (Martin, Irvine and Turner, 1984) indicated declines in Britain's world share of publications from 1973-80 in an additional IT-related field, computer engineering.

Irvine (1987) describes the National Science Foundation data base, and provides a guide to its use. From this source we can see that among the subfields identified (c100), only the two mentioned above are clearly IT-related. Another problem with these data should also be noted: publications are classified as belonging to particular disciplines on the basis of the classification of the journal in which they appear. So some lines of IT research, reported in, say, physics journals, will remain hidden in these analyses.

3.3 Government Support for R&D

3.3.1 General Support

The *Annual Abstract of Statistics* provides data on R&D expenditures in the UK in general terms, but goes into some detail on government-funded R&D. One table covers trends in central government expenditure, distinguishing between intra-mural and extra-mural R&D, with a mixture of functional and institutional classifications of the research area. (Intra-mural R&D is that carried out within government institutions, extra-mural research is effectively that which is contracted out. At present, the total for the latter is around twice that of the former, although this varies considerably by research area - thus almost all energy research was intra-mural for the first half of the 1980s.) Another table details this net expenditure in terms of a set of European Community standard objectives such as ''protection and promotion of human health'' and ''exploration and exploitation of space''; it is not really possible to identify an IT component of research from these data.

The main source for statistics on government support for R&D, and one which the *Annual Abstract* substantially draws upon, is the Cabinet Office's *Annual Review of Government Funded Research and Development*, published by HMSO. This draws on data provided by the DTI, and for international comparisons, the OECD and the CEC. This contains both general data and material on the activities of different departments. The *Review* appears to be improving with each issue, and the description of topics covered below mainly concerns the 1986 issue; with changes in programmes and government departments, some differences in classification are also likely from year to year.

The first section of the report covers broad areas of government R&D activity:

- government R&D expenditure by department (the DTI is the largest single source of funds), objectives, programmes, types of research (including an effort to distinguish between basic, strategic, and specific applied research and experimental development);
- nationalised industries;
- industry research supported by government (compared with other sources);
- special topics (e.g. evaluation, activities related to R&D, employment data);
- R&D in CEC countries and CEC institutions;
- international comparisons.

As we would expect by now, the greater proportion of the tables presented do not provide material that can be directly interpreted as bearing on IT R&D. However, we are provided with a detailed breakdown of publicly funded R&D carried out in various industrial sectors - including EDP equipment, telephone and telegraph equipment, and active components - in terms of the source of funding. (However, the full sectoral breakdown is not given for all funding sources - it is available for the DTI and SERC, for example, but not for the Ministry of Defence (MOD).)

The comparisons among CEC countries are presented in terms of research areas which, as we have noted, do not distinguish IT - they focus more on objectives such as ''pollution'' and ''infrastructure''. But the OECD comparisons that are also included do feature ''transport and telecommunications'' as a socioeconomic objective - however, it constitutes a small proportion of total government R&D.

As for the different government departments for whom breakdowns are provided, several of these feature R&D on IT-related activities. Thus:

- for the MOD, classifications include electronic components, electronic technology, tri-service electronic systems.
- for the DES, information on the Microelectronics in Education Programme's expenditure.
- for the Department of Health and Social Security (DHSS), data on IT R&D expenditure in the National Health Service.
- for the Home Office, telecommunications research contracted out and work on new equipment for police and the legal system.
- for the DTI, information on R&D programmes in the areas of IT, electronics, telecommunications, and mechanical and electrical engineering, radio regulatory R&D, and support for industrial training and education that includes microcomputers and software in schools, Information Technology Education Centres (ITECs), Microelectronics Applications Programme, and others. Material is provided on the Alvey Programme, of which more below.
- for the Research Councils, there are no IT components to the ESRC, or the Natural Environment Research Council. The AFRC does feature ''computing, statistics, etc.'' as one of its areas; the Medical Research Council features ''development of equipment and techniques''; and the SERC contains several IT-related categories including ACME.
- for British Coal, expenditure on automation, mechanisation and management information systems (MIS) is cited.

More information on the DTI's research activities is provided in evidence given to the House of Commons Trade and Industry Committee (1988, volume 2), which provides tables on trends in DTI expenditure on awareness, training and consultancy, and on R&D, broken down by the three Divisions of the DTI responsible - IT, Electronics Applications, and Telecommunications & Posts. Some information is also presented on expenditures on the Alvey Programme, and there are notes on collaborative programmes in the UK , and on the CEC's ESPRIT and RACE programmes.

The Advisory Committee for Applied Research and Development (ACARD) is a source of specific reports that occasionally carry statistical data. The 1986 report *Medical Equipment* provides some data on DHSS-supported R&D (and on trade in equipment, including electromedical equipment); the 1979 *Joining and Assembly* discusses robotics and automation R&D, and so on. ACARD and the Cabinet Office both presented evidence to the House of Lords Select Committee reports noted earlier.

3.3.2 Major Programmes

As programmes typically have fairly limited life spans, and as they involve various degrees of sectoral and international coverage, it can be difficult to apprise statistics concerning them. Two useful reports have surveyed IT R&D programmes in different countries. The OTA (1985) provides (for US readers in particular) a succinct description of R&D data for a number of countries, within which there is a brief account of UK government programmes and an effort to provide data on their costs over time. General Technology Systems (1986) attempts to classify national programmes in terms of three objectives: advancing IT products, facilitating the application of IT, and supporting economic adaptation to IT; not surprisingly, there is some difficulty in assigning programmes to these objectives. In addition, PREST/SPRU (1987) attempt to compare expenditure of precompetitive R&D in the IT field for six countries.

The major UK IT programme, Alvey, was explicitly organised as precompetitive R&D support. It is unusually well-documented: in its *Annual Report*, in a newsletter *Alvey News*, and in a series of studies carried out by evaluation teams based at SPRU and at PREST (University of Manchester).

The *Annual Report* for 1987, for instance, carries data on the number of projects, the funds committed to them, the participation in projects of firms, universities, polytechnics, and "establishments" (e.g. government research laboratories). Data are disaggregated by the main components of Alvey research - VLSI, software engineering, intelligent knowledge-based systems, man-machine interfaces, large demonstrators, and communications. Several types of evaluation data are also included, among them a grading of the performance of the different projects on the basis of reports from Monitoring Officers. (These are on a five-point scale from "excellent" to "bad", in which the whole programme achieves a pretty good approximation of a normal distribution, but the VLSI and intelligent knowledge-based systems (IKBS) projects are clearly skewed towards excellence, with a less marked skew in the other direction for the two other projects.) Chapters of the report go into more detail on project area achievements and, in some cases, expenditure. Detailed statistics vary from year to year; thus in the 1986 report data are presented on the numbers of professional staff in universities and industry involved in the programme.

Alvey evaluation is still going on, but an interim report has been published (PREST/SPRU, 1987). This contains a variety of statistics, some culled from the Alvey Directorate itself (and its earlier publications), and some the results of original research by the evaluation teams. Eight project areas are identified in this report: architecture, VLSI, computer-aided design, software engineering, man-machine interface (in some cases more detail is provided here), IKBS, integrated circuits, and large scale demonstrators. Among the statistics included are:

- a breakdown of applications for support from Alvey, broken down by project area and classified as accepted, rejected or under consideration.
- contributions to these research areas by the DTI, SERC, and the MOD.
- data on projects per participant, and partners per project, by type of participant.

For international programmes, it is usually necessary to turn to the reports produced by their central teams. The main European programme, ESPRIT, has documented its expenditure and status, for instance (ESPRIT, 1987). The *Alvey Programme Annual Report* for 1987 contains an article detailing UK participation in the ESPRIT programme. The UK is shown to be involved in almost two-thirds of the 205 projects, with a relatively higher involvement in some project areas (e.g. microelectronics) and, of course, lower involvement in others (e.g. computer integrated manufacture). Data are provided on the number and identity of firms, universities, and research establishments involved in more than one project.

3.4 Industrial R&D

The *Annual Abstract of Statistics* provides data on R&D expenditures in industry, with a detailed breakdown of manufacturing industry and totals for each of extractive industries, mineral oil refining, other treatment of petrochemical products, construction, and utilities and services. (For each sector or branch there is a further disaggregation of expenditure as to whether it is carried out in private industry or elsewhere.) Again, the details and aims of the expenditure are not provided, but the sectoral breakdown does provide data for electrical and electronic engineering in total, and within this for key IT sectors such as telegraph and telephone apparatus, electrical instruments and control systems, radio and electronic capital goods, electronic consumer goods, and the "core" IT-producing branch of active components and electronic subassemblies. Data are also provided for the EDP equipment as distinct from office machinery.

Chapter 4 will discuss the definition of the IT-producing sector. By far the largest amount of R&D expenditure comes from the radio and electronic capital goods sector, followed by telephone and telegraph apparatus, with others lagging far behind.

Thus the hardware end of IT production appears to be relatively well covered, though the software and services branches are hidden within other areas of economic activity - unfortunately, since telecommunications service industries, for instance, carry out considerable R&D internally (although they may also seek to externalise this R&D to equipment suppliers).

The *Annual Abstract* also provides data at constant prices on intra-mural R&D expenditure of a smaller number of manufacturing sectors, in which electronics is distinguished from electrical engineering and five other sectors. From these data it is apparent that electronics R&D has grown very rapidly, far surpassing that of other sectors, over the last two decades.

This point is noted in an interesting discussion of UK electronics R&D by Soete and Dosi (1983): they display 1964-81 data graphically, and from this it appears that chemicals has increased its R&D (in constant prices) steadily; other sectors have declined or stagnated, while electronics has witnessed substantial bursts of growth, first in the mid-1960s, then from 1975 on. Shortly after 1975 its R&D surpassed that of aerospace, previously the largest of the six sectors covered; by 1981 it represented about one-third of all UK R&D expenditure recorded.

Soete and Dosi go on to compare UK data with those from other countries. They note the important contribution of government - and particularly defence - R&D funds in the British case, and warn that private R&D expenditure in electronics, fairly constant in Britain, has been growing in competitor countries. They are also able to cite OECD data indicating that "electronics" R&D may be carried out by firms from non-manufacturing sectors (about 20% of recorded R&D, mainly from communications) and from branches of manufacturing such as instrument engineering. (The DTI has provided data for 1981-86 comparing, in current and constant prices, industrial R&D expenditure on products of the "IT and electronics industry" to "all products of manufacturing industry". (House of Commons Trade and Industry Committee, 1988, volume 2 p13.))

These data are also discussed and updated by Soete (1985a). In the same volume, but in less detail, Guy (1985) outlines information on R&D in telecommunications in the UK, while Rendeiro (1985) discusses that for instrumentation.

Returning to official sources, *British Business* fairly often carries R&D expenditure and employment data in its "business trends" section (since this section has its own index, it is relatively easy to trace the most recent data). The DTI's R&D surveys are covered here, prior to full reporting in *Business Monitor* issues. The *British Business* issue of 5 February 1988 provides trend data for the sample of firms studied in a 1986 survey, for instance. These firms, 74 enterprises, account for about 75% of recorded industrial R&D in the UK, and data are presented in terms of the product groups involved. Again, the most dramatic increases in R&D are seen to involve IT; in current prices, over the 1980s:

> "R&D performed on active components and electronic sub-assemblies almost quadrupled. R&D on electronic dataprocessing equipment, and motor vehicles and parts, more than doubled. R&D on pharmaceutical products increased by more than three quarters."(p28)

Data are also provided by industrial group in constant and current prices - interestingly, the electronics sector's marked increase is now less than that recorded for electrical engineering (which grew more than twice as rapidly) and aerospace. Constant price data suggest a fairly steady increase in R&D over the period 1975-86, although over a longer period of time (1967-86) the proportion accounted for by industry itself has declined and then risen again (to 64% as compared to 1967's 67% - the low was 1972's 60%); the government's contribution has grown and then declined (to 23% from a 1972 peak of 33%); and the proportion from overseas sources has grown fairly steadily.

Other data in this report cover sources of funding, and break down expenditure on R&D into current and capital items. The latter increased more rapidly, while salaries rose more slowly than the total. Employment data, with staff classified as "scientists and engineers", "technicians, laboratory assistants and draughtsmen", and "administrative, clerical, industrial and other staff" are also provided. The data suggest a decline in overall R&D employment since the early 1980s, although the first of these three categories actually increased.

The apparent declines in several categories of R&D picked up in the DTI statistics have been the focus of some concern, given that innovation is seen as a major component of continuing competitiveness. The 27 February 1987 *British Business* suggested, ominously, that there had been a 10% decline in electronics R&D between 1983 and 1985 (while most other sectors were increasing). But this was on the basis of provisional data; when final results were published in the 24 July 1987 issue, an increase in electronics R&D was shown, with no explanation for the divergent results or the basis for the correction.Walker (1987) notes the substantial changes within *British Business* data; notably, the R&D attributed to mechanical engineering dropped while that going to electronic engineering increased, which leads him to suspect that some military-related R&D is being transferred from the former to "electrical instruments and control systems" within the latter. The growth of the latter might alternatively reflect efforts to estimate the activities of small firms better. In either case it might be conjectured that statisticians, aware that these data may be politically sensitive, are putting extra effort into them.

In considering whether the statistical record might be incomplete, there have been some suggestions that R&D in small firms has been wrongly assumed to be negligible - especially with the emergence of new IT-based enterprises - and that more attention should be directed towards activities in this sector. Whether this would account for apparent declines is another matter.

It may well also be that an increasing proportion of IT-related R&D - especially in software and IT services - is doubly hidden: it is not only that the R&D activities are of an unconventional form and thus evade classification, but also that they take place in sectors that are poorly studied with respect to R&D. We know of no appropriate UK analyses, but in the case of the USA, Alic (1988) suggests that the service sectors of the economy are generally drastically under-represented in R&D data. Having made a plausible case that this is indeed so, he presents Battelle Institute estimates that suggest that R&D expenditures by US services are perhaps 10 times larger than official estimates, and constitute over 25% of total R&D. Alic argues that statisticians have directed insufficient effort to defining and assessing service R&D, and that the growing role of services, and of IT as a means of securing competitive advantage within services, means that this problem will not go away.

One final issue which should be mentioned here is the regional distribution of industrial R&D. Here CURDS has engaged in a number of studies, the results of many of which are reported in Goddard, Thwaites and Gibbs (1986). We shall consider some of their research on innovations later; for now we should note that they report results from a survey of three sectors in which the presence of R&D effort was recorded, and note regional variations in R&D employment. (This seems to be concentrated in the South-east.) In the same volume Sayer and Morgan (1986) provide a discussion of regional features of the UK electronics industry.

3.5 Innovation Data

Applied R&D is meant to culminate in a flow of innovations, usually into the marketplace, though they may also be destined for public sector use, for use within the innovating organisation, or - in the case of some software, for instance - as "public domain" or "freeware". As bibliometrics uses publications as an indicator of scientific outputs, so patents have been used as a measure of applied R&D outputs, and we consider these below. In addition, some researchers have attempted to develop innovation measures from other data, such as expert judgements or trade sources.

3.5.1 Patent Data

Patent Offices have explored the use of computers for organising their administration for many years, but more recently the potential of this information as a source of innovation statistics has been recognised. Pavitt (1987b) has reviewed the main sources, applications, and limitations of patent statistics. Among the limitations of patent data are: (1) not all sectors have equal propensity to patent their innovations (different methods of protection of intellectual property are appropriate in different sectors and for products of different types); (2) unlike the scientific publishing field, there is no global patent community to which we can (notionally) refer, and innovators will be more or less inclined to patent in specific countries depending upon their assessment of local markets; (3) the two preceding points converge in creating national differences in propensity to patent in any specific patenting system, although there are arguments (reviewed by Pavitt) for and against foreign patenting as a measure of innovative activity.

As with citation data, the leading patent data bases are produced in the USA, in this case by OTA; and, once again, researchers at SPRU have obtained copies of the data for analysis (Hamed, Patel and Robson, n.d.). The OTA data cover the US patent system, which is likely to be a good source for the study of other countries, on account of the size of its market for innovative products. Data are available on the country of origin of the patent, the name of the company involved, and on the type of product involved, with US and SPRU classifications available. These classifications provide many groups of IT products.

For instance, the US system features (at the three-digit level):

- telecommunications;
- digital and pulse communications;
- telegraph;
- telephony;
- electrical computers and DP systems;
- image analysis;
- and many more (there are hundreds of categories at the three-digit level).

The SPRU classification (by Dosi) conveniently groups product types into major headings, of which the following are most relevant:

- telecommunications (includes telecommunications, special radio systems, and other electrical communication systems);
- electrical and electronic components, devices and systems (semi-conductors, electrical devices and systems, lamps and discharge devices);
- calculators, computers, other office equipment;
- image and sound equipment (TV and facsimile, acoustics);
- instruments, controls and office equipment n.e.s. (photography and photocopying, machine controls, electrical instruments etc., other instruments).

The scope for using such data to analyse innovative activities at the sectoral and firm levels is shown in Pavitt's review (1987b), and the OECD (1986a). As part of their review of UK electronics R&D, Soete and Dosi (1983) present data on UK patenting in the USA in the "office and computing equipment" and the "communication equipment and electronic components" fields. The share of all foreign patents in these fields contributed by the UK dropped from over 20% in the early 1960s to less than 10% in the early 1980s (a worse performance than the average for UK patents, leading the authors to suggest that the UK's comparative advantage in these areas has fallen to the point where its existence is doubtful).

(This talk of "revealed comparative technological advantages" can be misleading, however: in this case one is inferring an *input* situation (local skills and resources: the ability to make IT innovations) from an *output* indicator (patents proving that one has actually done so!). The input is thus supposedly revealed by the output; this is notable, in that it is more common to find the reverse chain of inference in social indicator research, so that expenditures or labour inputs are taken to signify the volumes of, for instance, service sector output. Additionally, we might remark that the term "comparative advantage" tends to imply a fixed state that may simply not exist.)

Soete (1985a) goes on to document trends for the UK, USA, France, Germany and Japan in patenting in telecommunications, electronics and instruments from the 1960s to the 1980s; he argues that the "relative advantage" of Japan is apparent in all these fields, while France performs well in telecommunications. US performance is better than the UK's, Germany's worse, although neither shows much variation over time. Soete also notes the identity of the main national firms patenting in these fields. Rendeiro (1985) discusses Office of Technology Assessment and Forecast (OTAF) data on UK scientific instrumentation patenting.

SPRU researchers, of course, have not had a monopoly of the analysis of UK innovative performance using patent statistics. Narin and Olivastro (1987) follow Soete in comparing UK patenting patterns in the USA with those of major competitors. As well as studying levels of patenting, these researchers study patent *citations*, i.e. how often UK patents are cited in subsequent patents. Like scientific citation data, this is an effort to develop an indicator of the quality or impact of the outputs of R&D.

Among statistics presented by these authors are data on the five countries' patenting activities (with categories such as communications; sensor, detector and testing; and IT employed). Data are provided on the patent classes where the UK achieves highest citation ratios. The study concludes again that UK presence in most electronics and IT classes is ''minimal'', though activity is noted in fibre optics and opto-electronics. Much the same pattern is recorded in patent citations (with optical couplers also being an area of UK achievement). The authors specifically cite ''electronics, computers and communications'' as ''areas of notable UK weakness'' (px, Executive Summary).

3.5.2 Other Innovation Statistics

While patent statistics have received the lion's share of attention in recent years, there have been various other approaches to identifying innovative outputs. One method is to attempt to identify national leads and lags - in which year were firms of country X able to produce a 512k RAM chip, for instance? This sort of approach, which involves determining the distance of different countries or firms from a technological frontier, has rarely been performed systematically (although it would seem to have considerable scope in the IT field).

Another approach is the effort to accumulate data on large numbers of discrete innovations, finding ways of identifying innovations which are sufficiently comprehensive for trends over time and across sectors to be analysed without the threat that sample biases will be undermining the validity of any results. This is no easy task, but a number of attempts have been made in this direction nonetheless.

Soete (1987) presents one type of data which he describes as approximating innovation ''bibliometrics'': statistics on innovations that received press coverage (c6,000 per year), classified into product type and sector of origin and potential use. An interesting result from the analysis of these data is that there is:

> ''significant difference in diffusion user potential between the various sectors...(s)ectors such as plastics, instruments and electronics see their innovations used over more than 30 sectors...Most 'diffused' appear the following: control systems (0.04), electronic capital goods (0.05), measuring instruments (0.08) and computer software (0.08). Most 'concentrated': construction equipment (-) mining and extraction equipment (2.59), agricultural machinery (1.66) and textile machinery (1.11)''

The figures cited are Herfindahl indices of concentration/diffusion. There are no data for construction equipment owing to division by zero (p208).

A similar picture of the pervasiveness of IT-related innovations (recall the discussion of "information society" themes in Chapter 1) is provided by another data source. In a number of studies using the SPRU Innovation Survey, Pavitt has argued that a growing impact of electronics innovations across the economy can be observed, just as other science-based innovations (notably chemicals) have previously achieved pervasiveness. While we might have reservations as to the data quality in both this survey and the data cited by Soete, their similar results suggests a measure of construct validation.

The SPRU Innovation Survey consists of data on more than 4,000 significant innovations in the UK over the period 1945-83. These data were compiled from the early 1970s on the basis of questionnaires sent to experts in various industrial fields (over 400 experts in all), and then to the firms which those experts had identified as engaging in specific innovations. Such data clearly have some problems, and it is likely that earlier innovations may be under-represented, and that some sectors - especially services - are poorly treated. Additionally, concepts of what constitutes innovation may be poorly developed, or developed in contradictory ways. However, the researchers have made considerable efforts to validate their data. (Robson et al. (1988) compare results from their survey with US patent-based studies. This paper clearly makes the point about the growing importance of electronics-based innovations.)

Using these data, Pavitt (Pavitt, 1986, Pavitt et al., 1988, Robson et al., 1988) distinguishes between several types of firm/sector: science-based (among which most IT-producers fall), scale-intensive, supplier-dominated and specialist suppliers. This categorisation implies different diffusion patterns for IT among different types of using sector, and also suggests that IT producers will share behavioural features with other science-based firms. Pavitt et al. (1988) test this point, in a manner that is indicative of the sorts of data that can be derived from the survey. They show that electrical and electronics firms tend to perform according to expectations: there is a relative emphasis on product innovations (sold to other sectors) as opposed to process innovations (for own production), there are higher threats of technology-based entry (constituted by a high proportion of electronics innovations coming from outside the sector), innovative science-based firms are relatively large, etc. In contrast, instrumentation has the characteristics of a specialised supplier sector.

In this latter study, data are presented for the electrical/electronics and instruments sectors on the following measures:

- number of innovations recorded, and percentage of these that are product innovations;
- ratio of innovations purchased to those produced;
- proportion of innovations made by firms from other three-digit SIC groups;
- average size of innovating firms (employment);
- principal activity of innovating firms, i.e. whether in the same three-digit category as the product, whether in the same two-digit group, and if not the latter, whether a user or non-user firm;
- proportion of firms' innovations falling outside their own two-digit activities.

The main problem with these data from our perspective is that the 1945-83 period will contain many non-IT innovations in the electronics and instrumentation field, especially prior to the development of semiconductors (see Chapter 1). It is possible to analyse shorter time periods, and indeed in one table the authors provide decade-long disaggregations of the areas of innovation of firms in different sectors. They also discuss other indicators available in the data base, for example data on the source of the innovation (research, development, design, operating staff, etc.) For basic information on this survey see Townsend et al. (1981); Rendeiro (1986) cites data from this source on the sectoral composition of firms producing and using instrument innovations.

Patel and Soete (1987) also use these data, providing a detailed breakdown of the activities of innovative sectors (more than 20 innovations recorded as produced or used 1945-83). They provide data on the numbers of innovations produced and used, the number of sectors adopting product innovations and the sectoral source of process innovations, whether innovations are used in manufacturing and/or services, etc. Like Pavitt they use this to construct a typology (this time clearly at a sectoral level), among which are:

- pervasive sectors (with very widespread impact, e.g. instruments, electronics, computers, robotics);
- localised sectors (with little impact on others, e.g. radio and TV equipment);
- user-dependent sectors (producing innovations mainly for a single sector, like Pavitt's specialised suppliers);
- user-influenced sectors (including telecommunications: the authors note that its latter-day pervasiveness may be greater than these data suggest);
- and a number of innovation-using sectors.

There are many other potential applications of such data. For instance, Goddard, Thwaites and Gibbs (1986) report analyses of the regional composition of innovations in the UK based on the SPRU survey, and also report results (regional issues again) of a smaller survey of product innovations in three sectors: metal work machine tools, scientific and industrial instruments, and radio and electronic components, for the period 1974-77. Another survey considered the uptake of five process innovations, all of them computer- or microprocessor-based, and the incorporation of microprocessors into products. The authors conclude that the South-east features more product innovations, and has better access to foreign sources of innovation.

These efforts to establish non-patent forms of innovation data are of considerable interest, for several reasons, not least in that they allow for the analysis of sources of innovation and of process innovations that may not be patented. More generally, they are free of the confounding factor of sectoral differences in propensity to patent, which may interfere with any comparisons between discrete IT-producing sectors (thus software is unlikely to be patented) or between IT and other sectors. However, they carry their own limitations, in that there may be sectoral differences in press coverage or expert awareness of innovations. This seems particularly problematic for services - and the innovations recorded tend to be hardware-based. And it may even be that in sectors and periods of rapid technological change, reporting of innovations is somewhat depressed owing to observers becoming inured to change and raising their thresholds in judging what constitutes significant innovation.

3.6 Conclusions

The conclusions that emerge from this, the first of our set of reviews of statistical sources and of the data which they yield, are similar to those that will emerge from subsequent chapters. It is apparent that a wealth of data exists, and that as yet little effort has been made to pull together the many statistics that bear on R&D in IT-related areas. However, it is also apparent that there has only been a limited amount of effort devoted to the task of critically examining available data in terms of their adequacy to depict current IT developments. Our preliminary analysis here suggests that these two objectives may usefully be carried out hand-in-hand; although idealised models of the research process may suggest that we should first construct our conceptual categories and only then seek to develop appropriate indicators, it seems that in practice there is often a more dialectical relationship. In this case, interrogation of existing data - asking questions that derive from a first theoretical appraisal, of course, since neither data nor research questions drop out of thin air - can help in the elaboration and specification of the conceptual approach.

A number of outstanding problems are already apparent in using available data to examine IT R&D. As we have seen, often these activities are subsumed under headings that encompass a range of activities, not all of which are IT-related. Software activities are barely tackled in industrial statistics; and this applies to "output" measures such as patents as well as to measures of expenditures and other inputs. This latter problem is one that is particularly acute in the IT area, since the programmability and interactive capabilities of IT mean that many innovations will be hard to copyright or protect using traditional means.

IT in some respects here exemplifies a common difficulty with economic and technological statistics: though there has been a shift in the economy toward service-type activities (of which software is merely one instance), our statistics are still mainly oriented towards manufacturing sectors and their products. In this chapter we have noted the likely inadequacies of service sector R&D data, but later chapters will note similar problems in other areas of statistics.

4 The IT Heartland

4.1 Introduction: Defining the IT Sector

This chapter focuses on data and data sources concerning the "IT heartland": those industries directly concerned with producing IT. There have been many efforts to define an "IT sector", with authors taking more or less narrow, more or less electronics-based approaches. (Soete (1987) reviews several of these, although he does not completely distinguish in his account between an "IT sector" and an "information sector".) We shall discuss some of these approaches, highlighting sources that provide helpful perspectives and data on the heartland IT-producing sector.

In one of the best accounts of the newly emerging IT sector, focused mainly on the UK, Soete (1987) discusses:

(1) *An IT-producing sector*: Manufacturing activities such as data-processing equipment, telegraph and telephone apparatus and equipment, active components, radio and electronic capital goods, passive components, and other electronic equipment. Service activities such as telecommunications, computer services.

(2) *A predominantly IT-using sector*: Manufacturing: metal working machine tools, precision engineering, measuring and precision instruments, printing and publishing, photo cinematographic processing. Services: banking, insurance, other business services, R&D, radio and TV.

Soete provides data on trends in employment in Great Britain for these sectors over the period 1981-85. The "IT-producing sector" grew both in total and as a proportion of GB employment. However, in 1985 it constituted only 3.3% of employment, and the growth was low on the manufacturing side (c2% over the period) while that of services was actually negative (around -0.1%). The "IT-using sector" contributed considerably more to employment (15.3% in 1985) and grew in total, but while its services component grew rapidly (about 7% over the period), its manufacturing share actually declined (by almost 0.9%) In terms of contribution to Gross Domestic Product (GDP), this total "IT sector" provides more than the remainder of manufacturing, and Soete shows that both his IT manufacturing and IT services showed impressive and relatively stable growth over the period 1978-84 (during which there was a decrease in residual manufacturing output and a marked fluctuation in that of services).

This is an interesting study, and one which reviews a great deal of evidence on the development of IT (not all of it British: US data are used for diffusion trends). It provides a salutary note on the relatively small size of the IT-producing sector - and Soete's definition of this may be too wide in some respects (though in some ways also too narrow). But the definition of the "IT sector" as a whole is certainly too wide, especially insofar as it encompasses both IT producers and IT users. Quantitatively, a large share of the employment and output, and a large contribution to the growth trends, is being provided by user sectors such as finance and business services. The relation between their growth and their use of IT is well worth exploring, but may it not be an historically contingent one? As other sectors increase their IT-intensity, should they too not be considered "predominantly IT-using sectors"? (What is "predominant" in any case - using IT more than other sectors? depending on IT to a critical extent? being users based in the information sector?)

We would prefer to exclude IT-using sectors from a discussion of the IT sector, on the grounds that all sectors are potentially IT-users. If the IT revolution takes its expected course, all sectors will be, even if some are much heavier users than others. Attention then has to focus on the IT heartland, on those sectors that produce the core IT components and products that other sectors can use. Here too we may quibble with some of Soete's decisions: why include passive components, for example, which generally involve pre-microelectronic technology (as opposed to active components)? Why include "other electronic equipment", while excluding "measuring and precision instruments"? It will become apparent in the course of the discussion that many IT-using sectors are also engaged, to some extent, in IT production. Thus software is written extensively in large user organisations - meaning that Soete may have a point in that high IT-users are also often software producers. We will henceforth use the terms heartland IT-producing sectors to indicate those sectors *devoted* to these activities.

Let us consider how other authors approach the definition of this sector. The NEDO's Electronics EDC (and later its IT EDC) have tackled this in a number of reports (NEDO 1982a, b, 1983b, 1984). NEDO (1983b) adopts a definition used in several studies of trends in output, employment and trade. This resembles Soete's IT-producing sector: it constitutes "the manufacture and supply of computers (hardware and software), telecommunications and office equipment" (p2). In fact, the data on computers (not surprisingly) also encompass peripherals; but not all the office equipment is necessarily IT in an electronics- or microelectronics-based definition.

NEDO (1982a) also sees IT in terms of the convergence of computing, office systems and telecommunications. "The 'core' building blocks of IT are, broadly, the *supplying sectors* of computer hardware and software, data communications and telecommunications equipment, and electronic office equipment; and the *applications sectors* of administration and operational control...financial transactions...and information collection and distribution services" (p24, emphasis in original). This approach seems to be echoing Soete's producer/user distinction, but the statistical section of the report breaks down the activities of the UK electronics industry into components (PQ364), consumer products (PQ365.2), electronic capital equipment (PQ354 and 367) and IT (PQ366, 363, 338, 351 and SDQ9). Several significant qualifications to the data are noted: employment data for consumer products include records and tape manufacture; 40% of the electronic capital equipment sector is MLH 354 (scientific and industrial instruments and systems, of which around 40% is electronic, but accurate disaggregation is impossible with available data); of PQ351 photocopies only are included, and for SDQ9 (computer services) no reliable import data exist.

The latter NEDO report also delves deeper into core technologies and components that underpin equipment capability. It cites the following areas of activity (not all clearly demarcated manufacturing sectors): components and microelectronics; opto-electronics; displays; sensors; other devices and technologies (interconnect systems, human-machine interface systems); systems and software; computing technology; and CAD. Its Appendix A provides an interesting view of the segmentation of the UK electronics industry, and the text provides a lucid and brief, but unfortunately dating account of the UK electronics industry.

In what is probably the closest approach to that which we shall take, the "IT Industry" is defined by the Secretariat of the UN's Economic Commission for Europe as comprising five main sectors (one of which is further subdivided):

- semiconductor industry
- computer industry
- software industry
- telecommunication equipment industry
- telecommunication services (divided into regulated and unregulated).

This definition, it will be seen, follows that which we began to elaborate in Chapter 1: it includes the IT "heart" (semiconductors, manufacturing the key heartland technologies of ICs and microelectronics, and related products), and the wider IT "core" manufacturing and service industries involved in supplying computer and telecommunication goods and services, and enabling the use of these products by providing the software, networks, etc. which they require.

The relevant industry groupings within which these core IT activities are located are quite variable. At the two-digit level of the SIC these are 33 (office equipment and data processing: the computer industry is located here), 34 (electrical and electronic engineering: includes the telecommunications equipment industry, the semiconductor industry, and also instrumentation and consumer electronics) 79 (posts and communications: includes telecommunications services, except some VANS classified as computer services) and 83 (computer services: includes software industry, time-sharing computers, and some online services).

In the light of our definition of IT (Chapter 1) it could be argued that not all these sectors have always been IT sectors. For instance, certainly telecommunications has always handled information, but the industry existed long before modern electronics, let alone microelectronics. If Babbage had succeeded in building his mechanical analytical engine in the 19th century we might have been able to speak of a pre-electronic computer industry too, and even so the computer industry was initially based on valves - though its real take-off follows on the use of ICs. In many respects these two manufacturing sectors have been "informatised" themselves; IT has penetrated them particularly rapidly and deeply on account of their *raison d'être* being information processing. They are justifiably located within the "core" IT sector since their products are now practically always based on microelectronic components, and provide IT power very broadly to other sectors of the economy (as opposed to those sectors producing, say, industrial robots or machine tools, consumer goods or aircraft control systems). Our analyses of UK data suggest that they are outstanding in terms of their current consumption of integrated circuits (i.e. their embodiment of IT heartland products in their own products).

4.2 Statistics on the Heartland IT-Producing Sectors

4.2.1 Introduction: Basic Sources

As we have noted, annual Census of Production data for manufacturing industries, coded to the SIC (80) three-digit level, appear as *PA* issues of *Business Monitor*, *PQ* and *PM* series reporting quarterly and monthly data respectively. One of the *Business Monitors* dealing with service industries covers, as we shall see, an IT-producing sector. Chapter 2 described the types of data appearing in *Business Monitors*.

IT-producing sectors covered by *Business Monitors* include:

PA330 office machinery (PQ3301), electronic data-processing equipment (PQ3302);
PA344 telegraph and telephone apparatus and equipment (PQ3441); electrical instruments and control systems (PQ 441); radio and electronic capital goods (PQ3443); electronic components (other than active) (PQ3444);
PA345 electronic sub-assemblies and active components (PQ3453);
PA345 electronic consumer goods and miscellaneous equipment (PQ3454);
SDQ9 computer services (quarterly).

Notably, telecommunications services do not appear in these series, although a panel of VANS providers do provide data in SDQ9. Meanwhile, the list above certainly does not exhaust the set of industries whose output may have a large IT component - i.e. embodying microelectronics in their devices. Such cases include: PQ 351 (photographic and document-copying equipment), PQ 368 (electrical appliances primarily for domestic use: this mainly covers items like cookers and refrigerators), PDQ 369.1 (electrical equipment for motor vehicles, cycles and aircraft), and a whole series of industries concerned with the manufacture of machinery for handling production processes in other sectors, and generally falling within the grand category of "mechanical engineering".

Chapter 2 also drew attention to a series of other issues of *Business Monitor* from which data on IT industries can be extracted. These include *PA1002* (summary tables from the Annual Census of Production), *PA1003* (the size distribution of UK businesses) *PO1006* (the product concentration of UK manufacturers), and *MO12* (import penetration and export sales ratios for over 200 sectors of manufacturing).

Also of considerable interest is *PO1008*, the *Purchases Inquiry*. This provides data on the purchases of branches of industry (with purchasers disaggregated to four-digit level activity headings). This source can be used to analyse current purchases (i.e. not investment in fixed capital) by and from IT sectors of the economy. Let us consider it in a little more detail.

First, what are the limitations of the data? Three main limitations are apparent. (1) Only manufacturing sectors are displayed as purchasers, and no purchases of IT services are recorded. (2) The classification of purchases is not completely standardised across sectors, with more detail being given on those items that are believed by the statisticians to be more significant for the sectors in question. And (3) since we are dealing here with purchases that are either "consumables" or embodied physically into the products of the industry, some IT categories, representing investment goods, are rarely represented - thus, only the EDP sector is recorded as purchasing computer equipment, only the telephone and telegraphy equipment industry telecommunications goods!

What are provided, however, for a great many sectors - presumably those where the purchases are sufficiently substantial for it to be worth while recording them - are data on current purchases of a number of IT products. Sales of "active electronic components", and usually of integrated circuits within this, are provided for several sectors, for instance, and this gives us some insight into definitions of the IT-producing sector. Sectors recorded as purchasing ICs in the 1984 edition (the most recent published) are, in the order of magnitude of these purchases as a proportion of their total purchases:

- telephone and telegraphy equipment manufacture
- EDP manufacture
- consumer electronics
- radio and electronic capital goods
- electronic instruments
- alarms and signalling equipment
- electronic equipment for industry and commerce n.e.s. (Manufacture of active components itself is not portrayed as consuming ICs, but data are provided on its use of semiconductor materials.)

Using the *Purchases Inquiry*, it is possible to establish the purchases of passive electronic components and "other electrical and electronic equipment" (apparently excluding some basic electrical goods in most cases), which makes it possible to calculate indicators of the "IT-intensity" and "electronics-intensity" of different sectors. Around 20 sectors devote more than 20% of their current expenditure to electronic equipment as widely defined.

Business Monitor is a major source of information, as we have seen, on IT-producing sectors. But a number of other sources provide data in convenient form, and these should not be overlooked. Chapter 3 discussed sources of R&D data, and so these will not be considered here.

The DTI's evidence to the House of Commons Trade and Industry Committee (volume 2, 1988; some key data from the DTI and from Electronics International Corporation are displayed in volume 1) covers a range of IT topics. Most relevant to the present discussion are data on trends (variously from 1978-86 and 1980-86) in UK production, sales and trade in EDP equipment, telecommunications equipment, office machinery, electrical instruments and control systems, radio and electronic capital goods, electronic sub-assemblies and active components, components other than active, and electronic consumer goods etc.; some data are also presented on computer services and and overall "IT and electronics". We earlier discussed NEDO's approach to the "IT sector"; here we should note that NEDO (1983b, 1984) bring together earlier data on this topic, stressing especially the rapidly developing trade deficit in IT products as so defined.

Among the official publications that bring together data covering branches of the IT-producing sector, attention should be drawn to the Engineering Industry Training Board's (EITB) *Economic Monitor*. This is published three times per annum, and pays particular attention to trends in training and labour markets for the engineering industries. Many of its tables and charts depict "electrical, electronic and instrument engineering" as a distinct sector, and a section of the *Monitor* describes recent developments in output, productivity, training, employment, skill shortages and business optimism. Some tables in a statistical annexe distinguish between the three components of this sector, and data on office and EDP equipment may also be displayed. The EITB also produces *Sector Profiles* on an occasional basis, which assess various components of the engineering industry in more detail, again with a focus on the workforce and training. Lawson (1985), for instance, discusses developments over the period 1978-84 in the office machinery and EDP equipment industry, considering employment by occupation, sex, size group and region, and presenting some trends on training; there are also brief analyses of the output of the sectors, and of their trade performance.

McKinsey (1988), in one of three reports on UK electronics prepared for NEDO's Electronics Industry Sector Group, presents data covering seven sectors; these include electronic components, computers and automation, consumer electronics, software, telecommunications equipment and instruments, and defence and aerospace electronics. A great deal of the focus of this study involves comparing UK electronics markets with those in competing countries, and considering the circumstances of a number of leading companies in the UK, Europe, N America, Japan and Korea. Estimates are drawn from various consultants and from the target companies' own reports, and statistics include:

- 1976 and 1986 levels of electronics production in the UK and six other countries;
- trends in the UK electronics market and balance of payments deficit in this area 1976-86;

- the share of the UK and world electronic markets accounted for by the UK target companies;
- the profitability of the target companies *in toto*, and the UK companies' debt and cash positions.

The McKinsey report drew an angry response from at least one of the UK companies, but some of its conclusions, at least, are apparently substantiated rather well by these data. The UK electronics market is portrayed as being rather healthy, growing more rapidly than the world average and that of most competitors; but while the UK electronics industry has benefited from this, its competitive performance has declined. Thus non-UK companies have benefited particularly from the market growth, while UK companies have not fared notably well in international markets. In the course of developing prescriptions for strategy for the sector, the authors provide further interesting data on a number of topics additional to those mentioned above, for example, target companies' reliance on defence contracting, the geographic breakdown of their sales, and their size and sectoral focus (number of sectors in which active). The study thus proves a useful source on the major companies operating in the UK IT-producing sectors.

Moving to academic sources, a study by Soete and Dosi (1983) provides a convenient (if rapidly dating) summary of much official data on the UK electronics industry in general, and also contains some new reworkings of official and academic data. In particular, it provides sectoral breakdowns of R&D, employment, and labour and capital productivity, and provides forecasts of employment and occupational trends. The authors note various data limitations, and argue that the electronics sectors are displaying a pattern of innovation which may well diffuse to other sectors in the future. Not surprisingly, the application of IT is advanced in electronics itself, and takes the form of increased capital productivity, "materials-saving technical change" which can substantially reduce costs and increase growth prospects. Soete (1985a) also covers some of this ground, with Guy (1985) addressing telecommunications and Rendeiro (1985) instrumentation.

We now turn to sources of data on the main components of the heartland IT-producing sectors.

4.2.2 Electronic Components and Instruments

Business Monitor PA345 is a basic source on these branches of activity. However, it covers "miscellaneous electronic equipment", and this involves branches:

- 3452: gramophone records and prerecorded tapes.
- 3454: consists of two groups - (a) active components (this includes the IT "heartland" technologies of ICs, as well as thermionic valves (includes cathode ray tubes (CRTs)), electronic optical devices, diodes, transistors, piezoelectric and quartz crystals, etc.); (b) electronic sub-assemblies and components, mainly for electronic consumer goods (e.g. aerials, speakers, and tuners and tape decks when these do not form substantially complete systems).
- 3453: also consists of two groups - (a) electronic consumer goods (radios, TVs etc.); (b) other electronic equipment n.e.s. (Note that electronic consumer goods are distinguished from electrical household appliances, such as vacuum cleaners and washing machines, which form a separate sector; but some electronic consumer goods are missing from this group, e.g. watches (in 374), electronic organs and music synthesisers (492), hearing aids (3443).)

Thus the "heartland" IT-producing branch is mixed together with some very different areas of production in this basic source. Disaggregation to the four-digit level is provided for only some of the data - output and costs, capital expenditure, stocks and works in progress, and operating ratios. From these data it is apparent that branches 3453 and 3454 are substantially bigger than 3452 (though, in keeping with the image of the entertainments sector, 3452 notches up considerably higher value-added per employee). Branch 3453 is slightly larger than 3454 in terms of number of enterprises, sales of goods and output (1985 data); it has more than twice as many enterprises as 3452 but (reflecting the small size of enterprises in the latter) about eight times the sales and output. Interpreting data for the "heartland" IT-producing sector is made difficult owing to its being compounded in some tables with electronic consumer goods and the record industry, and even where there are four-digit disaggregations, it is confounded with the sub-assembly industry which is also oriented to consumer goods.

Some related branches of activity, furthermore, are treated in other *Business Monitors*. *PA344* includes as well as telecommunications equipment (of which more later):

- 3442: electrical instruments and control systems (covering electrical and electronic meters, instruments, control devices, etc.). (Inspection of other sectors reveals that electrical and electronic measuring and checking instruments are included here rather than in sector 371, and so are electronic photographic exposure meters - but not lasers - while electronic timing devices appear to be classified with clocks, watches and other timing devices in 374.)

- 3443: radio and electronic capital goods (including, as well as transmitters, studio equipment etc., X-ray and electromedical apparatus, navigational aids, and others). (Inspection of other sectors indicates that aerospace electrical and electronic equipment will be classified here or in 3442 rather than with other aerospace equipment in 364.)
- 3444: components other than active components, mainly for electrical equipment (resistors, capacitors, printed circuits, etc.).

Of these, 3443 has roughly the same number of enterprises but more than twice the sales or output, and substantially more value-added per employee, than the other two. It is exceeded only on the latter measure by the telecommunications equipment sector 3441 (which has many fewer enterprises but produces around 50% more than the other two).

Finally, *Business Monitor PA343* covers electrical equipment for industrial use, batteries and accumulators. Within this sector we find 3433, which incorporates *inter alia* electronic burglar and fire alarms and traffic signals. It will be recalled that "alarms and signals", together with consumer electronics and instruments, is one of the few branches recorded as consuming ICs. For some purposes we might wish to include this, too, in the IT-producing sector.

It will be apparent that documenting the IT-producing sector from these sources is no easy task. We are provided with some basic data, but the disaggregations are imperfect. Table 4.1 presents some comparative statistics (for 1985) on key branches here.

Business Monitor PO1006 (1980) shows that in the 1970s, there was a high degree of concentration in most sectors manufacturing, and most product groupings of, electronic components. The concentration seems rather less for the new IT products than for longer-established electronics, at this period, perhaps reflecting new entrants into less mature markets; thus the top five firms accounted for 95.5% of sales in valves and 86% of sales in diodes and rectifiers, but only 74.8% of sales in transistors and semiconductors and 74.0% of those in integrated circuits.

A useful source of comparative international data is the two-volume *Annual Review of Engineering Industries and Automation* by the United Nations' Economic Commission for Europe, published since 1981. The second volume of this report contains statistical tables with data similar to those included in *Business Monitors*. The first volume contains a more discursive analysis, with less systematic tables - some of which are, however, very useful. (for instance on the production of numerically

Table 4.1

IT-Producing Branches (1985)

	Number of Enterprises	Sales (in millions)	Net Value-added per Employee (k)
3302	887	3,453	7.6
3441	261	1,691	18.8
3442	805	1,094	15.2
3443	802	2,974	17.3
3453	528	1,359	16.9
3454	476	1,239	11.1

Note:
3453-Active Components and Sub-assemblies;
3454-Electronic Consumer Goods;
3441-Telecommunications Apparatus;
3442-Electrical Instruments & Control Systems;
3443-Radio & Electronic Capital Goods;
3302-EDP equipment.

Source: various *Business Monitors* (see text)

controlled (NC) metal-cutting machines in different countries, and on trade in electromedical equipment). The data are drawn from several sources, including enquiries to national statistical offices.

4.2.3 Computers

Business Monitor PA330 covers the sectors 3301 (office machinery) and 3302 (electronic data-processing equipment). It is notable that some microelectronic-based devices are excluded from "office equipment": facsimile machines (put in telecommunications manufacturing, 344), document copiers and microform/microfilm cameras and readers (which are assigned to 373). Sector 3302 does not include computer systems which are inseparable from industrial process control systems (assigned to 344), but *does* include computer peripherals and sub-assemblies (including specialised tape-recording devices).

The EDP component of this sector is revealed as being considerably larger than the office equipment component. There are roughly six times as many firms operating, according to the 1986 data, producing some 10 times the gross output with five times the number of employees. (One interesting feature of the branch comparison is that the average wages and salaries in the EDP branch are lower than those in office machinery, although value-added per capita is over twice as high in the former.)

PA330 presents trend data aggregated by the two sectors, and a number of comparisons between them on the same parameters. The basic statistics include, as usual, data on output and costs; capital expenditure; stocks and work in progress; employment levels and labour costs; regional distribution of employment, capital expenditure and output; and operating ratios. Given the dominance of EDP in the sector, even those data that are not disaggregated into the two branches may be taken as a rough guide to the EDP production.

Business Monitor PO1006 (1980) provides data on the industry and product concentration in computers. The top five firms accounted for 83.6% of sales in computer systems in 1977.

The EITB (1986) has produced a sector profile of the "Office Machinery and EDP Equipment Industry" which brings together data (mainly on employment issues) concerning Activity Headings 3301 and 3302 over the period 1978-84. (AH 3301 only accounts, it is noted, for a small part of the industry activity, and has displayed a precipitous drop in employment and a decline in output, while employment in AH 3302 has fluctuated over the period and output doubled.) Many of these data are derived from the EITB's own returns; other data on trade performance , output and sales are drawn from *Business Monitor* (MQ10) and *British Business*. The employment data are particularly interesting in that they are broken down by gender and by occupational group for the two industrial sectors. About 28% of the labour force are described as professional engineers, scientists and technologists, and technicians.

4.2.4 Software and Computer Services

A quarterly *Business Monitor*, *SDQ9*, describes the results of a quarterly sales enquiry of the computer services industry. This includes as well as software activities, computer processing - VANS and data-base services and remote processing of batch jobs, for example - and other related professional services (independent consulting, data preparation, facilities management, etc.)

SDQ9 warns that it presents the results of a voluntary enquiry, and thus does not provide comprehensive data. As a guide to trends, however, it is also limited in that the changing structure of the industry is reflected in changed composition of the set of contributing companies (around 200 companies contribute). Comparisons between an old and new panel (the new panel being established by a recruitment drive in early 1986) are available. Data on billings (to foreign clients, parents and associates, and other UK clients; data on billings to the public services are reported each fourth quarter) are provided on a quarterly basis. They are disaggregated into four main headings, in each of which there are two or three subheadings. These are:

- bureau services (data-base services; VANS; other services)
- software (bespoke software; software products; software support/ maintenance)
- hardware (hardware; hardware maintenance);
- other professional services (independent consulting; education and training; other computing services).

The software sector is roughly twice the size of each of the others, whose own sizes in terms of total billings are remarkably similar; bespoke software dominates the activities of the firms reporting here. Data are also provided on the value of software sales (including software "bundled" with hardware).

Information on the personnel is provided, broken down into full- and part-time staff, by the four headings listed above. The first two headings are of roughly similar size in terms of full-time employment, and this is about twice that of the latter two (again of roughly similar size). The software sector is remarkably dominant in its employment of part-time staff; perhaps this reflects the inclusion of the better-known "home-working" companies in the sample. More detailed employment data are provided each fourth quarter. These are broken down by full- and part-time workers, and into functions (consultancy, programming/analysis, computer operating, data control, data preparation, administration, selling, and others).

In the Introduction to this volume, we noted conflicting estimates stemming from the DTI and the CSA as to the size of software activities in the UK. In October 1988 it was reported that the DTI was considering altering its data production in this area "because of fears that the present system leads to an understatement of the output index...a DTI report on the latest figures for the sector...showed a sharp slowing in growth last year..industry output rose by only 5 per cent in 1987 compared with an annual average growth rate of 18 per cent over the 1978 to 1986 period...Almost all the measures of progress in the industry... showed a slowing from previous years...The DTI warns that the figures, compiled from...a voluntary panel of 220 contributors, do not provide a comprehensive picture of activity in the industry." (Dodsworth, 1988)

Business Monitor PA1003, based on VAT returns, also provides information on computer services (which, as we have seen, is somewhat wider than the software industry alone). There is a breakdown by turnover size of the number of companies active in the field.

As with several other IT-producing sectors, software activities are regularly reported on by industry associations. The CSA provides information on the software sector through a number of channels. Its *Annual Report* details revenues and trends in revenues by the business sector of member firms and by employment levels, trends in employment and business activities, and sales of hardware and overseas sales. In a management guide to using microcomputers - which provides some useful data on the microcomputer industry in the UK - Lewis (1984) provides data on the proportions of software packages devoted to specific purposes. (He covers available business software packages, used for at least six months in a minimum of five sites - but some US-originating software seems to be excluded.)

A series of official and officially commissioned studies on the software sector has appeared in the last few years. In 1986 ACARD produced its report *Software: a vital key to UK competitiveness*. This contains a number of tables drawn from the CSA and other sources: one figure shows that the growth of revenue in the sector is notably high even when compared to energy and finance. CSA data are reproduced on the sources of revenue for the UK industry, and other data display trade deficits (for 1983 and forecast for 1990), etc. However, this report was widely seen as depicting a gloomy future for the UK software industry. A subsequent report for the DTI (Coopers & Lybrand, Department of Trade and Industry, 1987) produced a more optimistic appraisal. It explicitly disagreed with the ACARD report's diagnosis that problems in the industry reflected its custom/service-based orientation (as evidenced by the high proportion of activity devoted to bespoke software) and that there should be a shift to a software products-oriented industry. For present purposes, the study is of interest in presenting considerably more statistical material - especially cross-national comparisons - than did the ACARD report. As well as setting out the size and structure of the market for computing services in different countries, information is presented on the concentration of the industry in the UK, France, and the USA, on the importance of overseas revenues to the leading companies in these countries; UK companies tend to be smaller than in France or the USA, and this is seen as potentially inhibiting overseas expansion (though the British firms are growing more rapidly than the French).

Many of the data in this report are attributed to IDC and Coopers & Lybrand's own research; their publication with a DTI logo and no disclaimer suggests that the figures are at least regarded as reasonable ball-park estimates. In some cases this is all they can be, since one aim of the study is to depict the next decade of evolution of UK computing services. (For instance, the sector is seen to continue to grow as a percentage of Gross National Product (GNP) - to over 1% - but with a slackening growth rate.)

A third major study has been prepared by the Centre for Business Studies at London Business School (Grindley, 1988), drawing upon a set of earlier reports prepared for the Alvey Directorate. A major objective of the study is evaluation of Alvey software activities - of which it is critical in the light of developments in the software sector. It also provides a detailed account of the software industry in the UK, and contrasts this with the US market and (in less detail) those of West Germany, France and Japan. Trends in the industry are identified, such as the shift from custom and in-house systems to packaged solutions, and a move to more complex integrated systems; neither of these trends is seen as giving much room for complacency on the part of the British industry.

Much of the data is drawn from sources such as the CSA or the National Computing Centre (NCC), and from consultancy reports such as those of IDC, with some original material on the age and size distribution of

UK independent software companies. The various tables presented in this report provide convenient summary views of the scale and structure of software markets and suppliers in the UK. We learn, for instance, that software purchases were running at around a third of the level of hardware purchases in DP expenditure in the UK in 1983 - and that together they add up to only a little more than the expenditure in-house on staff.

This last point raises an issue that is more significant for software than for any other IT-producing sector. This is that (despite the increasing use of packages) a large volume of software production and maintenance is carried out in-house, by programmers and systems analysts employed by IT-using sectors. These activities are largely if not completely neglected in most studies of computing services, yet they constitute a substantial volume of IT activity. Occupational data can throw light on these activities, at least insofar as they are carried out by IT professionals.

4.2.5 Telecommunications

Wall and Nicholson (1986) provide a guide to *Posts and Telecommunications Statistics*. Unfortunately their discussion of sources was evidently subverted while in its final stages of preparation by changes in telecommunications systems and regulations in the UK; thus much of the discussion refers to pre-privatisation BT and to more traditional telecommunications services. Nevertheless, it still provides an excellent pointer to many sources of information (e.g. on employment and output), and is a model of how such a guide might in future be constructed.

Recalling our earlier discussion, telecommunications equipment and telecommunications services - both basic and enhanced or value-added - need to be considered. In the words of the OECD (1988):

> "(t)he telecommunications sector, broadly defined, is both a service activity and a manufacturing industry. Telecommunications, which is limited in the present study to point-to-point communications...- and therefore excludes broadcasting - includes:
>
> - The production of equipment (switching, transmission and terminal equipment) which interconnect to provide the infrastructure and networks for telecommunications services;

- The infrastructure for the provision of universal telecommunications services on a national and international basis (voice, telex, telegraphy);
- The networks and equipment for enhanced telecommunications services (voice, data, video, and facsimile) which are based on the convergence of computer and telecommunications technology..." (p9)

We shall go along here with the exclusion of broadcasting from this sectoralisation. But it should be noted that the convergence of broadcasting and telecommunications - as reflected in the use of cable TV systems for telephony (e.g. Windsor Cable in the UK is offering telephone services to subscribers), and the use of broadcast media for data broadcasting (teletext systems are being used to transmit price data to UK stores) - may render this increasingly problematic.

In the UK at the time of writing, telecommunications equipment is manufactured by a number of private firms (not all of them clearly in the appropriate SIC sector); basic network services are provided by British Telecom and Mercury only, although several firms are providing private lines for business communications and the cable TV consortia's systems have the potential for use for telephony; and value-added services are provided by a large number of suppliers including BT itself (with, for example, Prestel and Telecom Gold).

Telecommunications Equipment

Equipment consists of three main classes, and again the OECD (1988) provides a useful definition:

> "- Transmission equipment (e.g. equipment for carrier systems, line apparatus for long-distance communications, radio relay equipment, microwave systems, apparatus for signal conditioning of satellites): that is, equipment which functions to forward information. Cables and wire (including fibreoptics) can be included under this heading or as a separate branch;
> - Switching equipment (e.g. exchanges, other switching equipment, switchboards, packet mode switching and circuit switched data network equipment);
> - Customer premises equipment (e.g. telephone handsets, key systems, private branch exchanges, data terminals) which is sometimes referred to as terminal equipment." (p10)

Customer premises equipment is known in the USA as CPE. A distinction is commonly made within the telecommunications equipment market between public switching equipment and private switching equipment.

BT is the main UK purchaser of public switching and transmission equipment. Its investment programmes have a substantial impact on annual statistics. The main development here over recent years has been the shift to digital exchanges.

Business Monitor PA344 covers the telephone and telegraph equipment manufacturing sector (3441), together with - as we have seen above - electrical measuring equipment, electronic capital goods and passive electronic components. *PO3441* provides quarterly data on telecommunications equipment manufacture. Inspection of these reports confirms the dominance of BT as purchaser of output of the sector (around three-quarters) and the major role played by the manufacture of public exchange equipment, which accounts for around half of the sector's output in recent years. (Private exchange equipment has been growing in importance and subscriber equipment declining; transmission equipment is the second largest area of output, accounting for around 20%.) The sales of exchange equipment are further disaggregated into electromechanical and electronic system types; for both public and private exchanges the latter have grown rapidly as compared to the former, overtaking them in sales in 1978 and 1982 respectively.

Business Monitor PO1006 presents data on the concentration of industries in telecommunications equipment supply, broken down by product sectors. For the 1960s and 70s, where we have data, it is apparent that there is a high degree of concentration in this sector. The largest five enterprises account for well over three-quarters of the market in most products, and 88.5% of sales from the industry sector, and so the near-monopsony of BT as customer is matched by an oligopolistic supply industry. (Guy, (1985) points out that this is by no means an uncommon arrangement in other countries.)

Apart from the official sources such as *Business Monitor*, the telecommunications equipment industry is documented in a number of ways. The Telecommunication Engineering and Manufacturing Association, (TEMA), claims to represent over 90% of the British industry, and publishes a brochure annually (*TEMA*) which provides statistics based on member company statements. These data include sales trends, by market (BT - by far the largest customer, taking some two-thirds of output, other UK customers, and exports) and by products (public switching - by far the largest product category and in recent years about

40% of output - and four roughly similarly sized product groups, each around 15% of the market: transmission, business communications, subscriber terminals, and other works and services). Trends are also reported of number of UK employees (falling) and sales per employee (rising).

Two international sources provide useful compilations of data and commentary on telecommunications in the UK and other countries. One of these is the OECD (1988) report from which we have already quoted. As well as providing data on investment and digitalisation of national (common carrier) networks, one chapter focuses on the telecommunications equipment industry. It contrasts the market share of the main suppliers of central switching systems (in all countries cited this market is very concentrated), and shows the distribution of such systems by type (from step-by-step and other electromechanical systems to digital electronic systems: Western European data for 1985 show France well in the lead for digital systems). Private branch exchange (PBX) markets for the UK, USA and three other European economies in 1984 are presented: the US market is larger than the four European countries together. Other data contrast Europe with other world regions, for example in a forecast of trends in various categories of the equipment market over 1983-90. In the Appendix, DTI statistics are cited to give trends (from 1978 to 1985) of sales, exports, imports, etc. of telephone and telegraph apparatus and equipment, with similar data provided for other countries; employment trends in the equipment sector are also contrasted across countries.

The Economic Commission for Europe (1986) provides for Britain, along with a number of other countries, an account of the structure and main features of the telecommunications equipment industry, drawing on a variety of sources; it also forms a useful setting of British data in a comparative context. The data cited include *Business Monitor* statistics for the first half of the 1980s on production, domestic sales and foreign trade of telegraph and telephone equipment, and employment in the equipment industry; and *Financial Times* data on the market value of selected UK telephone equipment groups (in order of magnitude these were for 1984/85: "other public switching", PBX equipment, System X, telephones, multiplex equipment, copper transmission system equipment, microwave radio, and optical transmission system equipment) and on sales of PBX suppliers to the UK market. One table also depicts the size of the total UK manufactured PBX sales (which grew from 33 million in 1978 to 150 million in 1983) and, interestingly, the increasing share of electronic exchanges in this total (from 9% to 99%, reflecting the application of new IT to telephony). The report attributes the decline in employment in this sector between 1981 and 1985, which accompanies a continuing rise in sales by domestic manufacturers, to the increased electronics content of the product and process innovations such as automatic assembly.

The Economic Commission for Europe (1987) also provides a convenient assembly of international comparative data on *trade* in telecommunications equipment. Exports, imports, and trade balances of "electrical line telephonic and telegraphic apparatus" (SITC 764.1 rev 2) are provided from 1978-84 for most OECD countries (among others). According to these data the UK moved from a net trade surplus of over $54million in 1978 to a deficit of over $40 million in 1984! Trade between the EEC and the USA is reported, and the main export markets of Japan, the USA, Canada, Sweden, and the Federal Republic of Germany - but not the UK though it features as a major market for the first three of these. Some similar data are reported for the whole sector "Telecommunications Equipment" (SITC 764 rev 2). UK official statistics on trade are published in *Economic Trends* and *British Business*; the long-term trend has been for a declining British share of the growing world market, with a steady increase in import penetration.

An analysis of the UK telecommunications subscriber industry is provided by Sciberras and Payne (1986). The study is based on interviews with senior management in OECD subscriber equipment firms (including new entrants from related industries); this included seven British-based firms estimated to supply over 80% of the national market. (This is a highly concentrated sector.) The focus of the study is on competitiveness in the sector; some data are provided on an anonymous firm basis, others form the basis for international comparisons of the British industry with others. Thus countries are compared in terms of the numbers of firms falling into various ranges on such parameters as volume of turnover in subscriber equipment; volume of production of PBXs, of telephones, of key systems; volume of investment in manufacturing equipment; R&D effort; employment of qualified scientists or engineers (QSEs), etc. A breakdown is also given on type of investment (automated insertion, handling and testers, in-circuit and functional automated test equipment (ATE), and other). The data rarely take a statistical form other than cross-classifications of this small number of firms, though rough-and-ready estimates of volumes of production and expenditure could be derived from them.

An earlier study by Turnbull and Hug (1984) provided a rather wider range of statistical material culled from secondary sources. Euromonitor estimates are provided of trends in the UK market for facsimile transceivers (sales volume and value, installed base), and telex (sales volume, installed base, value of new terminals installed), Mackintosh data on market size and total production of telecommunications equipment of several countries (including the UK), and other data on the breakdown of the business systems market between small and large PABXs, special telephones, key systems and others.

But probably the most rich readily available source of material on CPE activity in the UK is the Monopolies and Mergers Commission (1986) report on the proposed merger between BT and Mitel. As well as containing a great deal of information on the two companies concerned, this report contains several tables concerning the PBX market in the UK for the period 1981-84. Numbers of extensions delivered, broken down by size of equipment, and deliveries in terms of numbers of lines and of value of equipment, also broken down by size of equipment, are classified in terms of distribution through BT, independent distributors, and direct sales to end-users. (Size is graded into three groups: small - up to 16 lines, medium - 17 to 500 lines, large - over 500 lines.) These data allow for some analysis of short-run trends in dependency of manufacturers and end-users on BT, and of developments in the market in terms of system size (and thus, implicitly, the use of PBXs by organisations of different size). Further tables describe R&D expenditures of PBX manufacturers, and provide estimates of exports and imports of equipment. BT is a major actor in the PBX (private switching) market, acting as the main distributor of UK equipment output.

Network Supply

Telecommunications networks are highly concentrated. The main carrier in the UK is BT, privatised in 1984. Mercury Communications offers a mainly trunk digital network based on optical fibre and microwave, and mostly retailing to business users; it has a small percentage of the total market. At the time of writing only these operators are allowed to resell voice telephony traffic, although the position is being reviewed in 1990 (when further operators may be allowed). There are several suppliers of specialist data network services to businesses, among them Fastrak, Istel and Geisco; cellular telephony has Racal Vodafone's network, and steps are currently under way to enable operators to offer "Zonephone" or "Telepoint" services (a form of cellular telephony).

The dominance of BT means that our data on telecommunications services provision and use are very dependent on what BT makes available. Unfortunately, this is decidedly limited. The *Guide to Official Statistics* refers readers to BT itself if they want more data; it does not give any hints as to what sort of response they might expect! The main regular source of data from BT is the annual *British Telecom Report and Accounts*, which has been published since 1982. The main focus, like that of most company reports, is financial accounts - profit and loss, movement in reserves, etc. Of more interest to the project of mapping and measuring the information economy are data on the total numbers of employees in different divisions; on the turnover from different inland services (business and residential telephone rentals, subscriber call, apparatus, public call boxes, and finally private circuits, telex and miscellaneous) and from international services. Among the financial data are valuations of the tangible fixed assets broken down into land and buildings, plant and equipment, and assets in the course of construction.

It is often remarked that BT has been less forthcoming statistically since privatisation; a comparison of current data releases with the old *Post Office Report and Accounts* lends support to this. For example, the data on fixed assets in telecommunication in the 1980-81 edition broke plant down into inland and international plant, and the former into cables and transmission equipment, telephones and related equipment, exchange equipment, and telex and other miscellaneous equipment. Furthermore, the Post Office used to publish the "orange book" of *Telecommunications Statistics* which contained considerable data on telephone traffic, telegraphs, telex, exchanges (by type and size), trunk lines, etc. Unless there is a public service obligation to do so, of course, it is often hard to see why a private organisation would benefit from making available detailed material on its operations: apart from the cost of production and publication, some types of data might be considered to be a matter of competitive advantage or commercial secrecy. Placing material in the public domain *might* provide opportunities for academics and consultants to cast new light on telecommunications trends, but a large company will doubtless employ internal staff for just this purpose.

Prior to privatisation, *British Telecom Statistics* carried a rich quantity of contemporary and historical material. The 1983 edition presented almost 60 pages of tabulations. These covered trends in telephone activity: stations (broken down into business, residential, call office, BT and service stations, private service stations and radiophones); different types of exchange systems (displaying the displacement of manual exchange connections by the Strowger electromechanical system, and the subsequent rise of the electromechanical Crossbar and electronic exchanges); exchange connections; equipment and line plant; traffic. Data are also presented on telegraph, telex, and datel services, on BT's labour force (with its functional disposition), and on expenditure, income and fixed assets. Although these data are now no longer kept up-to-date, this volume gives an extensive historical perspective on the development of telecommunications activity in the UK.

In the absence of these publications, data have to be put together from a variety of sources. The Monopolies and Mergers Commission Report (1986) discusses BT's overall financial performance and its PBX activities in particular, but contains tables describing (mostly for the period 1981-85) BT's net expenditure on plant equipment (network equipment, telephone and associated equipment for supply to users, PBXs and associated equipment); turnover and profit and loss balances by categories of service (business and residential telephone rentals; subscribers' calls; apparatus supply, sale and rental; public call boxes; private circuits, telex and miscellaneous; international services); and the scale of PBX trading by BT (which shows a growing proportion of turnover to be accounted by PBX trading over the period).

Some indication of the sorts of data that might be made available on telecommunication services are provided by Economist Informatics (n.d.). As well as giving a good deal of information on the geographical structure of network services, this report provides data from BT on sources of revenue (in order of magnitude these are: local, rentals, trunk, other, international, office, telex, and "advanced"), and various data on regional telephone use (for the North, Wales and Scotland) in terms of call bill and rental per phone, and calling patterns (local and international). The north and south-east of England are also compared on various measures of business telephone use, and on telex, Prestel and fax use; and there are even some data on telephone use by economic sector and firm size. This is a rare instance of such statistics entering the public domain. (In this chapter we are concentrating on data on the supply industry; Chapter 6 considers some data on the diffusion of telecommunications equipment and services.)

A number of international sources are important in the telecommunications field, providing reasonably up-to-date comparative information for a range of countries. Chief among these must rank the International Telecommunication Union's annual *Yearbook of Common Carrier Telecommunications Statistics*. This provides data under a number of broad headings:

- Telephone service. This is the most detailed set of statistics, and covers system size (e.g. number of telephones connected to the PSTN; number of main lines; main lines connected to PBXs, to automatic exchanges; percentage of main lines equipped for direct customer dial overseas, and percentage residential; the connection capacity of local public switching exchanges; the trunk and international circuit ends connected to manual switching and to automatic switching exchanges); demand data (applications for main lines, waiting lists, etc.); and traffic (total, total national, total outgoing international, local traffic, national trunk (toll) traffic, and outgoing international subscriber dialled as a percentage of all outgoing international traffic).

- Public telegram service. Four classes of data are provided on national and international telegrams.
- Telex service. Number of subscriber lines, national and international traffic.
- Data transmission. All these data are "size" indicators: they cover the number of data terminal equipments on the PSTN and telex networks; the number connected to dedicated public data networks; and the number of private leased circuits.
- Employment. Full-time equivalent telecommunications staff, in total and disaggregated between operating staff, technical staff and others.
- Some basic demographic and macroeconomic data, making international comparisons of the raw figures easier.
- Telecommunications services' income, expenditure and financial results (in national currency, at current prices). These data disaggregate income, for instance, between telephone service (connection charges, rentals and calls), telegrams, telexes, and others; and expenditure between operational expenditure, depreciation, interest payments, taxes, and other.
- Telecommunications services' investments (annual gross construction expenditure), disaggregated into four categories.
- Finally, comparative ratios are presented: telephone main lines and sets per 100 inhabitants, telecommunications investment as a share of GDP and of Gross Fixed Capital Formation.

Moving to more discursive accounts - that nevertheless present abundant statistics - the Economic Commission for Europe (1987) describes the UK telecommunications services structure alongside that of other OECD countries. The British data are less rich than those for some other countries, but there are included historical data and forecasts for two aspects of digitalisation of the infrastructure. One chart depicts the growing digital transmission capacity of the UK, disaggregated into microwave, optical fibre and coaxial systems (the latter used to be dominant but are rapidly being overtaken by each of the more modern modes). A second graph displays the number of connections as it evolves over time, with the diffusion of successive switching technologies plotted on to it: there is a shift through manual, Strowger, Crossbar electronic and finally digital switching systems. (The data here parallel those in *British Telecom Statistics* cited above.) Again, this source is useful in situating UK developments within an international context. Comparative tables provide information on gross investments in telecommunications, investments in telephone services as a percentage of this, the share of GDP, of fixed capital formation, and of income from telecommunications services this represents, and other useful comparisons.

The Economic Commission for Europe (1986) also discusses the pattern of demand for telecommunications services, and presents an array of comparative data on this topic. These include telephones per 100 inhabitants; business telephones as a percentage of the total; main lines per 100 inhabitants; telephone calls per capita; total traffic and its annual growth (1975-84), national and local traffic as a percentage of the total; numbers of data terminals installed in 1975 and 1984; numbers of telex lines installed in these years, subscribers to cellular radio services, and so on.

A similar set of statistics, with a rather different comparative base of other economies, is presented by the OECD (1988). Among the comparative data offered are total income from telecommunications services (in constant price rates for 1974 and 1980, and as a percentage of GDP from 1974 to 1985); income from calls as a percentage of total telecommunications income; telecommunications investment (excluding land and buildings) as a share of gross fixed capital formation, and trends in investment (total and per capita) among common carriers; telephone main lines and telephone sets per 100 inhabitants (with data for London and Wolverhampton as well as selected cities in other countries also provided on telephone sets); waiting list for main lines (as a proportion of the total number of main lines); per capita traffic from 1974 to 1984 (there are startling differences in the number of calls per person in different countries - 407 in the UK in 1984, 1,508 in the USA, 1,718 in Switzerland!). The OECD report also contains a lucid brief summary of the main directions of change in national telecommunications networks, and a survey of the situation in different countries.

Guy (1985) also gathers together data from various sources to describe the UK telecommunications industry. The specific focus of his study is the relation between technological change, capital productivity and employment in the sector, but a varied range of data are assembled, many of them derived from pre-privatisation data sources. These include trends 1971-81 in R&D expenditure by the Post Office and BT, disaggregated into different primary objectives (development of new systems has been growing as a proportion of the total, to over 50% in 1981, as compared to basic research and sustaining and improving old systems), and by system function (switching and signalling has been growing, again to over 50% of the total, with a small growth in customer equipment R&D and declines in transmission, data and other). An early study, containing a great deal of interesting data on both posts and telecommunications, but whose statistics are generally outdated, is Walsh et al. (1980). Hubbard (1986) provides a brief and informative account of the UK telecommunications scene, providing data on the use of a number of products: telex, telephones, key systems, PABXs, and mobile telephones.

There has been considerable interest from market researchers and others in these latter areas of mobile communications and especially cellular radio. We shall consider data sources dealing with telecommunications facilities delivered to final consumers, such as cable TV systems, in Chapter 8, though we can mention here the study of the development of UK cable networks by Evans et al. (1983), and the *Annual Report* of the Cable Authority, which covers the numbers of franchises awarded to and operated by cable consortia, the number of homes passed by and connected to cable systems, and data on usage of cable TV. Some indication of the sorts of data dealing with telephone-related services can be given here.

British Telecom (1985) released some results of a market survey focussed on the use of radio paging (and the potential for using the technology among non-users); this brochure featured data on the diffusion of radio paging equipment and the use of telephones by people at work. Consultants and manufacturers frequently release estimates of the diffusion of cellular telephones across different European countries; the UK is relatively advanced with a national network and large user base. The Scandinavian countries and West Germany have more phones per capita - according to data from Ericsson (Milner, 1988) Norway has nearly three cellular phones per hundred population, around seven times the British figure, but the British market (which has grown from zero to around 300,000 subscribers in three years, according to further market data cited by Milner) is absolutely large.

Quality of Service

This is a topic which has received considerable attention in the UK following the privatisation of BT in 1984, although consumer groups have had a longstanding interest in the area. (Mitchell (1986) discusses the role of the consumer groups here, and cites the Consumers Association's user surveys carried out in 1969, 1975 and 1983.) Quality of service has concerned regulators in North America for rather a long time, and there is considerable effort there to develop relevant Quality of

Service Indicators (QSIs). For example, the Canadian Radio, Television and Telecommunications Commission (1985) outlines over 40 indicators and associated performance targets being approved for the British Columbia Telephone Company, covering the areas of service provision, repair, local service, long distance service, operator services, directory services, and billing. Such indicators are also applicable to other companies under federal jurisdiction. It is interesting to note that reference is made to both "objective" and "subjective" (i.e. user evaluations) indicators, and comparisons are drawn with practices for other telephone companies.

BT had stopped publishing QSI material at around the time of privatisation, but soon came under pressure to start again; this pressure was articulated by Oftel, and in late 1986 BT agreed to publish statistics again. The Director General of the Office of Telecommunications commented on BT's subsequent reporting practices, and provided some hint as to why there may have been some absence of alacrity:

> "BT delayed too long before publishing quality of service statistics in accordance with the commitment it gave me last November...quality of service declined in 1987 in consequence of the strike at the beginning of the year..." (Carsberg, 1987, p2)

Oftel had in the meantime begun to produce some of its own QSI data, reported in *Oftel News* (a survey of the effectiveness of public call boxes was published in September 1987) and in *British Telecom's Quality of Service 1987*. The latter, in addition to citing and discussing BT's own QSIs, provides both direct (survey) and by-product (complaints) data generated by Oftel itself.

Oftel's data include trends in:

- views of changes in service quality since privatisation;
- experience of faults in telephone service, types of fault, length of time for repair, engineers failing to keep repair appointments;
- length of time for telephone installation, engineers failing to keep installation appointments;
- complaints about telecommunications services received by Oftel, distinguishing between accounts, service provision, charges, service quality, operator/directory services, deposits, and others.

BT's own *Quality of Service Report* is now published every six months. The May 1988 edition provides QSIs (mostly in the form of trends over the past year) on:

- repairs (faults cleared within two working days);
- installation service (installation within six working days for business, eight working days for residential users);
- operator services (operator, and directory enquiry, calls answered in 15 seconds; one figure is also provided for proportion of callers unable to get through on first attempt)
- public payphones (numbers installed, proportions in working order - this is an instance of a QSI where a target has been set);
- network reliability (failures in local and trunk calls, and network faults per line per annum).

Not surprisingly the BT report is upbeat - challenges to meet, commitments fulfilled, and the title page of the October 1987 report carries a logo stating "Well on the way to recovery" - while Oftel's is rather more critical. Oftel is now relying on BT as a source for many data,but will continue to produce its own statistics in areas not covered by BT's mainly by-product data. The annual *Report of the Director General of Telecommunications* continues to discuss such issues, providing statistics on customer complaints (these were reported as having increased by nearly 100% in 1987). Both the BT report and *Oftel News* are sources of sporadic data on other aspects of telecommunications than QSI *per se*. The issue of *Oftel News* cited above carries an estimate of the numbers of cellular phone users in the UK; the BT report discussed below includes marginal information on the proportion of traffic carried by the new digital trunk network.

New Telecommunications Services

Telecommunications services must be the most murky part of the IT-producing sector to depict in quantitative terms; in part because they are new, in part because their products are immaterial, in part because of reluctance to release commercial information on the part of suppliers. The main classes of new services are variously referred to as VANS or VADS:

> "VADS are Value Added and Data Services. As with most important computer concepts the name is clumsy, the principles clear, and a formal definition virtually impossible."
> (*Vanguard*, 1988, p6)

Writing for the DTI, Coopers & Lybrand (1987) report varying estimates for the size of the UK VADS market, which they attribute to definitional differences; their discussion gives an inkling of the types of service included as VANS/VADS:

> "According to a PACTEL study for the DTI in 1986 the size of the UK VANS market in 1985 was £185m. This was made up of information services (value £96m), transaction services (£23m) and conveyancing services (£38m). This study also estimated the size of the UK on-line database market at £275m in 1985 and the UK videotex market at £52m. These could easily be included in the VADS market...Langtons by contrast estimated the size of the UK market to be between £20 and £40 million in 1985...this clearly illustrates the problems in measuring and defining the market consistently...This is not altogether surprising given the elements of network, hardware and software that constitute the market. What does emerge is that there is a significant market...dynamic and developing worldwide with the USA leading the way and Japan and other countries responding rapidly... Financial services is currently the leading user sector, comprising 90% of the European market according to Information Dynamics." (p4)

In a discussion of forecasts that might also be applied to market estimates, White (1988, p44) notes that there are "unique problems with VAN markets...it is something akin to forecasting *super novae.*" On the definitional issue: "(f)or want of a realistic generic definition, an alternative approach is to take 'generally accepted' examples of value added services - such as electronic mail and electronic document interchange - and simply sum individual forecasts for each sub-market. The flaw in this approach is that it is already clear that these existing markets are beginning to converge." (Another flaw of this method is that it provides much opportunity for double-counting.) The generic definition of VANS is rendered difficult by the fact that VANS tend to be defined differently in different regulatory environments; they are political as much as technical constructs. It can be argued that the concept of VANS was developed to expedite regulatory aims (to make separation of markets for anti-trust and related regulatory purposes more feasible), with the technical criteria fitted to this, rather than regulation being first based on the technical criteria.

The definitional issue is to some extent settled for us in the UK by Oftel's operating a VADS licence (previously the VANS licence). VADS would then be what are licensed by Oftel as VADS. Unfortunately, licence applications are now only required of companies or groups with over £1 million turnover from VADS (or more than £50 million from all activities), and so a financial criterion is added to the political and technical ones; this may render some small services invisible. Oftel has published (in *Oftel News* and elsewhere) data describing the types of service registered under the earlier VANS licence and the regional location of the licensed companies. However, it has been suggested that many of these applications are not really active services. Lists of companies holding the new VADS licence are available from Oftel library; at the time of writing these cover 23 companies (as opposed to 164 registered in October 1985). (OECD (1988) provides a brief discussion of cross-national differences in defining VANS, and some of the problems that these pose for comparative analysis.)

A valuable guide to the current VANS scene is Chang and Hitchcock (1987), who present a collection of essays reviewing various types of services - managed data networks, electronic mail, electronic data interchange, electronic funds transfer, videoconferencing and videotex - as well as data broadcasting. For each of these areas there is a directory containing details of the active suppliers; however, there are very few UK statistics included in the volume - reflecting the poverty of these data in the VANS field. A more recent, but brief survey of suppliers is Sarsons (1988).

Business Monitor SDQ9 covers VANS within its general focus on computing services, and within the subcategory of "bureau services". The other component of this subcategory, data-base services, will itself generally be regarded as one of the VANS, as the quotations above indicate. We are provided for each of these with billings to clients for work done, with these data further disaggregated into foreign clients, parents/associates, and other UK clients. Full- and part-time employment are recorded for bureau services in total only. These data are based on a voluntary panel, with the restrictions on generalisation that this implies, but they still constitute one of the few available statistical sources.

It is known that the DTI has been seeking to survey the VADS field more thoroughly, but has to date had little success in formulating an appropriate enquiry. A draft questionnaire which asked suppliers for a sectoral breakdown of their business received a poor response. Suppliers are believed to be chary of revealing data which might show that the field is less healthy than their promotional literature proclaims; but they also claim that it is practically impossible to disaggregate their activities by type of function in the way that official statisticians have requested. This does not seem to have prevented a number of consultancies presenting data on the size of different types of VANS market - electronic mail, radio services, data bases, etc. - for several Western European markets, including the UK. How reliable these data are is an open question.

4.3 Conclusions

The IT-producing sectors, as defined above, are unevenly documented. While there is a wealth of material on some of them, others - notably telecommunications services, and especially the newer services here - are poorly covered in available statistics. We shall see that this pattern is repeated where it comes to data on the diffusion of IT. As is noted in practically every chapter of this book, there are also frequently problems posed by the failure of some (and sometimes most) data to discriminate between traditional activities and those based on new IT (e.g. office machinery versus computers - though in this case we can often distinguish the two).

The examination of data and data sources in this chapter has proved helpful in further developing our understanding of the "information economy". Before concluding, however, we should stress one point that has emerged in several places in the discussion. As noted in Chapter 1, our notion of IT is inherently a "fuzzy" one. This means that the treatment above is not exhaustive of IT production in the UK. There are two aspects of this.

First, though we have attempted to focus on heartland and core IT production, some IT production is certainly going on outside the branches of the economy considered. Almost certainly the most significant activities of this sort will concern software, which is being written by systems analysts and programmers based in computer installations in all branches of the economy and not just in the computer and computer services industries. Occupational data (see Chapter 7) are one way of getting a grasp on such activities.

Second, new products with substantial IT components are being produced in many sectors. While some products such as robots and numerically controlled machine tools are often regarded as IT by commentators, our approach is to see them as having an IT component which adds to their functionality in their dedicated applications. As will be discussed in the next chapter, we might consider indicators of the IT-intensity of different sectors and products as more fruitful than attempting a strict demarcation between IT and non-IT products and activities. Perhaps more problematic will be the treatment of the "information industries" like broadcasting (and associated manufacturing sectors such as consumer electronics), where there is substantial blurring of traditional sectoral boundaries (in these cases, with telecommunications and with computers). Such sectors are the focus of the "Mapping and Measuring" research at the CCIS, Polytechnic of Central London.

5 Diffusion

Studies of the diffusion of IT across various sectors of the economy form one area where there has been considerable effort at generating new data. Much of the initiative here has involved non-official sources, in particular studies carried out by the PSI, but some official statistics have also been directed to this topic. The main limitations of recent official studies, shared by many non-official studies, are twofold: to date they have only concerned manufacturing industries, though this is liable to be improved upon in future studies, so that we have detailed comparative data for only a limited portion of the economy. Secondly, the focus of the research has been on computer- or microelectronic-based equipment, and thus there is little light thrown on use of telecommunications or of networking trends (though there are some glimmers in this direction). In this chapter we shall outline the main data sources that cover wider sectors such as manufacturing or private services, as well as those that offer scope for analysis of the entire economy.

We begin with two major official data sources.

5.1 The Census of Production Enquiry

The 1986 Census of Production covers Divisions 1 to 4 of the 1984 SIC; the so-called "production industries", energy and water supply (Division 1) and manufacturing (Divisions 2-4)) included for the first time questions directly focusing on IT-related activities. The IT questions were not asked of all industries falling within these divisions (e.g. construction firms) and the published data are also subject to some suppression on grounds of commercial confidentiality. The new Census of Production questions are not, unfortunately for present purposes, being asked every year, but it is intended to repeat them every few years; 1989 may be the next occasion. There are plans to extend the requests for data in future to cover the rather limited set of services studied by BSO. Some other services - telecommunications and air, sea and rail transport - were, additionally, to be the subject of a separate DTI enquiry. The remaining services, like public services, await future analysis.

The data produced in the Census of Production are twofold. First, firms were asked to specify how many staff were employed full-time on computer work. The specific question here was worded in consultation with the CSA, and an effort has been made to capture only professional staff (those with degrees or membership of professional associations), thus excluding, say, word processor operators. The employment data really focus on computer professionals, then, that is those people responsible for making computer systems work rather than those using them in applications - in other words, data roughly comparable to those concerning the computer services sector itself - though there is still likely to be some ambiguity here.

The second type of data elicited is capital expenditure on computers and associated data communications equipment. (For larger firms only there is also material on the hire or leasing of such equipment.) An additional question investigates the issue of leasing - which is a substantial proportion of computer expenditure. Data are obtained on payments for the hiring, leasing or renting of computer and associated data communications equipment. These questions make it possible to estimate the computer-intensity of investment in different sectors. Again there may be some ambiguity associated with the questions - when is an item of equipment regarded as a computer rather than a word processor or process controller, when does communications equipment become associated with data communications?

Results of these enquiries are published in *Business Monitor* at the three-digit SIC level. Some overall compilations and aggregations have been presented in an article ''Diffusion of Computers'' in the Business Trends section of *British Business* (February 10 1989, pp30-31). The data form a vital resource for tracking computer activities across sectors, at least in terms of investment of funds and professional staff. The *British Business* study presents comparative results. In terms of a diffusion index (relative to manufacturing Divisions 2-4), Division 3 (engineering and allied industries) was above average in capital and leasing expenditure, while Division 1 (energy and water supply) was below average for these measures but above average for computer employment. Division 4 (other manufacturing) was below average on all measures, as was Division 2 (particularly for capital expenditure).

The study goes into a finer level of detail on sectoral comparisons, too. Thus we learn that the largest spender on computer equipment was class 34 (electrical and electronic engineering), but in relative terms this constitutes only 16% of its (plant and machinery) capital expenditure. Class 17 (water supply) leads here with 29% of its capital expenditure on computers. Other IT-intensive classes are 33 (office machinery and DP equipment), 36 (other transport equipment), 37 (instrument engineering), and 47 (paper, printing and publishing). Manufacturing sectors with low IT-intensity by this measure include classes 21 (extraction of metalliferous ores), 22 (metal manufacturing) and 23 (extraction of minerals n.e.s.).

The study, finally, provides a number of aggregate statistics that are of some interest: around 81,000 computer specialists were employed in these industries in 1986 (almost half in engineering); capital expenditure on computers and related equipment was £704 million (again, almost half in engineering); hiring, leasing and renting payments were a remarkable £307 million (with more than half from engineering). Inspection of the detailed data, as is noted in the paper, suggests that leasing and buying are alternative ways of accessing IT power; some sectors are below average on one and above on the other, and vice versa.

5.2 Input-Output Tables

Input-output tables are very powerful tools for economic analysis in general, and it would be surprising indeed if they could not be brought to bear on mapping and measuring the information economy. The data used in these tables are derived from the Purchases Inquiry and the Census of Production together with other sources for those industries not included in these sources (see Section 5. 1, above). The achievement of input-output analysis is to bring data on the interrelationships of different industries together into a common table. Thus one of the basic input-output tables is the industry by industry table, which describes, for each industry, how much of its outputs is purchased by others, and how much of its inputs comes from others.

This arrangement of data allows for versatile analysis, and the input-output matrix is important in planning and forecasting in that it can be used to estimate the requirements that will be placed on other sectors by a change of activity in one sector. For the task of mapping and measuring the information economy, there are evident possibilities to assess the purchases from IT-related sectors by other parts of the economy, to calculate the contribution of these IT sectors to the final output of other sectors, etc. But there are inevitably limitations in input-output tables.

First of all, input-output data are not published annually for the UK, and only appear after some delay. (When this chapter was first drafted, in 1988, the 1984 tables had only recently been released; previously we had to rely on 1979 data, or else use the information provided in *Business Monitor PO 1008 Purchases Inquiry* for 1984, that gives a valuable but less coherent picture of industry purchases of commodities.) They are published as *Input-Output Tables for the United Kingdom*, and summary tables are presented in *Economic Trends*; some comparable European data are available (expressed in terms of the European System of Accounts) from Eurostat.

Secondly, input-output tables use their own aggregation of sectors drawn from the regular SIC classification. (Both 1979 and 1984 tables have taken account of the 1980 SIC revision, however, and so the data should be largely comparable.)

Thirdly, the input-output categories for services in the UK are far less disaggregated than those for manufacturing. In the 1979 tables, of 100 branches of the economy, only 11 (12 if we add "public administration etc., domestic service, ownership of dwellings") are services. Of these transport is disaggregated into four varieties while importantly different activities are made into bedfellows ("post and telecommunications", "banking, finance, insurance, professional and business services, hiring"). This severely limits the usefulness of the input-output tables as a basis for comparing services to other sectors. The 1984 tables, fortunately, do distinguish post from telecommunications, along with other improvements which give us some 14 services; but of course it is still difficult to develop historical comparisons. (The set of services for 1984 is: distribution etc.; hotels, catering, etc.; railways; road transport etc.; sea transport; air transport; transport services; postal services; telecommunications; banking and finance; insurance; business services etc.; other services; public administration etc.)

The fourth issue which we need to take up is how far input-output tables can be used to assess IT-related purchases by the various sectors of the economy. Given that there is no IT sector as such, it is necessary to consider what sectoral classes might be appropriate to use. Bearing in mind the caveat that (especially for earlier periods) the data are liable to contain some non-IT output under what is largely an IT sectoral heading, and that some areas omitted below may well produce new IT products and components within their products (e.g. aerospace), the following branches seem to be most relevant:

- office machinery and computer equipment
- telecommunications etc., equipment, electronic capital goods
- electronic components and sub-assemblies
- instrument engineering
- telecommunications services.

These distinct branches might be aggregated together in various ways, or expenditure on the products of each may be may be treated as indicators of different underlying aspects of IT activities. (For example, it is not necessary for the purchase of telecommunications equipment or services to coincide with the purchase of computer equipment; nor need the latter coincide with the use of electronic components for, say, process control.) Different types of industrial activity may utilise different IT inputs as signified by these branches. Nevertheless, it will be interesting to examine the "profiles" of purchasing from the different branches across the whole economy, as well as to explore the development of indicators of aggregate IT spend.

If we take IT investment to concern just investment in computer and telecommunications equipment (i.e. the first of the two categories above), we find that the UK data give a very similar picture to Roach's (1987) for the USA - around 80% of IT investment comes from services sectors of the economy, for instance. Likewise, the IT share of plant and machinery investment (around 25%) is very similar to that cited for the USA in 1985 by the Office of Technology Assessment (1988).

Table 5.1 displays some indicators for highly aggregated economic sectors developed from the input-output data. As well as the share of each sector's plant and machinery investment in IT, we present two Comparative IT Investment Intensity Ratios (CITIIR). A CITIIR of less than one indicates that an industry accounts for a smaller share of the IT spend than its share of total fixed capital investment expenditure. A CITIIR of greater than one indicates that the industry accounts for a greater share of IT spend than its share of total fixed capital investment.

The results confirm the importance of service sectors as IT-using sectors. Not only are they dominant users but a greater share of their investment is in IT. (As we can see, however, the telecommunications service sector is responsible for the high consumption of telecommunications equipment by services.)

The input-output data may be used for a variety of additional purposes. A few of these will be mentioned. For example, the data may be used for further analysis of the IT sectors themselves. Thus, we can use the industry by commodity matrix to investigate the degree to which the sales of the industry are confined to or concentrated in its core product - for example, we can see in the 1979 data that the office machinery and computers branch is also producing output (about 1% of its total) in the electronics components and sub-assemblies group. We can use the trade information to examine the dependency of sectors on imports of IT products; it should be possible to examine whether, for instance, electronics-intensive sectors import a higher share of their spend than others.

As with the Census of Production data, input-output tables are only telling us about expenditure during a particular period. They are flow rather than stock data, then, and we cannot tell from them how far there are amassed IT capabilities within sectors, although it is possible to

Table 5.1

Comparative IT Investment Intensity Ratios, 1984

Sectors:		**Indicators:**			
Input-Output Sector	**(1984)**	**PCINVCOM**	**PCINVTEL**	**CITIIRCOM**	**CITIRTEL**
1-3	Agriculture, forestry, fishing	0.6	0.1	0.13	0.02
4-11	Extractive sector	1.7	3.5	0.37	0.87
12-25	Manufacturing	4.1	4.0	0.92	1.00
26	Construction	0.5	1.4	0.10	0.35
27-45 (less 36)	Services	5.7	4.6	1.26	1.15
27-45 (less 36 and 37)	Services other than telecom-munications	5.8	1.8	1.28	0.45

Source: Calculated from Input-Output Data, 1984.
Mark Matthews is thanked for his assistance in this exercise.

Definitions:

PCINVCOM = % of sectoral plant and machinery investment in computers

PCINVTEL = % of sectoral plant and machinery investment in telecommunications equipment

CITIIRCOM = comparative IT investment intensity ratio for computers

CITIRTEL = comparative IT investment intensity ratio for telecommunications equipment impute stock data from flow statistics. But it is quite plausible that there are considerable fluctuations over time in IT spend, and - more problematic in many ways - that these fluctuations are not consistent across branches of the economy. For example, it is likely that financial firms engaged in particularly high levels of expenditure immediately prior to "Big Bang".

To examine how far these and related factors are posing real problems, it will be useful both to examine the new Census of Production data as it builds up into a time-series, to see how consistent a picture the newer data yield with the earlier input-output IT measures discussed above - and to compare both types of "flow" data with the "stock" data yielded by the PSI studies and others (discussed below).

5.3 Information Technology Trends

While most of the studies reviewed in this chapter seek to estimate IT diffusion in various sectors of the economy by taking samples of all establishments operative in these sectors, an alternative approach involves looking at IT users only. This is an approach with a long history: in the mid-1960s and early 1970s, for example, the Department of Employment (1965, 1972b) was carrying out surveys of users of computers in offices. These are interesting studies, not least for the demonstration that banking and financial services were dominant users over 20 years ago and that in 1972 the top three user sectors were all services (public administration and defence, distributive trades, and joint financial services). The forecasts of computer usage for coming years contained in these reports, and the details of the establishment of and working conditions in EDP installations also make fascinating reading.

In these studies it was relatively straightforward to establish the universe of computer users and survey them. The 1972 study, for instance, obtained responses from an estimated 82% of office computer users! (Even so, difficulties were being experienced with "very small computer systems" - costing less than £20,000!) At present, there are three main efforts to define the universe of computer installations, a topic of considerable interest for those marketing IT hardware, software and consumables. Unfortunately, this high level of interest results in the managers listed by these three sources being bombarded with mail, not a small proportion of which involves questionnaires, and response rates to surveys are now notoriously small from these samples. Two of the three efforts result in published lists of computer installations, which could be used as data sources for statistical analyses of the share of different sectors in computer use: one is published as the magazine

Computer Survey, the other as VNU Publications' annual *Computer Users' Yearbook*. (These sources carry some information about the applications and other IT equipment used at various sites.) A third directory of computer installations is maintained by the NCC, and this has been used as a basis for published survey research.

The NCC published its first edition of *Information Technology Trends* in 1986, after several years of reporting surveys based solely on NCC members. While the sample on which statistics are reported is thus wider than the NCC membership (c2,500 organisations, mostly large and established computer users), it is still recognised to be heavily biased toward large and medium-sized organisations and computer installations.The NCC sample was based, in addition to membership, on responses to a survey of a stratified sample of organisations included on the NCC's National Computer Index (this has around 30,000 records, just over 2,100 cases were sent questionnaires). A relatively low response rate (12.7%) was obtained (that for member organisations was also only 26.2%); against this must be set the fact that the data presented are very rich and detailed. Discussions with NCC suggest that the Index itself is fairly representative of large computer installations (around 80% of machines costing more than £500,000 are captured, 60% of those between £100,000 and £500,000, 30% of those between £50,000 and £100,000, and a low proportion of cheaper machines).

Data are presented from some 843 organisations, spanning manufacturing, utilities, and public and private sectors. The classification of sectors in most of the report is not according to a strict SIC-type system: it reflects expediency (problems with the sample size in some instances) as well as the conceptual interests of NCC staff. For most tables where an industrial disaggregation is presented, this is as follows: process industries, engineering industries, other manufacturing, distribution, transport (includes communications!), finance, local government, education and research, public utilities, other non-manufacture (business services and media), computing, and other sectors (central government, unions, and charities). Data are also disaggregated by organisational size.

The survey thus possesses considerable virtues (wide coverage of sectors and, as we shall see, an interesting range of variables) and poses substantial problems (bias toward large users and probably enthusiasts - those willing to fill in the detailed questionnaire - and non-SIC coding sometimes limiting comparability). It is company rather than workplace (establishment) centred, and the respondents are usually senior managers in charge of DP or IT services. The main focus of the survey is the organisational patterns of use of IT, but many of the data have relevance to other concerns.

For instance, several sets of data provide information bearing on the patterns of diffusion of computer hardware across the economy:

- (1) The value of installed equipment, further disaggregated by the manufacturer of the computer system; other tables show the value of equipment as a proportion of turnover, and as a function of number of employees.
- (2) Current and forecast numbers of visual display units (VDUs)/ terminals, other user interface devices, personal-computer-based terminals, networked microcomputers and stand-alone microcomputers.
- (3) Number of terminals per hundred employees.Results to this enquiry are provided in a more detailed - 26 sectors - industry breakdown. Not surprisingly, computing is the most terminal-intensive sector (with over 50 per employee), followed by banking/ finance and education (over 30 per employee), and then oil and coal and research (over 20).
- (4) Current and forecast numbers of user interface devices in different locations: senior managers' offices, sales/marketing departments, other offices, shopfloors/warehouses, and "point of sale".
- (5) Current and forecast proportions of organisations with micros connected to Local Area Networks (LANs) or external databases, or with terminals connected to mainframes via a Wide Area Network (WAN).
- (6) IT staff, and development staff, as a percentage of all employees; spending on IT staff per employee per annum. While most of the measures show IT use to be more common in larger firms, terminals/employee and IT staff as a proportion of employees are variables that fairly consistently decline with greater firm size. Thus large firms are more likely to use IT, and to use more IT, than smaller, but they are not necessarily more IT-intensive.

These data can all be used to gain a better picture of sectoral patterns of IT use, with the caveats noted above. There is surprisingly little information on the applications to which the technology is put, although to some extent this can be gleaned from the information cited above.

Other types of data focus very much upon the organisation of IT use across industries. As well as data on how computer policies are controlled in the sample, there are a large number of items bearing on the role of IT staff and the development of end-user computing. Together with the statistics (mentioned earlier) on the use of LANs and WANs, these data promise to move us beyond simply quantifying the presence of computer facilities in the sample, toward telling us something about the technological trajectories of IT usage.

It is commonly asserted in the trade press and elsewhere that a shift to networking is a key feature of current developments in IT (''the convergence of computers and communications''). Similarly, it is held that end-user computing is making received notions of IT activities, based on mainframe computers with few terminals, obsolete. The data on networking indicate large cross-sector variances. But there is a general expectation of substantial and rapid growth in networking between 1986 and 1991 (both in the proportion of organisations reporting networking and the numbers of micros networked); end-user computing (which is disaggregated between managers, administrative, technical, clerical/ secretarial and other) in practically all cases. (The exception is in process industries, where the ''other category'' of end-users is expected to fall.) Thus the descriptions of IT trajectories noted above seem to have some basis in reality - or at least are reflected in DP managers' expectations, which presumably are shaping their behaviour and planning.

The main problem with these data, and the non-statistical information presented in *Computer Survey* and *The Computer Users' Yearbook*, is that they concern known users of computers only. They do not tell us about the intensity of computer use in different sectors, since they do not include non-users; although if we were to assume that the complete universe of users was being sampled, it would be possible to relate computer activity to the total employment, output, etc., of the sectors. And they are lists of users based in large part on intelligence gathered historically, with consequent biases toward conventional computer use rather than more novel IT applications, and towards large systems rather than minicomputers and microcomputers.

5.4 Broad Cross-Sectoral Studies

5.4.1 Microelectronics in British Industry

From the beginning of the 1980s, the PSI has been engaged in a set of studies that fall within the rubric of mapping and measuring the information economy. The first studies we describe, those led by Jim Northcott, are primarily focused on manufacturing industry; a later study by W W Daniel does permit a rather broader view of IT diffusion across the economy.

Northcott's studies were based on the recognition that despite considerable speculation on the ''impacts'' of IT, there were really few data concerning actual rates of change. In keeping with the themes early dominant in the speculative literature, a major focus of the research has been on employment implications of the new technologies; a second theme is the pattern of applications of IT. IT is essentially defined in terms of microelectronics-based products and production processes.

Surveys were conducted in 1981, 1983, 1985 and 1987, with similar surveys modelled on this research now appearing in a number of other countries. Telephone-based surveys were employed, since efforts to use postal surveys met with response rates too low to serve as convincing data sources for a diffusion study. The early surveys involve c1,200 manufacturing establishments, grouped into six size bands (with 20-49 employees being the smallest). The most recent survey also includes 200 small firms with under 20 employees. As far as possible the same firms were followed up from survey to survey, but the relatively high rate of attrition meant that it was necessary to top up the sample with replacements matched to the original cases.

At the time of writing, the most recent publication is a book-length comprehensive overview of the 1987 survey, with many comparisons with earlier data (Northcott with Walling, 1988). It is noteworthy that these authors conclude that the "speed of penetration of microelectronics through industry has been much faster than with most other new technologies. In 1977 only 3 per cent of the establishments in the survey sample were using it in their products and only 8 per cent in their production processes, and for UK manufacturing as a whole the proportions were smaller still...Since then, however, the proportion of UK manufacturing establishments with microelectronics applications in products doubled in the three years 1978-81 and doubled again in the next three years 1981-84, while the proportion with applications in processes more than trebled in the former three year period and nearly doubled again in the latter one." (Northcott with Walling, 1988, p45).

The PSI studies make several attempts to go beyond a simple counting of the number of establishments using microelectronics, so as to measure the extent of use, and the types of use, of microelectronics. Concerning the extent of use, Northcott asked respondents what proportion (by value) of the output of the establishment involved the product innovation, and what proportion of their processes were controlled by microelectronics. While these are bound to be fairly imprecise indicators, the trend across surveys is a rather impressive one, at least for process innovations, where the percentage of processes controlled by microelectronics is reported to have grown steadily from 23% in 1981 to 32% in 1987.

The studies also go into considerable detail about the particular type of applications in which microelectronics are used (design, control of individual machines or processes, integrated central control systems, automated handling, automated storage, and testing and quality control) - this gives some opportunity to consider the degree to which IT is being used for systems control in an integrated fashion. There are also data on five distinct types of IT process-control equipment (CAD workstations, computerised numerical control (CNC) machine tools, programmable logic controllers, pick-and-place machines, and robots), and on the types of microprocessor used in products (the 1981 survey suggested that people did now know about the "chips" used in processes) - distinguishing between standard industrial microprocessors, custom chips and semicustom chips.

As with the earlier studies, Northcott's recent work presents many tabulations and data-based illustrations. At the level of manufacturing as a whole, for example, data are provided on the trend in, and level of application of, microelectronics in products and processes, as we have seen. These data are presented both in terms of the sample data, and in the form of national estimates prepared by weighting these data up to give a picture of the whole UK manufacturing sector. Thus, by 1987 one factory in eight (13%) was using microelectronics in its products, and 59% of factories in their processes. Since the technology tended to be used more by larger firms, this meant that up to 84% of employment was in microelectronics-using establishments. This does not mean that 84% of employees were working with microelectronics themselves, however. As we have seen, only around one-third of the processes in users' factories were controlled by microelectronics to date.

It would clearly be possible to plot these data as trends, so as to arrive at forecasts for future diffusion rates of the new technologies. In fact Northcott asks users to outline their future plans. And he also investigates the scope for applying microelectronics in non-using establishments, asking those who do not see room for such applications to outline their reasons for believing this. (For process innovations, the reasons seem to be mainly to do with small size or small production runs; for product innovations they tend to concern peculiarities of the product type - e.g. the scope for incorporating microelectronics in yogurt pots does not seem very wide!)

As well as trends over time, these data provide material for analysis of diffusion trends across different types of firm. As noted, there is a strong trend for larger establishments to make more use of microelectronics. (In process applications, this is nearly 100% of establishments with 1,000+ workers, as opposed to under 50% in factories with under 50 workers, and under 20% for those with under 20 workers.) It is interesting to note that smaller factories using microelectronics tend to use them for the same proportion of process applications as do the larger establishments.

Industries vary considerably in their levels of application. Table 5.2 displays data on the 10 manufacturing branches into which Northcott groups his results. It is interesting to note that there is little correlation between the sectoral incidence of product and process applications, and also that the engineering industries are incorporating microelectronics in their products practically as rapidly as they are applying them themselves. It is also interesting to compare these data with the Census of Production results discussed at the beginning of this chapter; there is clearly not a complete match, since while paper and printing industries appear as leaders in both studies, electrical engineering seems relatively lagging in the Northcott study - while the meta-extracting sectors come out much more favourably than their investment patterns would suggest. Nothing could underline the need for both financial and technological measures of IT application more clearly than such apparent inconsistencies!

In these studies, disaggregations are also provided by region and by the ownership of the firm. The PSI studies also go into the perceived benefits and difficulties of using the new technologies. The main difficulties have been skill shortages, with one-fifth of users also reporting economic difficulties and roughly similar proportions having problems with software and with sensors.

However, benefits are even more widely reported. Around three-quarters of product innovators report major benefits from improved product performance and a widening of product functions; a similar proportion of process innovators report benefits in the form of improved product quality and process control. Majorities report other improvements, too, such as improved flexibility and efficiency. Such results suggest that there will be no turning back from the "microelectronics revolution".

Finally, the most recent survey also reports data on the use of other new technologies by establishments. Microelectronics, at 63% of establishments (a weighted estimate) are far more widely diffused than new plastics (7%), fibre optics (6%), new metals (4%), new ceramics (3%) and biotechnology (3%). In part, this is because, in the terminology of Chapter 1, microelectronics are a more fundamental heartland technology, with applications underlying a wider range of industrial processes, than these others. But in part, too, it reflects the relative immaturity of the other new technologies - we are further away from the new materials or biotechnology revolutions than from the IT revolution.

Table 5.2

Use of Microelectronics in UK Manufacturing, 1985

Sector	**Proportions Using Microelectronics in:**	
	Processes	**Products**
Paper & printing	75	0
Food & drink	69	0
Chemicals & metals	69	0
Other metal goods	63	2
Electrical engineering	60	59
Mechanical engineering	58	36
Textiles	57	0
Other manufacturing	51	2
Vehicles	47	18
Clothing	44	0

Note: Data are presented in weighted-for-establishment form, and cover establishments with 20 or more employees.

Source: Northcott with Walling (1988)

Other topics considered in the Northcott studies will be taken up in later chapters. They include skills and training; implications for jobs; and the role of external help and government support.

These studies represent a rich source of data on diffusion of microelectronics within manufacturing, although the use of IT in office systems and telecommunications in these sectors (for example, for document processing - though probably not for computer-aided design) is liable to be overlooked. The other main limitation in the data is the absence of service establishments from the surveys. However, to overcome these limitations would have meant developing questions more appropriate for service-type applications. These would be considerably different from those pioneered by Northcott, which focus on process applications of IT which are mainly specific to manufacturing.

From a social scientist's perspective, the data analyses tend to be rather basic ones; there is little of the sort of detailed multivariate statistical analysis that one would have thought could be applied to the data, although the extensive tabulations are probably more than sufficient for most policymakers' requirements. There are some innovative approaches in the research, for instance the effort to specify the extent of use of the new technology, the percentage of products and of processes incorporating or controlled by microelectronics. Incorporation of microelectronics into products was assessed as a proportion of the value of output involving products using microelectronics; in products, the respondent was asked to indicate "roughly" what proportion of processes are controlled in that way. The explication of the latter question states that what is sought is a "*broad* indication of the extent of use of microelectronics - whether, for example it is a relatively minor, isolated and unimportant application; or whether the entire production process is completely automated; or whether it is somewhere in between...importance...may be regarded as.. . the percentage of production costs...represent[ed]." (Northcott with Walling, 1988, p231).

These studies permit international comparisons, as in Northcott, Rogers, Knetsch and de Lestapis (1985), where French and German data are compared to British; there are interesting differences in the branch pattern of diffusion across the three countries.

While discussing studies of manufacturing industries, we should mention the report by Attenborough (1984), which assembles data on the diffusion of a number of new technologies in UK manufacturing. Comparative statistics for a number of other industrial countries are presented. Chapter 6 will present material on studies of specific manufacturing systems such as robots, numerical control, and flexible manufacturing systems.

5.4.2 Workplace Industrial Relations Survey

Daniel's study, although also conducted from the PSI, emerges from a different background to Northcott's. Daniel (1987) presents results of the 1984 Workplace Industrial Relations Survey (WIRS), based on interviews conducted with a sample of 2,019 workplaces in Great Britain. As suggested by the title of the study, much attention is focused on industrial relations, but there is also interest in technical change. A distinction is made, among changes having occurred in the last three years, between "advanced technical change" (new plant, machinery or equipment including microelectronics), "conventional technical change" (not incorporating microelectronics) and "organisational change" (not involving plant, machinery or equipment). In addition to the concern with change, there are other questions dealing with the "technical stock": the computer facilities of the establishment (in-house mainframe, link to computer elsewhere in organisation, link to computer outside organisation, in-house minicomputer, in-house microcomputer, use of computer bureau service), and the use of word-processing equipment.

Daniel presents results disaggregated by size (and again larger firms are more liable to use IT), but in terms of a sectoral breakdown the study is relatively disappointing. Several sets of data are disaggregated into private manufacturing, private services, nationalised industries and public services, but this makes for very restricted possibilities for comparison. Work under way at CURDS (by Steve Johnson; for a first report of the CURDS analyses, focusing on regional aspects of diffusion, see Goddard (1988)) suggests that since the raw data are coded to the four-digit SIC level, rather more detail can be meaningfully extracted; some 10-branch analyses have been prepared. (These show that while Daniel's tables suggest a low service sector use of IT, some services are exceptionally high users, others exceptionally low.) Given that this survey is to be replicated and extended in the future, it will be worth exploring further.

5.4.3 Computers in Manufacturing Surveys

The journal *Engineering Computers* runs an extensive survey of the use of computers for engineering purposes in British manufacturing; in many respects this forms a valuable complement to the PSI manufacturing surveys, since its focus is somewhat different. (It also covers very small firms - under 20 employees.) The sample size is in the high hundreds, and telephone interviews and questionnaires are employed together. Some basic data are published in the *Computers in Manufactur-*

ing Survey, with more analytic studies appearing in the journal over a period of time following the survey.

Data are presented on the population of mainframes, minis and micros, on applications (management, design, production engineering, etc.), and on purchasing intentions in both cases. The survey report presents data in a form liable to be most interesting for sales staff; articles in the journal present lucid appraisals of the development of increasingly integrated systems in manufacturing. These do not always, however, feature sectoral disaggregations.

Another survey with a similar orientation is the *British Industrial Computing Survey*, run annually by the research firm Marketing Direction in collaboration with the publishers of *Industrial Computing*, in which magazine results are presented. (Again the full tabulation of the results is available at commercial rates.) The data are produced by a postal surve; the 1988 data are based on 470 replies to a questionnaire sent to a random sample of the magazine's circulation list; the respondents are directors and senior managers.

The validity of the sample used in this study is rather difficult to establish from the reports published in the magazine, but there can be no doubt that this survey throws a good deal of light on the use of IT in manufacturing industry. Considerable data are presented on the use of different types of CAD system, of workstations, of voice and of vision recognition systems, of robots, and other components of computer-integrated manufacturing.

Data presented on the 1988 survey, in the October 1988 issue of *Industrial Computing*, cover a wide range of topics. The applications to which computers are put; planned expenditure on computer hardware, software and services; market shares of different suppliers; computerisation plans and objectives; awareness and use of standards such as the Manufacturing Automation Protocol (MAP) and Technical and Office Protocol (TOP), and attitudes concerning networking; and expected payback periods are all covered. To cite a few results: in line with other surveys, large companies are found to be more highly computerised, to use CAD and similar systems, and to be embarking upon networking strategies; staff decreases are reported by a large minority - 27% of users reported job losses, 58% reported no change in numbers employed; improvements in productivity and competitiveness are the outstanding factors in computerisation strategies (''opening new markets'' and ''flexibility'' are well down on the list); and reasons for not implementing open systems networking include the insufficient development of the standards (50%) and insufficient expertise (34%).

5.4.4 A Study of Private Services

Given the relative paucity of material on the service sector, it is welcome that at least one study has made an attempt to address the gap. In a doctoral dissertation, Yap (1986) presents the results of a mail survey of *private* services: some 3,000 establishments were approached, yielding 638 usable service sector responses, presenting data on their circumstances in late 1984. (The study is also reported in part in Walsham and Yap (1985) and Yap and Walsham (1986).) One interesting feature of the study is that the actual response rate was 716, since 78 manufacturing establishments also responded; thus some service-manufacturing comparisons are possible (though not pursued in the studies cited). Yap reports analyses in terms of five sectors: wholesale distribution; retail distribution; transport and communication; business and financial services; and miscellaneous services. However, the raw data allow us further to distinguish a sample of manufacturing establishments, as noted, and also to differentiate between business services on the one hand and banking and financial services on the other. Yap and Walsham generously made their data set available for re-analysis while we were preparing the present report, and we draw below upon some of the results which this yields (these will be published in detail in a separate report).

The research elicited a great deal of information on computer usage by the responding establishments. Yap requested information from respondents as to the numbers of units of offsite and onsite mainframes, and of minicomputers and microcomputers in use at the site; and also asked whether use was made of computer bureau services.

The survey finds considerable variation in whether or not computers are used in the establishments: over 90% of banking and business service establishments use them, as opposed at the other extreme to 60% of transport and 54% of retail establishments. The variation is actually more marked than this, since computer users range from the owner of a single microcomputer to establishments equipped with several mainframes and other systems. The data set allows us to assess the use of different types and combinations of computer; and, since there are questions concerning when computers were first used, to plot diffusion curves. The picture obtained from the latter exercise is one of an approach to saturation of computer use in the more advanced sectors, with use still accelerating through laggard sectors in the early 1980s; and in terms of the different generations of computers, a set of overlapping diffusion curves, with mainframes being overhauled by minicomputers and then more recently by microcomputers - which are by far the most prevalent systems, of course. Minicomputers fall in prevalence between micros and mainframes.

The sectors with highest use of mainframes (manufacturing, banking/ financial, and business services) also tend to be highest users of mini and microcomputers. They also have the highest ratio of microcomputers to mainframes, which we can treat as a rough indicator of application of IT to production as opposed to administrative tasks. In this respect manufacturing industry appears to resemble the information-processing services more than others. Repeatedly these three sectors emerge as the most computer-intensive of the groups surveyed.

Yap and Walsham (1986) develop a measure of computer capacity, formed from a weighted score of computer use (assigning 5 points to each mainframe, 3.5 to each mini and 1 to each microcomputer). Such an indicator can be a useful way of aggregating data on different types of computer, without adding up mainframes and micros as if they were equivalent (although contemporary micros may actually be more powerful than mainframes from only a few years ago). Our analyses indicate that for the whole sample, the sectoral ranking in terms of computer capacity is practically identical with that reflecting incidence of computer use, and it still remains the case that the most prevalent user sectors tend to be those user sectors with most capacity.

Some indication of computer usage patterns is provided by other sets of questions. Most directly, data are available on whether or not computers are used for each of 14 applications. (These do not, however, cover either the extent of use for these applications, or the type of system which they are running on.) While many of the most common service applications are covered, such as financial planning, payroll, project control, and sales analysis - together with some applications that are more manufacturing-oriented, such as CAD and production planning - there are also notable omissions here (such as transactions processing), and we do not have much idea of the types of software used (it would have been valuable to have information on the use of databases, spreadsheets, etc.). While there are significant variations in computer applications across the users in different sectors, some applications are very widely popular - notably credit checking, sales analysis, and billing.

Other computer data concern computer-related employment, classified into five groups; some data on the overall employment in the establishments by broad occupational categories are also provided. Together with information on different configurations of computers installed at establishments, these data allow us to move toward identifying a number of distinct types of computer installation in use across British establishments. Even within sectors, even among users with apparently similar levels of computer capacity as measured by the Yap indicator, there are in fact several significantly distinct patterns of computer use.

For instance, a high-capacity user in banking may use a few mainframes - with or without other systems - or be reliant on a large number of networked microcomputers.

Yap's data also cover word processor (WP) usage, with questions on year of first use of WPs, and on the numbers of general purpose and of dedicated WPs in use. Data are reported on the degree of benefit achieved by the use of general purpose computers, personal computers for professionals and managers, and WPs (in terms of a five-point scale from "much less" to "much more" benefit than expected.) There is a slight tendency for benefits to be more than expected, although the most frequent answer is "the same as expected".

Fourteen other ITs are studied, together with the use of a number of telephone facilities. The 14 are (roughly in order of prevalence): photocopier, electronic typewriter, computer, telex, audioconferencing, radio paging, microfiche/microfilm, viewdata, facsimile, automatic telex system, Group 3 facsimile, electronic mail, LAN and optical character recognition equipment. As well as the presence/absence of these items, data are elicited on their extent of use; and levels of use of telephone equipment facilities - call logging, stored numbers, automatic redial and audioconference - were also assessed. In terms of sectoral variations, Yap himself demonstrates that finance and business services were the highest users of all ITs in 1984; manufacturing tends to be a relatively low user of technologies that are oriented to office work, however, and so it does not emulate these services in this respect in the way that it did for computer usage.

As in the PSI studies, establishment size (measured by turnover or by overall employment) was positively associated with use of computers and most of the other ITs. Yap and Walsham (1986) present one set of results relating organisation size to IT usage. They use their measure of computer capacity, and find for the whole sample and for the various sectors a strong relationship between computer capacity and the number of employees. In aggregate, computer capacity increased approximately with the square root of the number of employees, but financial and business sectors had higher capacity than other sectors (p273). The researchers further compare these results with those of a more mature technology, the telephone - here the number of extensions increases roughly in line with the number of employees.

This study is clearly not on the same scale in terms of sample size as those noted earlier, and it suffers from some shortcomings of sample associated with the low response rate, and a rather gross aggregation of the economic sectors of the users. But it has obtained information on a rather wide set of features of IT use in services, and as such the raw data can be exploited further - and replications of the study would yield useful trend data. The study was concerned with predicting the extent of IT use, and the reports that come from it present useful information on, for example, the occupational profiles of users and non-users of computers in different services.

5.5 Other Dimensions of Diffusion

The discussion above has concentrated on the diffusion of IT products and applications across sectors of the UK economy. However, diffusion can be addressed in other ways than by cross-sectoral comparison. Most notably, regional diffusion is a topic that interests many commentators, in particular proponents of regional policies who fear that particular regions may be neglected in the "IT revolution". An often related concern is with the diffusion of IT across firms of different sizes, which is obviously of concern to proponents of small firms policies. Both the regional and firm-size topics are tackled with empirical data by studies in Amin and Goddard (1986) and, as we have already noted, in Northcott's PSI studies. The latter (Northcott with Walling, 1988), in particular, demonstrates considerable variations in microelectronics usage by size and region, with several of the measures being disaggregated into 10 regions of mainland Britain. Thus, for example, the "North-South divide" in 1987 is not strongly marked in terms of process applications, but product applications are notably low in Scotland and the North.

The diffusion *process* itself has mainly been the topic of case study analysis, where the role of various innovators and the benefits of new technology have been described. One topic that has been attracting large-scale empirical analyses is Information Systems Planning, that is documentation of the degree to which decisions concerning the introduction of new IT are explicitly related to corporate strategy in general. Most, if not all, of the studies in this area are based on small samples. Hochstrasser (1987) presents an array of impressive charts based on a sample of 11 companies; Parker and Idunduin (1988) report a survey eliciting responses from 45% of the UK's top 100 firms. A review of the relevant literature, and a comparison of practices in Australian and British firms is provided by Galliers (1987). Surveys of computer strategies and IT plans of large users are provided in various consultancy reports: for instance, Price Waterhouse's annual *Information Technology Review*.

5.6 Conclusions

This chapter has indicated both opportunities and problems in the analysis of IT diffusion. Opportunities are marked here, in part because so little has been done; there is considerable scope for new survey research, of course, but there is also scope for considerably more analysis of existing data sources.

Official statistics have not been explored in any great depth as of yet - current SPRU work will, it is hoped, help to correct this. Additionally, a number of non-official sources can be exploited to a greater extent than has so far been the case - the SPRU use of Yap's data, and the CURDS use of the WIRS data set are cases in point, and it should in principle be possible to engage in multivariate analyses of several of the other data sets described above, so as to extract further information from them.

The existence of a great many problems with available data obviously will place limits on such analyses, but should be cause to develop better data as well as to push existing data to their limits. Among the most outstanding of these problems, we will simply list the following: the lack of attention to, or detail on, services' use of IT; the concentration on IT as "stand-alone" hardware, with relatively little attention to software, systems, and networks; and the very little effort that has gone into assessing technological capabilities (rather than simply levels of expenditure or possession of equipment in certain grand categories).

6 Major IT Applications and Application Areas

This chapter continues the theme of diffusion, but deals with data and data sources covering only a narrow set of IT applications, or a narrow set of industries. Of course, many applications are restricted to particular industries, and so there is of course some overlap, and judgement has been exercised as to where particular instances will be placed in this chapter. (If an application is specific to, say, retail, we shall cover it under that heading, for instance; if it is generally applicable we shall cover it in the first subsection. Some user sectors have received sufficient concentrated attention to warrant consideration on their own account, especially public sector activities.) We should also bear in mind that some of the topics discussed here are also covered in some of the surveys discussed in Chapter 5; furthermore, some of the employment-focused studies discussed in Chapter 7 also throw light on diffusion trends.

6.1 Major applications

6.1.1 Integrated Circuits, Computers and Software

Several market research firms address the scale of the IC market, though their reports often focus on Europe as a whole rather than the UK. The DTI commissioned studies from Butler Cox and Michael Shortland Associates in 1986 (reporting early in 1987) on the comparative status of the UK market for semicustom chips, preparatory for an awareness campaign designed to encourage electronics firms to recognise the scope for application of these ICs. (The research reportedly indicated that the UK has a more developed market here than West Germany or France, but that many small firms seem unaware of the potential. Recall that Northcott's PSI studies, discussed in Chapter 5, included questions about the use of such chips.)

In addition to the user surveys discussed in Chapter 5, there is an almost continuous stream of reports on the computer market. These are more motivated by interest in the relative success of different manufacturers and models than by desire to map the diffusion of computers in general, and are widely reported in the computer press. Some surveys are very broadbrush, others focus on specific classes of computer, e.g. laptops, multi-user microcomputers.

In Chapter 8 we examine home computer market statistics; in both this case and that of business/professional microcomputers there is considerable scope for confusion concerning whether claims about market share are based upon:

- information received from suppliers (manufacturers and importers), distributors, or trade associations;
- actual sales, sales plus rentals, or deliveries to the trade;
- annual figures, estimates of annual figures based on a shorter period of time, or figures explicitly dealing with a shorter period - and in all cases, the precise start and end points for the period.

Unhappiness about the inaccuracy of such data has often surfaced. For instance, Mason (1985) cites marketing managers of computer companies complaining that problems with these data make decision-making difficult, and presents data from three companies indicative of their divergence, even though all three are using dealer samples. (This is reproduced as Table 6.1 below.) The implication is that sample sizes are too small for reliable estimates, and that use of short periods (or presentation of unsmoothed data) may lead to even a few large orders showing up as apparently major trends.

These problems are presumably particularly acute where microcomputers are concerned, for the market is volatile, the range of dealers and selling agreements is wide, and suppliers can have clear incentives to represent their sales as more buoyant than in fact they are. But there has been controversy over market research in the mainframe field too; in 1986 ICL attacked the validity and interpretation of a telephone survey carried out by Strategic Resource and Information which indicated that substantial numbers of ICL mainframe users were planning to switch to other suppliers.

More generally, it is quite possible that both microcomputer and mainframe statistics are weakened by their focus on new equipment. There is little evidence in the UK on the scale of the second-hand market in IT goods, although in the USA data are available on markets for both used computer and used telecommunications equipment. There is a tendency to assume that the rapid rate of technological change, and the associated cost reductions in equipment, mean that second-hand sales will be insignificant for IT goods. However, several journalistic reports (e.g. Berman, 1987) suggest that second-hand equipment appeals to many users not only for its cheapness (this may indeed be less important for microcomputers than in other market sectors, although there is persistent criticism of mainframe suppliers for inflationary pricing of new releases), but also for the speed of delivery, for the ability to retain com-

Table 6.1

Divergent Estimates of the British Microcomputer Market (1985)

Market Research Company	Romtech	Context	Wharton
Period of Survey	August	June-August	August
Sample Size	250	257	100
PC Makes:			
IBM	45%	28.1%	54%
Apricot	17%	20.4%	4%
Apple	8%	10.5%	13%
Olivetti	7%	7%	7%
Compaq	3%	5.2%	11%
Others	20%	28.8%	11%

Source: Mason (1985)

patibility with existing (but obsolescent) systems, and for the sake of familiarity.

Similar statistics of sales are produced on computer software. Romtec, for instance, produces data on spreadsheet sales (reported in *Computer News,* October 15 1987). Frost and Sullivan present estimates and forecasts for business graphics software for the UK and Europe *(Computer Weekly*, May 1 1986), and so on.

Several computer magazines and newspapers engage in reader surveys, that demonstrate more about the installed base of equipment, and patterns of use of software, than about current purchases (though some feature levels of expenditure and purchasing intentions). Thus *Computer Product News* (1985) presents results of a survey of its readers, disaggregated by country, documenting patterns of use of different professional microcomputers, minicomputers, mainframes, development systems, and data printers, for example. *Computer Weekly* carries out surveys of DP expenditure, together with market researchers IDC; in an article published on December 4 1986 data are provided (from a number of sources) on:

- levels of and trends in hardware expenditure disaggregated by broad category of expenditure (hardware, maintenance, software and services (sic), DP supplies, line charges, external expenditure, salaries, overheads)
- hardware expenditure disaggregated into a large set of different hardware items (e.g. communications equipment - which featured the highest growth rate, supporting arguments of a trend to networking - printers, terminals, etc.);
- software expenditure, disaggregated by user industry sector and supplier sector (system houses, independent vendors' packaged software, independent vendors' custom software, and processing services);
- software expenditure by application sector (10 categories of application are cited) and supplier sector;
- trends in software and services expenditure by types of supplier;
- and comparisons between UK DP expenditure levels and those of other countries.

Computer Weekly forms a good source of both original and secondary material on computer and DP activities - for instance, the survey carried out with Datapro on the use of different software languages and the sources of applications programmes, among UK mainframe and minicomputer users - the sample size was over 2,100, from a target group of 10,000 installations (Barrett, 1986). Another newspaper that frequently reports useful statistics is *Computing*, whose surveys of DP managers (carried out with Price Waterhouse) cover issues such as hardware and software expenditure plans, salaries, staff recruitment, the use of leasing, centralisation/decentralisation of DP activities, the issues worrying DP managers (project deadlines are a recurrent concern!) and methods of financing. Such surveys feature quite large samples, but typically have relatively low response rates, and it is evident that the samples are biased toward large computer users. However, as indicators of trends in corporate computing they form useful complements to publications such as the NCC's *IT Trends*. *Computing* and the NCC's Microsystems Centre carry out some joint surveys, for instance into microcomputer hardware, software and peripherals usage. The NCC itself publishes market analyses and reports on market trends, including estimates of the numbers of products and suppliers entering the market.

Surveys of IT budgets are also produced by consultants, e.g. Price Waterhouse's annual *Information Technology Review* (unusually, free of charge!) whose 1987 edition is particularly interesting for drawing attention to the likelihood of underestimating IT expenditure by relying on the data provided by DP managers. In a survey of 750 installations, the study reports that over a third of total DP expenditure is "illicit", stemming from end-user departments rather than DP management. (Communications-related expenditure accounts for almost half as much again as DP expenditure, furthermore.) Similar problems may well be raised in terms of IT staff being recruited elsewhere than in DP departments. Another interesting feature of this study is that it considers the role of IT managers within companies, concluding that there is an increase in their importance in terms of corporate location (e.g. report ing to the board).

Other types of data are presented less frequently in the media, although it seems likely that this will change with the growth of academic research in the IT area. Among studies that have been published recently we can cite Lee (1986), who studies the use (or non-use) of structured techniques for software system development in UK companies.

6.1.2 Word Processors and Office Equipment

Despite being a major market, and thus receiving some attention in terms of the sales of specific types of office equipment, it seems that office work tends to suffer from some of the lack of statistical interest that applies to the service sector more narrowly defined. It will be recalled that the cross-sectoral studies of Chapter 5 did not, on the whole, focus on office technology. However, there were some notable exceptions: Yap devoted considerable attention to office equipment, while WIRS contrasts change in offices with change on the shopfloor.

Daniel (1987) notes from his analysis of WIRS data that the use of IT in offices appears to be proceeding faster than that on the shopfloor: in the preceding three years (1981-84), more than twice as many establishments had experienced advanced technological change in their offices as had experienced change on the shopfloor (35% of the establishments as against 15%). This differential was less marked in the private sector establishments, where the diffusion of IT was more rapid (41% as against 31%). One-quarter of the establishments used WPs at the time of the survey, these being more common in the private than the public sectors, in manufacturing than in services. Daniel found no clear relation between organisation size and use of WPs, though there was a strong relationship between the number of non-manual workers on site and their use.

The Yap survey (Yap, 1986) included questions on the use of both conventional and IT-based office equipment. For one set of items - terminals, printers, dedicated WPs, general purpose WPs, electronic typewriters, copiers, phone extensions, and telex and fax machines - data are provided on the number in use, and can be related to the number of employees (or just to office employees) to give per capita estimates. Telephone and postage bills are elicited, and for a number of other items data cover their presence or absence, and a qualitative judgement on the degree of use. (These include LANs, electronic mail, videotex, radio-paging, and new telephone facilities, among others.) Yap and Walsham (1986) contrasted the "mature technology" of the telephone with the new technology of computers: the number of telephone extensions increases roughly in line with the number of employees at establishments (roughly two-thirds of employees had telephone extensions), while computers are less diffused and computer capacity increases with the square root of the number of employees. Some other "new" technologies, such as telex and fax, tend to be restricted to a very few per site, rather than to be multiplied within establishments.

Our own analyses of these data suggest that WPs of one sort or another, terminals, and electronic typewriters had by 1984 reached a level of penetration of about one per 10 employees, with some sectors (e.g. banking and business services) easily exceeding this. (In contrast, manufacturing establishments in this survey appear to have relatively few items of office equipment per employee, and retail and transport services are also not office-IT-intensive.) New telephone facilities (such as automatic redial and call forwarding) appear to be widely dif-

fused.
Apart from these surveys, there are various other studies that bear on one or other aspect of office automation, but generally with a limited focus or sample. An interesting early study is Steffens (1983), which describes a survey of 231 companies (from a set of 1,060 establishments which were known to have established computer bases - i.e. the sample excludes both newcomers and non-adopters). The questionnaire addresses a set of office ITs rather similar to Yap's, as well as paying special attention to WPs. Attention was given to the reasons for investing in new office IT (staff costs were ranked highest most often, but increased complexity of management information was close behind), and to organisational obstacles to its use in general (staff shortages, again, were a major factor here) and by management (unfamiliarity with facilities scored highest).

Another limited sample is that used in the Eosys studies of office automation carried out for the magazine *Computing*. The sample of managers responsible for office automation in the survey reported in the September 13 1984 issue only comprised 136 users, and these seem to be biased towards DP staff. However, the study is interesting in the light it sheds on such issues as the need for systems compatibility, and problems in the use of electronic mail. By 1985 the sample "of managers with responsibility for office automation" was down to 110. *Computing* (March 6 1986) reported trends across their surveys from June 1981 to June 1985. Swann (1986) considers a number of studies seeking to survey office equipment, including, as well as NCC and Steffens's material, reference to some consultancy and academic surveys.

The magazine *Business Computing and Communications* (1987) presented a survey of management views concerning desktop publishing. (The response rate was extremely poor: only 141 responded from a target sample of 2,000 managers of director status in large companies.) Though a surprisingly large number claimed that their firms were using desktop publishing, there was widespread ignorance of the system, and management responsibilities seemed to be diffuse and fragmented. Another small sample of managers (118 of 1,500 from organisations with over 750 employees) provided responses to a survey on information presentation. This survey found rather little access to computerised information by boardrooms, and fairly long lists of improvements in the quality of information were desired.

6.1.3 Robots and Numerical Control

International comparisons of robotics have long been recognised to be made more difficult by the different definitions of what constitutes a robot - in particular, Japanese data are believed to overstate the numbers of robots on account of including rather simple pick-and-place devices along with the more complex equipment which other countries are likely to focus on exclusively. (See Economic Commission for Europe (1985) for a discussion of definitional issues.) While robots are mainly employed in manufacturing, there are signs of their application in service industries, and so we shall discuss them here rather than as a sectoral technology. (Cf. Macilwain (1988), who does note that robot makers have been slow to enter service applications.)

The BRA reports annually on the number of robots installed in the UK, and the applications to which they are put. The BRA's annual *Robot Facts* provides analyses of robot sales and installations by application type (spot welding, injection moulding, etc.) and by sectoral use (among which the automobile industry is easily dominant). The regional distribution of robots is presented, together with comparisons with data for other countries. The BRA has also presented data on attitudes among different groups of personnel to the use of robots, since the comparisons suggest that UK industry is relatively slow in using this technology (and tends to purchase less sophisticated systems than its competitors do). Some of these data are also reported in the BRA's journal *Industrial Robot.*

Northcott et al. (1986) conducted a major postal survey of robot use in the UK for the BRA. As with other PSI studies, their report is extensively illustrated with graphs and tables concerning the 1985 population of some 3,200 robots in 740 user companies. Some of the results are evocative of earlier studies: for instance, robot users tend to be larger plants (in terms of employment and turnover). In terms of broad industrial groupings, the distribution of robots is:

- mechanical engineering (23%)
- vehicles, aircraft and shipbuilding (22%)
- electrical, electronic and instrument engineering (15%)
- other metal goods (13%)
- other manufacturing (13%)
- plastic products (9%)
- chemicals and metals (5%).

The study provides considerable detail on the process of introduction of robots, on the use of shift working (to capitalise on the value of the technology, two or even three shifts are common), specific applications (arc welding is most common), the numbers of robots per plant (57% of users have two or more), and so on.

Tidd (1988a) describes a smaller but more recent postal survey of over 100 robot-using firms (in 1987), paying particular attention to the use of robots for assembly - thus he presents data on the proportion of the final product assembled by robot, on the specific assembly tasks undertaken, and on the sector of use. Other results include the number of robots per plant, the time taken to implement the system, and perceived benefits. Tidd (1988b) goes on to compare robot applications in the UK and Japan in some detail. On the international diffusion of robotics, see Economic Commission for Europe (1985) and Edquist and Jacobsson (1988).

Machine tools are widely used in the manufacture of metal products, and we deal with them here rather than in the sectoral discussion below because data on CNC machine tools are often included along with data on robots. A study that provides an excellent introduction to trends in the technology, outlines international and supplier profiles, and goes on to analysis differences in CNC use in Germany and the UK is Sorge et al. (1983).

The magazine *Metalworking Production* has mounted a series of surveys of numerically controlled machine tools in the UK. The fourth survey was in 1976/77, the fifth in 1982. A large volume of data is published, dealing with number of tools of various types (and of various vintages) installed; comparisons are drawn with other countries (West Germany, France, USA and Japan). The distribution by sector, and their source (domestic or imported) is reported. One of the main features of the results is the shift, within a rapid growth of the equipment (and displacement of non-NC equipment), toward more capable equipment. Issues in the definition of a machine tool are discussed (it should be non-portable and have its own power source), and data on robotics are also included.

6.1.4 Computer-Aided Design and Expert Systems

Though CAD is particularly pertinent in engineering and other manufacturing sectors, it is also used extensively in architecture, construction, and some other professional services. Thus Peat Marwick McLintock (1987), in a study conducted with the Construction Industry Computing Association, provides data on the use of CAD (and various other ITs) by large construction-related firms (architects, surveyors, contractors, etc.). The survey found IT already highly diffused among big users in this sector: 95% of respondents used computers for financial and management accounting and office systems. It is likely that follow-up studies will allow trends in IT application to be monitored.

Research at SPRU into CAD has built on a survey of a relatively small number of firms (just over 30) using CAD (Arnold and Senker, 1982). Arnold (1984) goes on to provide an extensive discussion of the market, dealing with suppliers as well as users. Arnold supplies data on suppliers' market shares and estimated sales for the UK. He also presents international comparisons of CAD use - while admitting that definitional problems are serious here - and of government support programmes.

In a recent paper, Simmonds and Senker (1988) describe follow-up surveys now under way, and summarise some market research data on the size of CAD markets. An earlier study (Arnold, cited by Brady and Liff, 1983) attempted to specify users of CAD in the engineering sector by their Minimum List Headings; for 1981, 149 engineering users were located, almost half of these (71) in electrical engineering, and with mechanical engineering lagging behind (39) but still in front of vehicles (25), instrument engineering (8), shipbuilding (4), and metal goods n.e.s. (2).

More recently, there have been a number of efforts to survey the field more thoroughly. For instance, *Computing* newspaper, together with CAD/CAM Business Associates, undertook a survey of over 120 CAD-using companies, addressing such questions as their CAD expenditure, training costs, development work being undertaken, and user satisfaction and concerns with various features of CAD systems. (The report was summarised in *Computing,* January 9 1986.) The *Engineering Computers* survey was used by Potts (1985) to outline patterns of CAD use in the engineering industry. Extremely rapid growth was recorded - for draughting applications the number of users had grown by 50% in one year, with a further 100% growth forecast for 1985/86. Growth in other applications (including the dominant one, design calculations) was also rapid.

Bessant (1986) reviews studies of CAD in the UK, provides data - compiled from supplier information and trade literature, and thus prone to reporting problems - on the major commercially available systems (application areas, capabilities, numbers sold), and gives a sectoral breakdown of application areas of the larger CAD systems (those based on minicomputers or workstations). Another source of (international) data is the magazine *CADCAM International.*

CAD will also be a feature of some of the new manufacturing systems discussed in Section 6.2.1 below. As with robots, there are serious definitional problems in the CAD field. The term is used to cover systems of very different sorts: mainframe-based, workstation-based, and relatively primitive (by current standards) microcomputer-based systems, with capabilities ranging from simple draughting to 3-D design with high-resolution colour graphics and integration with inventory and production systems. The problem here is largely a matter of generational improvement in what is expected and delivered from expert systems, together with the emergence of "cheap and cheerful" models for a wider range of users. Experts on CAD interviewed for this report looked back with regret to the easily definable market of the early 1980s! One problem is posed by microcomputer-based CAD systems; these are probably easily dominant in terms of numbers of items sold, but are barely visible in sales data. The challenge of such systems has led major suppliers to respond by reworking their own software into versions that are simpler, or that can be run on smaller machines; available statistics may not discriminate between different versions of the software.

Although in both cases the heart of the matter is an absence of an agreed minimum definition, the problem emerges even more acutely when we turn to "expert systems". The term has been, of course, an IT buzzword - together with the related idea of "artificial intelligence" (and, in the UK at least, "Intelligent Knowledge-Based Systems") - and this has led to it being seized upon in order to promote all sorts of software products.

There have been relatively few empirical studies that can flesh out the enthusiasm of advocates of expert systems, who are arguing that already these are solving important problems in industry and public services. (One problem in this field is commercial secrecy: expert systems are of strategic importance, and details of their development are liable to be withheld at least until the technology matures.) *Business Computing and Communications* (March 1987) is one exception, having carried out a survey with PA Management Consultants of 257 large UK-based companies; over 50% reported using or attempting to develop such systems. Guy (1987) reports survey results based on just 27 users of expert systems - and even here found considerable diversity in the scale of system in use, with the number of rules involved ranging from a few dozen to over 5,000! A more substantial review of research by Jahoda et al. (1988) examines developments in the USA, West Germany, France and Japan as well as the UK; while criticising unrealistic forecasts of market growth, and expressing doubt concerning the level of accuracy of several consultancy reports cited, this study is able to cite a number of studies that give some indication of the scale and direction of expert system activity in the UK. It suggests that this particular IT is still rather uncommon.

Expert systems seem to be attracting attention in larger companies, however. Price Waterhouse's 1988/89 *Information Technology Review* asked its panel of DP managers of 750 computer installations (with five or more staff in the DP department - an estimated 15% sample) to describe their use of expert systems. Some 11% of this panel claimed to be using expert systems, with 2% using over fiveof them. Responsibility for the systems largely rested with the DP department, but a shift to end-users was forecast. The study addressed perceived obstacles to expert system development, with corporate lack of awareness of potential and difficulties in technical experts' finding suitable applications both being mentioned by more than half of the panel; and expectations of the future role of expert systems show a small minority expecting them to be important in the next three years, a larger minority thinking that they will never be important, and the bulk of respondents opting for their achieving importance "sometime".

6.1.5 Telecommunications Services and Systems

Chapter 4 outlined the general paucity of statistics on telecommunications services, and the diffusion studies reviewed in Chapter 5 added only a little to this. The liberalisation of telecommunications equipment and service markets in the UK has led to considerable development of consultancy and market research activities in this area, and as usual the trade press is a good place to find reference to reports emanating from such sources. However, it has to be admitted that the trade press in this area is relatively undeveloped - at least, compared to the computer field, which hosts several weekly magazines. Among the publications found useful in the course of this study, we should cite: *Lines of Communication*, *Network*, *Telelink*, and *Videotex Viewpoint*. As in several other IT fields, however, many of the reports discussed in such sources concern "Europe" rather than the UK.

Telephony

We considered some sources of data on telephone system supply and usage in Chapter 4. Data on the pattern of use across business and residential users are available, along with data on growth in the number of installations, but there are remarkably few available statistics on more detailed features of the diffusion of telephone services. One exception is Economist Informatics (n.d.) which provides some regional and sectoral disaggregations. Even so, these data are not always presented in a very helpful format: for example, we are provided with a sector-by-sector chart of the ratio between Scottish business users' telephone use (call bill per phone) to the UK business use as a whole, but we are not provided with the overall distribution of use across sectors in the UK, (though another chart does provide data of this sort for north England - but we can be fairly sure that this will not be typical of the UK). Some data are also provided on telex and fax use in the north and south-east of England, related to establishment size (as indexed by the number of telephone lines installed!). This is one case where the use of new technology does not seem to increase with size in any regular manner - indeed, telex use seems more prevalent among smaller sites in the South-east.

With the liberalisation of the telephone attachment market, and the growing sales of various novel types of telephone and attachment, market research has been brought to bear on the topic of customer equipment as well as on expenditure on network services (see Chapters 4, 8). Thomas (1987), for example, presents a study commissioned by the Telecommunications Industry Association, and drawn from a data base of material on European telecommunications. The source of the data is unspecified, but probably involves suppliers; the data project the installed base, from 1987 to 1990, of one- and two-piece telephones (the latter broken down into business and domestic markets, with the business base predominating somewhat at 27 million as compared to a domestic base of 20 million in 1987), cordless (655,000) and cellular phones (140,000 mobile, 40,000 hand-held), telephone answering machines (1.75 million), fax machines (110,000) and PABX systems of various kinds.

Mobile phones and radio paging

Mobile telephone use has received considerable attention from the press and from market researchers, perhaps because it is a very profitable and rapidly growing sector, perhaps because it represents a fashionable yuppie technology. We have already identified some relevant data (in Chapter 3); other public sources include a *Financial Times* survey supplement (April 28 1987) which reproduced international diffusion statistics from the *European Mobile Communications Report,* and an earlier article in the same newspaper (Thomas, 1986) which presented data from CIT Research on the use of cellular radio (including cellular car phones), private mobile radio, and radio paging, with a breakdown of the proportion of workers in different occupational groups using each system. Although the sample studied is not made explicit in this report the structure of diffusion across occupations seems plausible - over 80% of directors use cellular phones, less than 20% of other occupational groups, while radio paging is much more evenly distributed.

In contrast to the numerous studies showing firm size to be correlated with use of IT, British Telecom's (1985) radio-paging survey provided no evidence for variations in the use of this service across firms of different sizes. (It is interesting that two sets of BT data - see those on fax and telex cited above - behave in this way. Is it a feature of the technology, or of the organisation doing the research? In this current case, there may be problems with the sample: the research was done on a sample of working adults, and the published data tell us little about the volume of radio paging engaged in by firms of different sizes; and Yap (1986), reports a size trend for radio paging - and a lower level of use overall - in the services sector.)

Telex and Facsimile

These telecommunication services have grown considerably in popularity in recent years, despite the development of sophisticated electronic mail systems. In the case of fax, in particular, the ease of use of the system, and the ability to transmit graphics and signatures, have weighed heavily. The introduction of fax facilities on some personal computer systems is probably a minor, but not insignificant, boost to the system. Some of the growth in telex traffic, in contrast, is probably due to the availability of telex services from within electronic mail systems. While neither telex nor fax are necessarily based on "new" IT, microelectronics-based terminals are now standard, and many new features are being added to the equipment.

The growth of these markets has led to much interest on the part of market researchers and consultants. There have been numerous descriptions of the growth of the markets - for instance Barton (1987) and Moggridge (1987) outline statistics from the British Facsimile Consultative Committee suggesting a rapid growth leading to c150,000 fax terminals by the end of 1987; with the population still dominated by Group 3 machines (considerably more limited than Group 4 machines, which utilise digital lines). However, we know of relatively few studies that address the pattern of diffusion of the technologies: the exceptions have already been cited (Economist Informatics, n.d.; Yap, 1986).

6.1.6 Data Communications and New Telecommunications Services

Data communications are of growing significance in many companies, as means of intra-corporate communication and as methods of access to other organisations. Data communications are also the basis for VANS/VADS services. We shall first consider some general features of users of data communications, and then move to specific services. Cable TV and related consumer services are discussed in Chapter 8. Electronic Funds Transfer (EFT) and Electronic Funds Transfer at Point of Sale (EFTPOS) will be treated as sectoral technologies, under retailing and banking. Other new telecommunications services, such as data broadcasting, could also be covered here, but in general data are nonexistent - for data broadcasting Chang and Hitchcock (1987) are only able to provide statistics on use of one of the two services in operation in the UK, for instance.

We shall discuss the following categories of new telecommunication services here: videotex, electronic mail, and data bases. They share in common the property of being computer-mediated, interactive, and accessed by terminals or microcomputers, unlike most of the telecommunications services discussed earlier. A review of British experience with VADS is provided by Coopers & Lybrand (1987); and in 1988 the DTI has been publishing a series on the use of VADS such as electronic data interchange in various sectors of the UK economy. These studies, entitled *The Use of Value Added and Data Services in the ... Sector* cover textiles, wholesale food distribution, electrical industry, construction, educational supplies, pharmaceuticals,brewing, aerospace, agrochemicals, and transport. Some of these studies are more surveys of potentials than of practice, but they often contain useful data on communications activities in the various sectors.

Data Communications

Finkelstein (1988) cites data from a Logica Telematica report concerning annual UK shipments of one type of equipment that is particularly relevant here - network terminal points (modems or interfaces to specialised networks). The data are classified into the type of network involved: perhaps surprisingly, analogue leased lines are currently in the lead - which suggests that in-house communications rather than access to external services are the major application - but it is forecast that connection to the Public Switched Telephone Network (PSTN) will dominate by 1992. Antonelli (1986) discusses the international diffusion of modems, including UK data.

The 1987/88 edition of Price Waterhouse's *Information Technology Review* features data from a 1986 survey of 750 IT managers from UK companies with five or more IT staff in their DP departments. The questions include: the allocation of responsibility for different communications services (focusing on, but going beyond, data communications); the main problems faced with implementing communications systems; current and planned use of Mercury services, and plans for implementing Open Systems Interconnection (OSI).

A source that may be of increasing value in the future is VNU Publications *The Data Comms Book* (an annual in the same series as *The Computer Users' Year Book*). Currently its main contribution is to provide comparative information on communications products and their suppliers, with information on users typically focusing on qualitative accounts of the problems and opportunities they face.

Videotex

Within the videotex format, a variety of IT-based services can operate. Videotex often supports limited data-base access, messaging and electronic mail, some forms of computer conferencing, teleservices such as telebanking, teleshopping and telebooking, etc. These applications need not be restricted to the videotex format, however, and we shall consider some of them later. But there has also been attention directed to videotex itself, as a medium for information and communication services that requires little training and that has been extremely successful in sectors such as travel and insurance. *Videotex Viewpoint* provides news coverage of this field.

The main public videotex service, Prestel, releases data on the number of users and their composition as residential and business users. These are published on Prestel itself on Page 65659, although it appears that the quality of the data has declined (in terms of both frequency of updating and accuracy - figures seem to be rounded up more than previously). This source also provides information on the number of pages of information available, the rate of page accesses, and the rate of messaging.

Schofield (1988), in a brief news item, comments that Prestel has, after "an 8 month delay...finally updated its quarterly figures, and now claims 90,000 users for June 1988. This is surprising for three reasons. First, it shows growth of 1,444 users/month, compared with 540/month over the previous year. Second, the number of Prestel frames has dropped from 310,000 to 257,420. Third, the number of frame accesses per week has dropped from 9.1 million to 7.5 million...some large information providers have switched from using Prestel computers to using their own, accessed via a Prestel gateway. The frames and accesses are thus lost to the Prestel monitoring system..." (p25).

Sporadic information on the popularity of specific services is available on Micronet (a computer hobbyists' section of Prestel), but on the whole there is remarkably little data on the use of the service - especially when compared to the statistics provided for the equivalent French and German services. (A useful source of comparative information is

Mayntz and Schneider (1987); see also various statistics in Miles (1988a).) It would appear that the failure of Prestel to meet early expectations of a mass consumer market continues to evoke some reluctance to publicise its level of activity which, however healthy it may be, still falls far below forecasts for demand growth. In contrast, Prestel was reported on quite intensively in its early days - cf. Kania (1984), reporting on research carried out near the launch of Prestel.

A large number of private videotex systems have emerged in the UK, however, and it appears that sales of videotex terminals are considerably higher than Prestel membership figures alone would imply. It is extremely difficult to define a comprehensive sample of private systems operators (let alone their users); there may be problems in defining the relevant system type (are public display systems such as those used to indicate train arrivals and departures to be included, even if they are non-interactive?), and services may change their type (e.g. such railway station systems may be connected to interactive public terminals); a few systems have been set up by hobbyists intent on pushing their home computer systems to the limit, and many systems are probably employed in schools and colleges as small-scale information services installed as much for educational and training purposes as anything else. (Nevertheless, even some school systems can be quite large-scale, with dozens of terminals linked in to a minicomputer.)

Nevertheless, there have been two efforts to survey private videotex in the UK. Yates-Mercer (1985) reported estimates of private systems which put their number in early 1984 variously at 250 and 400. She was herself able to locate 242 organisations which were or had been involved with such systems, of whom 155 were running at the time of her survey. Further bodies were planning to install systems, and some 44 failed to provide data. Her study classifies users by economic sector, examines the date of implementation of pilot and operation systems, and describes the use of hardware, software, and bureau services. In research currently under way at SPRU, Jagger and Miles have obtained data on over 400 systems (early 1988), and have further received completed questionnaires from well over 100 of these. As well as replicating most of the Yates-Mercer questions, they have investigated the use of the systems (for messaging, transactions, information, etc.), the users' orientation toward and use of various VANS, the origins of the innovation (technical department, financial department, etc.), and obtained information concerning satisfaction with various aspects of the system, improvements desired, and future plans. Results of this study are published in Jagger (1989).

Electronic Mail

The use of electronic mail services has not so far been charted adequately, to the best of our knowledge. The fragmentation of the market into services provided by several different suppliers (of whom Telecom Gold and One-to-One are believed to hold the largest market shares), and the "bundling" of electronic mail (sometimes termed "email") with other VANS means that it is difficult to obtain a comprehensive view of its diffusion. Press reports quite frequently document the growth in membership of the main services - *The Guardian*'s weekly computer section seems to be a good source of such news. Chang and Hitchcock (1987), in their directory of electronic mail suppliers, provide where possible the registered users with each service, and the book also contains an essay by Jones outlining the growth in Telecom Gold use.

There are clear reasons for suppliers of these services to seek to push use estimates upwards, since unless one is dealing with a closed group of other users, the value of a particular service will be in large part determined by how many other people one can access on it. It has been suggested that one way in which email use is exaggerated is through providing large numbers of company employees with mailboxes.

Data Bases

The European Community news magazine *I'M* (*Information Market*) frequently carries statistics (drawn from a number of sources) on the use of online data services and other telecommunications facilities; sometimes the data reproduced span a wider range. For instance, the most recent issue to hand (no 52) notes on its cover page the number of hosts connected to the French Minitel service in December 1987, provides a chart of the schedule for introducing ISDN for 13 countries (including the UK), gives various figures on the content and hosts of data bases, and reprints Dataquest estimates of the number of terminals linked into various kinds of network in the EC. As will be apparent, many of the data are not specific to the UK, and often report figures at the European level. *Information World Review* is another magazine (in newspaper format) oriented to the online and data-base communities (it also covers such areas as CD-ROM), and this frequently features valuable data.

A useful review of the information services industry is provided by O'Brien and Channing (1986). These authors review the main consultancy reports on the size and structure of the market, and provide one table estimating revenues from "on-line database and videotex activities" in major Western European countries (including the UK), the USA and Japan. They also seek to describe the industry structure and identify the main actors involved in service provision in the different countries. Hartley et al. (1986) focus on the UK online data-base industry, and are able to cite a number of statistical sources - including data from *I'M* on the occupational composition of users in different countries - but the study mainly involves description of organisations and services.

East (1987) describes a study that he is conducting into the use of online data bases in the UK, modelled on the Information Market Indicators produced in the USA. This is one of the very few UK statistical studies of users of new telecommunications services to reach the public domain. Currently public libraries, universities and polytechnics are being studied, and it is planned to extend the research to government-funded establishments and to users in the private sector. Based on analysis of invoices from service hosts, East is calculating connect time and expenditure on individual data bases. In the paper cited he presents data for libraries on their overall expenditure on online, the range of expenditures, the frequency of use of, and the expenditure on, individual data bases, the subject areas accessed, etc.

I'M and several other sources frequently carry material on telecommunications tariffs in different countries. The June-August 1987 *I'M* (no 48, pp6-7) compares and contrasts time and data charges in different EC countries, using these to estimate the costs of searches on data bases in different countries charged by the telecommunications operator (over and above any charges from the host). Prices vary widely across Europe, with little consistency in tariffing practices. For comparisons of costs of different types of telephone call, see *IPTC News* (International Press Telecommunications Council) June 1987.

6.2 Sectoral Studies: Manufacturing Industry and Private Services

6.2.1 Manufacturing

We have already touched on a number of surveys which focus on manufacturing industries, and sometimes within these on engineering. (See Chapter 5, and the discussions of robots and CNC above.) For a number of early studies of IT in manufacturing, including studies of CAD, CNC, robotics, assembly technology, maintenance, the printing industry and manufacturing in general, see Senker (1985). A set of surveys of IT in Scottish manufacturing industry (and some services) is being produced from Glasgow Business School. These include studies by Boddy (1987) on financial services, Buchanan (1987) on chemicals and allied industries, McCalman (1987a) on electronics, and McCalman (1987b) on mechanical engineering; the number of companies involved in each sectoral study ranges from 21 to 30.

But other IT-related innovations in manufacturing have received increasing attention; among the most important of these must be the emergence of Flexible Manufacturing Systems (FMS). However, FMS is yet another of the terms which has been stretched beyond recognition by many interested suppliers - just as "flexibility" itself has become a selling point for promoting IT systems. Bessant (1984) cites a number of divergent definitions of the term FMS, and concludes that it really indicates more of an approach to common manufacturing problems than a specific combination of ITs. The various definitions "involve the notion of making small batches economically through...some combination of machine tools *and* handling systems operating under computer control" (p4, my emphasis). FMS thus brings together, at a minimum, "elements of machining, handling and overall production management", to which may also be added "testing and inspection, stock control and management, design...and marketing" (p8). This more comprehensive list seems to be taking us toward what is often referred to as Computer Integrated Manufacturing (CIM), which brings together the whole range of key company activities.

(Potts (1987) uses *Engineering Computers* survey data to outline the areas of application of computer-aided production management packages - noting that around 65% of engineering companies have installed one component of such systems, but that integrated systems are rare. Another use of data from this survey is provided in *Computers and Manufacturing Technology* (June 1986), which outlines trends in the use of various sorts of production control-related systems. Senker (1986) discusses results of a small-scale survey of engineering users of CAD/CAM and computerised production and inventory control systems.)

Wobbe (1987) presents a collection of studies of FMS in Europe, which includes diffusion studies funded by the CEC's FAST Programme, for Denmark, France and West Germany (with surprisingly little discussion of definitional issues). Shorter studies are included for a number of other countries, including two papers dealing with small-scale surveys of UK experience. Dodgson (1987) presents results of a study of 40 small engineering firms (these are not representative of the UK as a whole, being based in the south-east of England), and actually focuses on CNC systems. Haywood (1987) outlines some results from a study apparently involving some 38 FMS systems (the methodological description refers to some 50 interviews, but some of these involved suppliers and others), and notes that by the end of 1986 over 100 systems or cells were installed or planned. (Compare this with Bessant's (1984) identification of only 8-10 UK FMS, out of a world population in excess of 100 - with Japan in the lead, followed by the

USA.) Among the results of his analysis are these: FMS tend to be used by larger firms; the cost of systems has been declining rapidly (but is still usually in the millions of pounds); the systems are generally used for low batch sizes (58% deal with batch sizes of 10 or fewer); and users are beginning to come from still larger medium-sized enterprises and from a wider range of branches of manufacturing.

Bessant, together with Haywood and other colleagues at Brighton Polytechnic, is continuing to carry out telephone surveys of UK FMS users. While it has to date been relatively easy to accumulate a comprehensive set of users (since the absolute numbers remain small) on the basis of reports in the trade press and recipients of DTI aid, the wider diffusion of FMS may reduce the adequacy of future samples! Further reports may be expected from this group (e.g. Bessant and Haywood, 1986a,b).

Despite the evident difficulties, there have been some attempts to amass data on the diffusion of FMS and related industrial automation technologies on a cross-national basis. Arcangeli et al. (1987) reproduce a number of tables which draw on a wide range of sources (whose quality is almost certainly most accurately described as variable). These tables, featuring the UK alongside other countries, include:

- several classes of computer per thousand workers;
- stock of robots and FMS, absolutely and per capita;
- sectoral distribution of countries' FMS stock.

Another study, by Edquist & Jacobsson (1988), discusses the diffusion, in industrial and newly industrialising countries, of a number of "flexible automation techniques": CAD, robots, CNC, and FMS. The authors amass a considerable volume of data, and go to some pains to tackle - or at least explicate - definitional problems. However, the international coverage is very uneven from IT to IT, and one looks in vain for data on UK FMS in this study. Economic Commission for Europe (1986) is another wide-ranging international study, in this case providing a concise discussion of definitional and other aspects of FMS, including the structure of the supply industry (no fewer than 11 different definitions of FMS are cited!) There are a few statistics presented here which show UK FMS in a comparative light, notably Table III.1 which analyses the distribution of FMS by application area across 12 countries. NEDO Advanced Manufacturing Systems Group (1984) considers a subsection of FMS, flexible machining systems, and mainly deals with the UK scene - with a set of case studies - but again provides some international comparisons, statistics, and a discussion of definitional issues.

6.2.2 *Service Sectors*

While we have noted the general paucity of data on service industries, it would be wrong to think that no attention has been addressed to services and IT. In the following subsections we consider a number of services, but first we should mention some efforts to appraise the whole sector (or at least its private components). Chapter 5 introduced the Yap (1986) survey, and so we do not need to refer to it again here. But a number of studies from the Technical Change Centre also centred on services. This Centre is now defunct, but its publications are still available from the PSI, London, as well as being held by numerous libraries.

Several of these studies deal with specific services, but two take a broader approach. Barras (1984) deals with technical change in services, and while he presents a good deal of interesting data and argument concerning services investment and capital stock, the data do not specifically deal with IT. Swann (1986) describes the sectoral adoption of IT, but again has little new data (other than case study material) to add on use of services. Her focus is on possible employment implications of new technology in these sectors.

6.2.3 *Banking and Financial Services*

As we saw in Chapter 5, these are very IT-intensive branches of the economy; their high expenditure levels have attracted a great deal of consultancy and market research, especially in the heady days of the "Big Bang". A number of trade magazines and newsletters are useful routes to this material, and to reviews of technological developments, for instance *Banking and Financial Technology*, *Electronic Banking and Finance*. Numerous technological developments have been implemented or are in advanced stages of planning in these sectors, ranging from the early use of computers in "back-office" administration through networking of branches, the development of Automated Teller Machines (ATMs), experiments with telebanking, and the prospective use of EFTPOS and "smart cards".

As well as studies specifically devoted to these sectors, in recent years their buoyancy has led to their prominence in various more general surveys - as the bright spot in DP managers' salary expectations (*Computing*, June 26 1986, discussing the current Price Waterhouse survey of DP department activities and views), or as a drain on skilled IT labour for the rest of the economy (Rajan and Fryatt, 1988). DP and computer activities in finance (especially back-office activities) are thus often covered in the computer trade press; sometimes these reports include statistical data of one sort or another, most commonly on staffing issues, but sometimes on other topics. For instance, Tilley (1988) cites a MORI survey of 46 financial institutions of whom 63% said they were considering contracting out their major computing projects and only 13% expected projects to be completed on time!

Press reports have discussed the use of credit cards and related cards; usually these are discussed in aggregate terms (e.g. "(a)bout 25 million cards are on issue in this country...compared with about 7 million in France, the next most prolific user of plastic (in Europe)", but one recent report (*The Times* May 16 1988, p32, from which the quotation just reproduced is taken) did give a breakdown of the use of Access cards by seven categories of retailer - statistics covered the number and proportion of outlets, and the volume and proportion of turnover involved. An early study (Marti and Zeiliger, 1982) contains still-useful discussions of the shift to "paperless money", and presents data on the ratio of back-office to front-office terminals in banks, on ATM diffusion, and on a range of related trends in handling money. But perhaps the most useful recent source of information is the Report of the Review Committee on Banking Services Law (1989), which addressed the implications of IT for banking law. Among the data cited here is evidence for a rapid substitution of ATMs for counter services where it comes to cash withdrawals: while at the beginning of the 1980s counter services predominated, by 1987 almost twice as much money was withdrawn from ATMs. Other data compare trends in paper, plastic (ATMs and credit cards) and electronics (EFT, EFTPOS) as media for transferring money, and consider the relative importance of different "payment instruments" (cheques, postal orders, direct debit, credit cards, etc.) A substantial growth in IT-based transactions is consistently apparent.

More broadly, Rajan (1984) represents one of the broadest studies of new technology in financial institutions - banking, insurance and finance - with a postal survey of 196 organisations and 35 detailed case studies. For each branch, he provides an account of the main stages of technological development and major current innovations, together with a range of statistics on related topics - especially employment-related issues - and judgements on obstacles to innovation (as usual, skill shortages rank highest here).

Tarbuck and Arnold (1985) provide a review of studies carried out through the early 1980s of IT in services. In the case of financial services, they are able to cite data on ATMs installed by 1981 and planned for 1982, and to relate these to the number of bank branches. The Rajan study cited above also provides data on trends in ATMs, and adds to this similar data on counter terminals. Chang and Hitchcock (1987) describe the networks of the two shared ATM systems (Link and Matrix) with a little data on current and projected ATM installations and card membership. (Although data on current diffusion are only provided for Matrix in the directory portion of this report, data on Link are provided elsewhere in the volume (p124).) Comparative data on ATMs, EFTPOS terminals and the use of credit cards in European Community countries are reported in essays in Muldur and Pastr (1987), a collection which includes several useful studies of new technology in financial institutions. Omdal (1987) presents data on national and Eurocheque ATMs in 15 European countries in 1987 and 1988. Simpson (1987) presents and discusses trends in the development of the Banks Automated Clearing System (BACS), a major EFT operation in the UK dealing with bulk automated payments between financial institutions ("the largest automated clearing house in the world"), and with operations such as direct debiting.

A study of a management IT - Marketing Information Systems - in major banks, building societies, charge card operators and insurance groups (though totalling 27 institutions in all, this forms a fairly comprehensive sample of major firms in several of these branches) is presented by Stone and Clarkson (1987). The authors argue that these management systems are becoming increasingly important in the firms surveyed, providing for their sample data on: membership of ATM networks, levels of sophistication of computer systems, and of activities such as customer account sorting, postcoding addresses, and demographic profiling. The paper provides useful information on the structure of ATM networks and related services.

Two of the Technical Change Centre studies mentioned earlier deal with financial services: Barras and Swann (1983, 1984). The studies (of insurance and accountancy, respectively) have a similar format, attempting to identify the trajectory of IT innovation in the branch concerned, and to draw on case studies to discuss issues in the choice and management of technology, and the employment and organisational implications. The sectoral data provided do not, however, deal with technology as such (but rather with employment, output, etc.), and while the qualitative discussions are very revealing, there is little evidence as to the representativeness of the small samples studied.

Finally, some of the most successful VANS have been online financial information services. The *Financial Times* (December 19 1986) carried some rare quantified information on the relative development of the five major suppliers of these services, presenting charts depicting their level of use by six sectors: banking and credit, investment and insurance, auxiliary banking and finance, service organisations, public companies, and public sector organisations). The data draw on a Romtec survey, and show very uneven use of the services across sectors, with 90% of banking and credit companies using them; the main suppliers are serving quite segmented markets, rather than displaying across-the-board success.

6.2.4 Retail, Wholesale and Distribution

Many technological developments are being introduced in these sectors, ranging from EFT and Electronic Point of Sale (EPOS) systems to automated warehouses. Some have received considerably more attention than others, reflecting in part the scope for suppliers' market expansion. We consider a number of distinct ITs below.

Computer Weekly (September 11 1986) describes a study of the distribution and transport industries carried out with Romtec. While this presents charts of use of micro, mini and mainframe systems, and of mini and micro software and use of independent consultants across 10 branches of these sectors, it is not clear what sort of survey and sample has been employed (and much of the text is clearly drawn from suppliers' views). However, reference is made to a 45% sample of the 150 major retail chains, all of whom were computerised.

Point of Sale: EPOS and EFTPOS

The cashpoint in retail outlets has moved through a number of stages: from mechanical to electronic till, to EPOS systems where numbered articles are scanned by laser readers and data on sales fed directly into the cash register (which may or may not be integrated into the store's stock ordering and marketing systems), and EFTPOS systems where cashless shopping is accomplished by the use of machine-readable cash cards.

Marti and Zeilinger (1982) cite a number of statistics on new retail technology. These include the percentage of new shops (disaggregated by size and whether part of a multiple or a cooperative system) with electronic cash registers in 1980; major stores operating laser scanning systems in 1981 (number of lanes involved, and the supplier). They also present data on the transactions carried out by various methods (cash, cheque, credit card, etc.) and give estimates of the time taken for transactions using the different methods. Tarbuck and Arnold (1985) provide data from early 1980s surveys of the introduction of EPOS (laser scanning) systems.

A *Financial Times* supplement on retailing technology (March 28 1988) carried reports of several studies by consultants and suppliers of EPOS systems. These include ICL estimates of the number and growth of EPOS installations (from 142,000 in 1988 to 410,000 in 1993), a Coopers & Lybrand survey of *major* retailers and high street multiples (46% of these have installed EPOS terminals, and pie charts of penetration by sector are provided), and ICL surveys of retailers that suggest that at present 75% of retailers have either not considered EPOS or not formulated a strategy for it. Mehta and Watts (1986) discuss and reprint data from a Butler Cox report on new shopping technology, which draws on a study of the 102 biggest retailers and a study of suppliers. Data cover the areas discussed above (e.g. expectations of installing systems, perceived benefits, penetration by sector of retailing), together with some material on the shares of different suppliers and the installed bases in different European countries (where France is clearly in the lead).

As a burgeoning market, EPOS/EFTPOS is attracting its share of conferences, and the proceedings of the 1987 conference organised by RMDP (1987) carry several articles laden with statistical data (and forecasts). These include information not only on the hardware market, but also on the shares of different types of operating system and programming languages in retail software packages; surveys of shoppers' and retailers' views of EFTPOS; and the international diffusion of laser scanners in retail (Japan is in the lead).

Electronic Data Interchange (EDI), Teleshopping, etc.

EDI, sometimes known also as Trade Data Interchange, comprises the exchange of commercial documents (e.g. bills of trade, invoices, orders) within a computer-communications system. Only a minority of the EDI service suppliers in Chang and Hitchcock's (1987) directory provide data on the number of users. Like electronic mail, the value of the service depends upon how many of one's suppliers and clients can be reached through it, although the services are liable to be more sectorally organised (i.e. it does not matter who is not on the service as long as one's chief trading partners are).

Teleshopping is computer-mediated home shopping, usually run through videotex systems in the UK. Despite several efforts to get such services off the ground, success to date has been very limited and statistics correspondingly hard to come by (Davies, n.d.). Information on developments in this field - and those of related teleservices - is provided in the *Teleservices Monitoring Studies* produced by the Oxford Institute of Retail Management, Templeton College.

The travel industry is one of the great success stories for videotex systems, and has been discussed in numerous studies (e.g. Feeny, 1987, who presents a study involving a small sample - 26 - of travel agents). The newsletter *Travel Data* covers IT for the industry, and is a useful source of further information. *Retail Technology* provides a similar function for high street stores in general.

6.2.5 Other Services

Whitaker (1986) outlines the results of a 1986 survey based on a random sample of the membership list of the Hotel, Catering and Institutional Management Association. Only a usable 17% response rate was obtained from a target sample of 900, in part because of the presence of retired members in the list - and the Association will no doubt be limited in terms of its representativeness of the sector as a whole. Nevertheless, the study presents useful trend analyses and comparisons between hotels and caterers of different types (as usual, larger firms tended to adopt IT first and to have experienced greater levels of diffusion). The study covered a range of ITs, of which the most prevalent were electronic cash registers, microcomputers, and computerised switchboards (all installed at 50% or more of establishments). Minicomputers and EPOS systems had penetrated between 20 and 30% of sites, while computerised heating, vending and security equipment were making some inroads. Whitaker pays some attention to how far the commonest applications of computers (stock control, accounts, payroll, etc.) are integrated, and finds partial integration to be common but full integration rare.

6.3 Public Sector Information Technology

Although the public sector was one of the earliest large users of computers, and is probably still the largest single user of most IT hardware and services in the UK, it is widely admitted that it is hard to obtain a comprehensive view, or even a good overview, of the diffusion and use of IT within it. Some official sources exist that do purport to provide relevant data, but these are often contradicted by other official sources. Thus estimates of IT expenditure by Local Authorities (LAs), for example, range from £280 million to £480 million, out of total LA spending of around £40 billion per annum. To some extent, as with other inconsistencies we have encountered, such discrepancies may reflect the point in time at which surveys are held - particularly as the use of IT in this sector is said to be growing by nearly 25% per annum. But the usual problems as to the definition of IT are joined, in this case, by problems in defining the public sector itself.

We shall discuss three main public sectors below: central government, local government, and public services. But first we can note some sources that do cover a wide span of public activities. An interesting data source is CIPFA's (1986) *Computer Audit: The State of the Art in the Public Sector*. The participating organisations in this study included not only local authorities, but also regional and district health departments, utilities, central government and quangos. Some 452 organisations responded (45% of those invited to), covering a good range of the above categories.

The primary concern of this survey is with the resources developed for conducting computer audits, and it was conducted by the CIPFA Computer Audit Working Party. (Computer auditing covers the auditing and review of computer security, controls in "live" systems, procedures for developing systems, procedures for acquiring facilities, and overall management of computing resources. Data are presented, for instance, on staff and finance provided for auditing as a proportion of DP resources, on the qualifications of auditors, etc.) But the survey also contains some information on computing trends: respondents indicated their current and proposed future use of development software, word processing, viewdata, electronic mail, and LANS. Data are also provided on the size of their computer budgets and their experience with data-base software, online enquiry systems, micros, and commercial software packages.

Many of the large-scale surveys of computer users cover public organisations, but rarely are they singled out for specific analysis. *Computer Weekly* (July 2 1987) does just this in one of its surveys with Romtec. This reports on the type of suppliers of microcomputers and larger machines, expenditures and expectations of expenditures on hardware, hardware maintenance, software and services, and on plans to develop custom software. Some but not all data are disaggregated into central government, local government, higher education, hospitals, police and fire services, and others (mainly research institutions). The last category is the largest spender, followed by local and then national government; total expenditure expected for 1987-88 was £1,710 million, the greater proportion of which was on hardware. One-fifth of total IT (probably this should read DP) employment in the UK is believed to be based in public sector organisations. But financial limits are reported to be causing severe problems across the public sector. Brady (1986) provides a review of IT in public administration in the UK that reproduces a good deal of statistical information.

6.3.1 Central Government

One reason for difficulties in mapping and measuring IT innovation and diffusion in the public sector is the latter's high degree of fragmentation. In addition to the ministries (MOD, DHSS, DTI, Departments of Employment, of Environment, etc.), there are some 80 other departments and agencies - including, for instance the Land Registry Office, the Scottish Development Agency, the Driver and Vehicle Licensing Authority, and many more.

The Central Computer and Telecommunications Agency (CCTA) is, as its name suggests, a major source of information on central government IT use. Part of the Treasury, it was originally the Central Computer Agency, which took over management services, technical support, financial approval and procurement functions from other bodies. It later took responsibility for telephone networks and office machines. The CCTA's role has been defined in terms of enabling departments to achieve efficiency and effectiveness in the acquisition and use of IT. This role originally took the form of approving departmental expenditures and offering advice on the purchase of equipment and the implementation of new systems, especially where interdepartmental facilities were involved. But with increased emphasis on delegation of management responsibility, and with the diffusion of minicomputers and microcomputers into a widening range of public sector applications, the Treasury began to give individual departments a price ceiling, under which they could make their own decisions on IT purchasing. Responsibility for financial approval was transferred to the Treasury Expenditure Divisions in 1985.

Until 1986, the CCTA maintained a list of major computer installations in central government (responsibility for this has apparently shifted to the NCC, which maintains a large directory of public and private computer installations.) Such a list is a useful resource for analysis and market researchers, but, as already noted in other instances, knowing the whereabouts of mainframe computers indicates little about the current diffusion of smaller computers and other IT applications. The CCTA's role is one of providing advice to departments, with the provision of statistical information on the use of IT being decidedly a by-product of this. As we shall see, it is a useful source of data.

Most of the published information on central government IT falls into one of two categories: (1) detailed analysis of individual departments' current uses of, or plans for, IT use, and (2) aggregate statistics for all of central government.

In the latter category the CCTA publishes an annual fact sheet, *Facts and Figures about Information Technology in Central Government.* This includes the total departmental IT expenditure broken down into staff costs (some £400 million in 1986/87), departmental computer costs (£525 million, composed almost equally of equipment and running costs), telecommunications (£500 million split equally between operational and administrative headings) and external support (£155 million, almost half of which is accounted for by consultancy). The figures are unfortunately not disaggregated into distinct government departments or agencies.

Statistics in the 1986/87 report indicate a growth of 12% over the previous year, as the total reached nearly £1.6 billion. (This is as large as the figure for central and local government establishments from the *Computer Weekly* survey cited above; presumably the latter is unlikely to have received thorough returns from, say, MOD properties.) This is cited as putting the spending on IT at 1% of total public expenditure. The value of the installed base of IT is estimated at between £5-6 billion.

Under the category of computer costs, the CCTA provides a breakdown of spending on hardware and software for administrative IT, by the type of contracts awarded (this includes purchases, rentals, and standing arrangements). Expenditures for external IT services are also disaggregated, into consultancy, turnkey projects, and bureaux and facilities management. There are 18,500 staff reported to be working on administrative IT, of whom 10,000 are within the "IT functional specialism". The fact sheet also covers the value of purchases with suppliers for major government contracts - until 1980 the UK government aimed at preferential treatment for the "national champion", ICL, and the fact sheet shows that it is still the most significant single supplier. It also contains a "view of the future", which is less tentative than one might expect: e.g. "Firm projections, based on departmental plans, give a figure of 155,000 terminals by 1992; with a probable growth to 240,000 by 1995" (no pagination). The 1987 estimate is 65,000 terminals, that for 2000 is 350,000.

Further details of Civil Service computer staffing resources are also available from the CCTA's *Annual Report of Staff in Administrative Computing*. The 1986 edition indicates staffing figures for Administrative Data Processing (ADP) functional specialism, clerical and DP grades (figures cover both staff actually in post, and vacancies notified). Resignation rates and sources of entrants (in-house or external recruitment) to various grades are also collated. Some 17,364 staff are covered, with disaggregations by Civil Service grade and by functions such as management (764 staff), programming (4,380), systems (2,900), operations (3,051), operations support (756), data preparation (4,153) and training (1,361).

These data are not disaggregated by department or agency. In order to arrive at the published aggregates, the CCTA presumably obtains (or estimates) data on all the above-mentioned areas for each department. This implies that individual departments have provided figures; as far as we know, however, such data are not published in many of the annual reports of departments (at least not in a format that makes them easily accessible). The reasons for not disaggregating data so as to provide details of individual departments' IT spending may be simply that the CCTA sees this as none of its responsibility; or it may not wish to be seen as classifying departments into some form of league table; it may be seeking not to draw attention to activities of the MOD or security agencies; or a combination of these factors may be at play. (But then, a separate row of figures in military employment is featured in the main table.) According to information from the CCTA library, the *Annual Report of Staff in Administrative Computing* is currently a restricted document. What purpose this restriction can serve is unclear, and 1986 data have in any case been made available in an undated report from the Society of Civil and Public Servants, *Civil Service Computer Staffing Resources - a Programme of Action.* The CCTA has provided additional data in its *IT Series,* where *Progress Reports on Information Technology and the Civil Service* have given data on terminals in use, on telecommunications as compared to computer costs, and on the CCTA's own administrative costs.

Another body which on occasion provides data on particular departments' activities, and on particular issues, is the National Audit Office (NAO). The NAO's role is that of auditing and certifying the appropriation accounts of all government departments, of providing Parliament with independent evidence on the "economy, efficiency and effectiveness in the use of resources in the departments and other organisations examined" (quoted from p8 of *The Role of the National Audit Office,* National Audit Office, 1987c).

In 1987 the NAO published two reports relevant to this study. *Inland Revenue: Control of Major Developments in Use of Information Technology* (National Audit Office, 1987b) provided data on spending on computers, telecommunications and associated accommodation, internal IT staff and the use of external consultants. *Computer Security in Government Departments* (National Audit Office, 1987a) documented known cases of computer fraud in government between 1981 and 1986, as well as cases of computer disasters such as fires and floods in government between 1984 and 1987; these are quite possibly more adequate data than are available for private sector organisations. This latter report included some data on IT costs in central government (see Table 6.2). The reports of the NAO are discussed by Parliament's Committee of Public Accounts, so this means that further evidence - sometimes statistical - can be found in Hansard and the proceedings published by the Select Committee. In 1988 it produced a review critical of the Alvey Programme. The House of Commons Trade and Industry Committee (volume 1, 1988) presents a discussion of government IT expenditure which draws heavily on CCTA data and on answers to parliamentary questions; statistics include current and projected workstations for civil servants in various departments, IT expenditure in 1987/88 in different departments, a breakdown of overall government IT expenditure, and the nationality of the top 20 hardware and software suppliers.

Occasionally government departments have published documents outlining their IT strategies, and it seems likely that similar documents (or at least statements of intent) have been prepared for internal discussion (at least) by the IT steering committee of each department. If this has not yet been accomplished, such documents are likely to be forthcoming, in the event that the Treasury accepts the arguments which move assessment of IT spending from individual project assessment to a "portfolio" approach. One source of information on future plans, related to those systems whose development is contracted out, is the publication of the projects' names and those of the customer departments which put out operational requirements for competitive tender. A summary listing of these was published monthly by the CCTA in the newsletter *CCTA News*. From mid-1988 *CCTA News* has ceased being published as a separate entity, and is replaced by a regular newssheet in the magazine *Government Computing*. For a while, as an experiment, one interesting feature of this newsletter was its listing of surplus kit that government departments wish to sell; apart from telling us something about their strategies, this demonstrates the vitality of at least one second-hand market! (Recall the discussion earlier in this chapter.)

Another set of CCTA publications should be mentioned here. This is a series entitled *Information Technology in the Civil Service*, which contains several different types of report. Numbers 8 and 11 (1984 and 1985) describe the CCTA itself, its staffing, finance and activities; several other reports review specific types of IT products, and some of

Table 6.2

IT Costs in Central Government

Net Purchase Costs of Hardware, Software & Other Support, 1985-87, by Department

Department	Percentage Share
Ministry of Defence	31.7
Inland Revenue	15.9
Department of Health & Social Security	11.2
Universities and colleges	6.7
Others (none greater than 4%)	34.5

IT Cost Trends in Main Expenditure Areas, 1984-86
(£ millions)

	1984	1985	1986
Staff	225	345	405
Purchases	270	285	330
Telecommunications	765	1,035	1,185

Note: estimates derived from bar chart

Source: CCTA data reproduced in National Audit Office (1987b)

these reviews carry surveys of users or of experiments with new technologies (e.g. 1 - telephone extension logging (1983); 2 - electronic typewriters (1983); 7 - multiuser office systems (1984); 10 - laptop computers (1985); 13 - optical disc data storage (1986)). CCTA (1984) presents a study by Eosys of government administrative telecommunications - in 1981/82 the bill for these was £108 million, of which 90% was telephone charges and only 10% involved text and data. Several of the other reports in this series contain methods for evaluating systems, and discussions of standards (especially OSI).

6.3.2 Local Governnment

Fragmentation may be a problem for mapping and measuring IT in central government, but it becomes endemic when considering LAs. With over 500 LAs in England and Wales alone, each of which operates a range of services with considerable autonomy in decision making, the task is clearly formidable, and it becomes more so since local government operates as a "vertical market". There is no single group which represents (or could provide an overview for) all of local government. There exist, or have existed in the recent past, London Boroughs, Metropolitan Districts, Metropolitan Counties, Shire Counties and Shire Districts - each with their own professional associations and journals. (Reorganisation of local government, like that of national government, thus makes the establishment of time series problematic.) Each individual service is also represented by different bodies - e.g. those for the social services, planners, housing officers, chief education officers, rating officers, and chief executives.

LAs produce audits, and standard returns which are required by the Department of Environment (revenue output forms), and these contain breakdowns of capital expenditures. But these are not particularly reliable sources of information, in part for organisational reasons: many LAs' computer departments are under the authority of their Treasurers, and their budgets are not necessarily separated out from other financial functions. Revenue budgets may include IT expenditure under various headings - central services overheads, computerised computer development functions, overhead accounts, etc. - none of which are broken down by application.

The accounting problem has become even more convoluted as LAs have followed the trend to "end-user computing". The application of IT has spread outward from the central support departments into the "enabling" and "caring" services of LAs. As user departments embark upon their own IT activities, their IT purchases may not be considered as central resources, and data will rarely be disaggregated into hardware, software, etc. IT expenditure is liable to be hidden under various categories with little or no common recording procedures between services (let alone between LAs). And in some instances the budgets may be massaged in order to hide embarassing cost overruns, whether for development, installation or debugging.

Like central government, LAs are major computer users: the first was installed in 1957, and by 1980 around 90% of LAs had mainframe facilities of their own (Brady, 1986, citing Local Authorities Management Services and Computer Committee (LAMSAC) data). Among the first to attempt any systematic measurement of IT in LAs was the Audit Commission; this body plays a role for local government somewhat similar to that carried out by the NAO in central government. Operating with both district and private auditors, the Audit Commission conducted a survey in 1984/85 which was designed by the NCC and published in 1986 under the title *Computing in Local Government: An Audit Survey*. Over 40% per cent of existing authorities replied to the survey, which covered computer strategy; the structure of computing facilities; controls over the cost of computing; the management of the development of systems; and the use of resources.

The survey was conducted by auditors, and some of the assessments provided are based on their subjective judgements, others on LA responses to enquiries. LAs were asked about the degree of consideration which had been given to the development of strategies, the extent to which documentation existed, and the estimated growth in terminals and micros. The development and implementation of IT strategies was related to the acquisition of computer facilities, the extent to which the facilities were deemed adequate, where feasibility studies had been undertaken and suppliers' proposals appraised, and so on. The status of computing was also assessed, and the extent to which the responsibilities of computing departments were adequately defined, and material was presented on staffing numbers and average computer budgets (by type and size of authority and as a proportion of authorities' total budgets). On development the survey looked at the use of standards, approval procedures, project control, and user involvement. Results are presented by type of LA.

In addition to this overview the Audit Commission has, like its counterpart in central government, also been looking periodically at computer fraud. Surveys published in 1981, 1985 and 1988 (forthcoming) cover a wide spectrum of public and private computer users, and investigate categories of fraud such as unauthorised submission and alteration of data.

Another computer audit survey, published in 1986, has already been referred to (since it was not solely concerned with LAs): CIPFA's *Computer Audit: The State of the Art in the Public Sector*. As with the Audit Commission survey, results are presented as averages for each category of respondent.

A third organisation which has produced and disseminated data on IT in LAs has been LAMSAC. For several years it has published an *Index of Local Authority Computer Applications*; this is aimed at facilitating the interchange of software and experience among LAs, and contains the availability of transferable systems in use by LAs. Included in the survey are addresses and contact names in participating LAs, with a short description of their principal hardware, a listing by application of those programs available for transfer, the languages used and the operating systems for which they are suitable. Details are supplied of which authorities are experienced (and willing to share their experience) with IT in different application areas (e.g. careers advice, museums, school meals administration, and rates.). Finally the *Index* also contains details of the use by LAs of software developed by third parties and defined as proprietary software.

LAMSAC also operates several databases, among which LAMCIT lists the hardware (no software included at present) held by each LA, and the departments to which each system is linked. It includes contact names and addresses, the total number of computing staff employed, and some of the applications. The *Municipal Yearbook*, too, lists the major computer systems in each LA; although this is restricted to the identification of principal systems only, it does provide information on the "population bands" and addresses for each authority. (Apart from LAMSAC's data, *The Computer Users' Yearbook* and *Computer Survey* also contain details of many LA, and central government, computer sites.)

The most recent, and potentially the most important, source of data on IT in the public sector is the survey entitled *IT Trends 1987* (not to be confused with the NCC's *IT Trends*). Conducted by SOCITM this survey is intended as a step toward an IT Statistical Information Service which would provide time-series and comparative data. The first survey concentrated on the input of resources for IT in local government and includes returns from 26% of LAs (these are believed to cover most of the major users). Topics on which information is provided include:

- the management of IT, covering elected member involvement, corporate IT steering groups, the role of the central IT manager, technology agreements, and the existence of IT strategy documents - 53% of all LAs are reported to have an IT Panel or Subcommittee, for instance;

- central IT services, covering central computer equipment, network services - such as the use of fax, electronic mail, PSS and LANs - ancillary services, system development - including the use of 4GLs and of formal standards for system development - and services such as computer time and consultancy provided to external bodies;
- staffing for central IT, covering staff in post, vacancies, investment in staff, turnover, internal staff movement, additional remuneration and additional allowances for staff;
- finance for central IT, covering investment in central IT, profiles of central IT budgets (disaggregated by staff, equipment and software, training, establishment expenses, and external services), costing policies and the charging policies used for attributing services to user budgets;
- departmental use of IT covering dedicated minicomputers, work-stations, and departmental IT staff. Poor information was received in response to this question, indicating that central DP departments felt out of touch with departmental activities.

Data are disaggregated by type of council, and an appendix contains key facts from all the participating authorities. SOCITM hopes to extend the survey to include information on output, as well as input, in future studies. What is most striking about the current study is the scale of IT applications in LAs - thus over two years facsimile has grown from nil usage to an almost universal service, electronic mail is in use by a third of LAs, videotex by 12%, 4GLs by 60%, and so on. SOCITM concludes with a number of proposals for future elaboration of the data.

Befitting its role as major supplier to local as well as national governments, ICL has recently published a study on IT in local government, which provides many statistics and estimates (ICL, 1988). Trends and forecasts are provided on LA IT expenditure (£353 million in 1987 on equipment, software and services, not including salaries or secondary expenditure - these figures are not drastically different from those in the *Computer Weekly*/Romtec survey cited earlier); and expenditure is disaggregated into personal, departmental, corporate and networking systems. It is suggested that at present some 0.96 of gross revenue budget is spent on the central IT budget by LAs, a figure very close to the average for all other industries (put at 0.97%); and this is forecast to rise (so that the 1990 equivalent of the £353 million cited above is forecast at £613 million!). Table 6.3 outlines some of the estimates and forecasts cited in the ICL report; the forecasts may, of course, reflect a certain element of wishful thinking.

Local government IT has attracted its share of academic attention, notable among which is Barras and Swann's study (1985). Much of the material in this report, which attempts to identify trajectories of LA computing, is based on a sample of 12 LAs. However, more comprehensive data are cited from LAMSAC and other sources, and there is a useful bibliography.

A final source of information on IT in local government is the *Directory of Local Government Private Viewdata Systems* compiled by the London and South Eastern Library Region (LASER) to assist LA information and library staff interested in developing community information services. For approximately 90 sites (all those known at the time of the survey) details are provided on how long each system has been in existence, aims and applications, hardware and software used, database size, funding, and contact names. *Videotex Viewpoint* has published the main results of the survey.

6.3.3 Public Services: Education, Health, Etc.

Other public services are often considerable users of IT, and some are pioneers of particular applications. However, documentation of their activities - other than planning documents - is very scattered and uneven. Material on some services frequently appears in computer and communications trade literature, while others are barely covered. Perhaps surprisingly, one accessible source of information on practices and plans for computerisation in public services is the study of data privacy by Campbell and Connor (1986). The magazine *Government Computing* frequently carries articles describing IT activities in public services.

(a) Education

Chapter 7 will outline data and sources on IT-related education, training, and qualifications. Here we consider applications of IT within UK education. Before turning to particular branches of education, one technology whose main use to date has been in education and training - interactive videodisc - can be mentioned. The National Interactive Video Centre (1987) provides data on the markets for applications of this technology: 58% is here listed as training and 11% as education, with point of sale applications taking a 23% share. This annual report also provides data on the number of programmes produced each year in various application types in the UK, together with other material on hardware sales and activities. The Centre supplies information about the use of the technology, and about specific activities such as the "Interactive Video in Schools" project.

Table 6.3

Local Government IT Expenditure (Great Britain)

Local Government Finance *(£ billions)*	**1983/84**	**1987/88**	**1990/91**
Total revenue	32.2	35.0	34.9
Capital	5.2	3.5	3.3
Total	37.4	38.5	38.2

IT Expenditure *(£ millions: % of total IT spend in parentheses)*	**1983**	**1988**	**1993**
Personal	7.0 (4.2%)	64.0 (15.8%)	225.0 (22.2%)
Departmental	6.0 (3.7%)	48.0 (11.6%)	224.0 (22.1%)
Corporate	144.0 (90.6%)	274.0 (67.5%)	468.0 (46.2%)
Networks	2.0 (1.5%)	21.0 (5.1%)	96.0 (9.5%)

Source: CIPFA and ICL estimates from ICL (1988)

(1) Schools and Local Education Authorities

Schools are using microcomputers both as a tool for teaching IT-related subjects, and as a general-purpose teaching aid; furthermore, the personal computer may be used for school administrative functions. The magazine *Educational Computing* carries news on these topics.

The *DES Statistical Bulletin* for December 1986 provides some results of a survey carried out in 1985 concerning the adoption and use of microcomputers in primary and secondary schools. But Lancaster (1988) provides a more detailed study, drawing on two surveys of headteachers of the 199 secondary schools in four local education authority areas. He reports data on the subjects in which computers are used (science subjects still dominate) and the administrative applications (option choices and pupil records are most important, but almost 20 applications were recorded). Respondents generally evaluated the benefits of computer use favourably. The extent of use increased over the period studied (1984-86) but the pattern of use changed little. The first survey in this study elicited replies from 165 schools, an 83% response rate; the follow-up survey achieved responses from 136 of these, an 85% response rate. The four education authorities were selected according to several criteria, among which was whether they were more or less innovative than average (as indexed by the number of advisors employed per capita).

Streatfield and Jones (1987) present the results of a questionnaire survey of 89 local education authorities (a response rate of 82% of the authorities, all of whom had been contacted), following up an earlier (1983) survey. The focus of the study was on the administrative use of computers, and data concern use by schools and colleges as well as that of the authorities themselves. Eighty-five per cent of respondents reported themselves to be attempting to manage the development of computer-aided administration in their schools. The study provides detail on the hardware and facilities operating and planned by the authorities, and on their use of communications systems such as the Times Network for Schools and LANs.

There is little in the way of data on the use of such computer-communications systems by schools. Pain-Lewins (1988) provides a survey of the use of electronic communications systems (Prestel and the Times Network for Schools) by schools. The questionnaire was sent - by electronic mail! - to 124 Times Network Systems managers, but only 11 responded. (Electronic mail permitted the author to inspect whether the message had been read: after six weeks, and despite a reminder, over 25% of recipients had not read the questionnaire, which in itself says something about their usage of the system.) Case study material does show, however, that a small number of schools are innovative users of these services.

(2) Higher Education and Research

A Working Party on Computer Facilities for Teaching in Universities (1983) sought information on universities' use of computers for educational rather than research purposes. When it came to assessing the pattern of use of computer facilities: "Not all universities replied. Of those that replied only a few were able to provide adequate information..." (p3). Nevertheless, a table is presented outlining use of central and departmental facilities by students from different subject areas: at this point in time science and social science students each used c25% of the facilities, when teaching use only was considered. Anstey (1985) gives an analysis of trends in university computing advisory services, providing material on, for instance, increases in the numbers of users eligible to use such services, and trends in the use of advisory services (these have not kept pace with the increase in user numbers - the author argues that this is because access to advisory services becomes more difficult for users with the shift to more widely distributed computing).

Research tends to be a greater consumer of computer resources than does teaching, in higher education. The journal *University Computing* carries articles covering computer use in that sector of higher education. *Network News* (a newsletter published by the Computer Board and Research Councils' Joint Network Team and Network executive) regularly carries statistics on the usage of JANET (the Joint Academic Network, which provides computer links between UK universities and also includes a number of polytechnic sites). A detailed study of academic networking, providing data on JANET and other services, is presented by Holligan (1986).

(3) Libraries

Librarians are notable, even notorious, for documenting their activities, and in consequence a variety of material on IT use in libraries is available. Several bodies are active in the area, notably Aslib (the Association for Information Management) which supports an Information Resources Centre; another information source is the Library and Information Technology Centre, Polytechnic of Central London; and The British Library's R&D Department has published widely in the area.

The first two information sources mentioned above both, in 1987, published overviews of library IT issues. A *State of the Art of the Application of New Information Technologies in Libraries and their Impact on Library Functions in the United Kingdom* report was published by the Library and Information Technology Centre, Polytechnic of Central London. This report describes the range of new library applications of IT in considerable detail, but also includes some statistical data. Several of the Appendices are rich in data - Appendix 5 describes for university, polytechnic and public (but not business) libraries, the types of automated cataloguing systems used and the customer base for integrated library systems; 6 presents data on automation plans and costs for different types of library, and also covers items such as the number of machine-readable titles on catalogues; 7 covers data bases accessible through Blaiseline (the British Library online data base), with the number of records held; 8 deals with interlibrary loans. While much of the text of the main report deals with system characteristics (and is designed to assist librarians in their choices), Chapter 5 in particular does provide information on the use of data bases by libraries (some 13% of libraries are reported to use online services in the mid-1980s), on the use of Prestel and private videotex systems, on the availability of personal computers to public access, etc.

The Aslib Information Resources Centre report (Sippings and Ramsden, 1987) is based on a survey of Aslib members - a 24% response rate was obtained from a postal questionnaire mailed to 1,500 members, including LA, government, academic, industrial, research, private and other libraries in June 1986. Two earlier surveys had focused on online activities. The Aslib study broadens the scope of the survey to include data on library automation, software and a range of other topics. Numerous tables are produced on the use of computers (71% of users are micro-based; only four users reported using CD-ROM) and communications, including questions on activity levels (e.g. hours/year spent online) and on problems confronted. East and Forrest (1988) present a detailed set of statistics of online use for public and polytechnic libraries, and report that they are currently developing similar data for universities. The data cover expenditures of 19 public and nine polytechnic libraries - in each case over 20% of those providing online services - and outline their expenditures in using various data bases.

Finally, the British Library *Library and Information Research Reports* constitute a wide-ranging set of studies on library and information science activities. Many of these reports draw on small case studies or are reviews of groups of IT systems or of research and literature in a specific field. Some topics have been approached statistically, although in several of the instances cited below the two preceding reports will carry more up-to-date and in some cases more comprehensive figures. The studies that seem to be most relevant cover the use of Prestel in libraries (Yeates, 1982; Sheldon, 1982); the use of microcomputers by academic libraries (Burton, 1987, discussing data on a sample of 475 libraries); surveys of library computer software suppliers (Tagg and Templeton, 1983); studies of an electronic publishing system (e.g. Pullinger, 1985, 1987); and studies of the "information workforce" (Angell, 1987; Moore, 1987; TCC, 1983). *British Library Research Reviews* is another series worth inspecting for detailed discussions of topics relating information, training, and IT.

(b) Health

Surprisingly, there seems to be little in the way of overall analysis of IT activities in the health care sector in the UK, although the National Health Service remains the largest central government employer. In part this may be because of the fragmentation of responsibilities between national government and health authorities, between hospitals (and hospital boards) and other forms of medical practice (general practitioners (GPs), etc.). In part it is because of the proliferation of different IT applications in health care - from medical information systems to computer-aided diagnosis, from office automation to laboratory equipment, from networks to electromedical devices. The scene nowadays is far removed from that of the 1960s - in 1965 only five regional hospital boards were using computers, and this for routine administrative activity (DHSS, 1975). Information on the R&D under way on IT use in the health sector can be obtained from the annual *DHSS Handbook of Research and Development*.

One area that has received rather a lot of attention is the use of personal computers in general practice. In 1982 a scheme was launched to promote microcomputer use among GPs. Around 150 practices had subsidies towards the costs of buying and installing micros, and the staff and doctors in these were surveyed (more than once), with interim and final reports being issued by the DHSS (1984, 1986). The surveys covered such issues as physical alterations required to use the systems; training and documentation; patterns of use (e.g. in patient registration, repeat prescribing, recall and screening); the reliability, usability and suitability of the systems; staff attitudes; organisational innovations. The studies revealed, among other results, that the doctors themselves were more enthusiastic about the systems than their staff - but then, the decision about computerising was most often one that involved only the doctor. Problems with using the new systems (especially around data entry and the inadequacies of documentation) and success factors (practices with established manual filing systems and systematic application of the IT across the group being most successful) were also discussed.

These surveys, which feature many tables, are believed to be capturing between a third and a half of all practices using personal computers for their activities (i.e. some few hundred out of around 10,000 practices in the mid-1980s). Around 600 doctors and 1,000 ancillaries were involved. A later study (Fitter et al., 1986) took the best responding practices from these surveys and compared their practices - two years after the introduction of personal computers - with those of 27 non-users. This study discusses the development of computer-based activities, the evolution of attitudes, and the implications of IT for the practice of management and the delivery of health care. Finally, DHSS (1986) provides a report reviewing different systems for general practices, which draws on a survey of 107 practices' experiences.

6.4 Conclusions

This chapter has covered a wide range of sectors and cited a large volume of material. We are aware that the coverage of economic sectors and types of IT has been very uneven, and suspect that in part this has been due to our inability to locate and access relevant material, as well as reflecting an undoubted concentration of research attention on specific subjects. The IT applications in many sectors are extremely diverse, furthermore, and assembling any coherent picture from a multiplicity of sources can be very difficult. This is apparent, for instance, in the relatively well-documented areas of public sector IT.

When it came to considering the diffusion and use of specific ITs, it is noteworthy than problems of definition arose frequently. Just what is a robot, or an expert, CAD, or FMS system? Rapid change in the power of IT, and suppliers' tendency to jump on fashionable bandwagons, have together exacerbated these issues. Increased IT power has meant that a variety of cheaper systems have appeared, often emulating on microcomputers what a few years ago was restricted to mainframes and dedicated systems. And it has also meant that advanced features are often becoming standard, and that very different generations of system are lumped together into the same definitional categories. It may be that it is only with relatively mature and well-understood products, featuring incremental technological change, that relatively stable statistics can be produced. And even here technologies may ''demature''. And while CNC is sometimes cited as just the sort of mature technology on which we may develop statistics, how do we handle the integration of these machine tools into FMS cells?

Given these problems, it is no wonder that statisticians have been wary about attempting to classify the new technologies into neat frameworks. However, while we can sympathise with their reluctance to enter these fields - and these are indeed areas ripe for unofficial research and the activity of industry associations and academics - it might be appropriate for them at least to make more effort to scrutinise and criticise the definitions used by regular unofficial sources.

Chapter 7 Work and Employment

This chapter focuses on data and data sources which concern the implications of IT for work and employment. (For a general guide to employment data, see Buxton and MacKay (1977).) We begin with the relatively straightforward issues of employment in IT-related occupations, and the implications for training of the diffusion of IT across the economy. We then move to studies which are more concerned with the use of IT: studies of employment "impacts" of new technology, and of technology and industrial relations issues.

7.1 IT Employment

Chapter 4 outlined data sources concerning the IT-producing sectors themselves, and these sources (e.g. *British Monitor SDQ9*) provide data on employment in the computer, software, telecommunications and related industries. (Eyeions, (1986) discusses some of these data.) However, a great deal of attention has been devoted to the workforce involved in producing, servicing, and using such hardware and software across the economy - at least, to the professional workforce, if not to the workers involved, say, in keying data into terminals. This attention stems from several interests over and above the official statisticians' desire to document patterns of occupational change. One such reason is the perception that skill shortages exist in many of these jobs, and that these may inhibit the diffusion and effective use of IT. A related reason is that levels of remuneration have become very important factors in firms' abilities to attract and deploy these skills.

7.1.1 IT-Related Jobs

It is not very easy to obtain data on IT employment from official sources. Indeed, as more jobs involve working with IT-based equipment and systems, it may be argued that just as all sectors of the economy are coming to be IT users, so increasing numbers of jobs have an IT component. In Scandinavian countries there are efforts to examine this through Labour Force Survey investigations of the equipment used by workers in their activities, but we know of no similar efforts for the UK.

We have argued that microelectronics can be thought of as a heartland IT, extending through a core of computer and telecommunications technologies, into a vast range of IT-using technologies. Likewise the IT-producing sector has a heart producing semiconductors, chips and related components, and a wider core that includes computer and telecommunications goods and services. Similarly, we can identify some occupations as clearly being core IT occupations since they involve directly working with heartland or core technologies - occupations such as computer programming and data entry, and much of electronic engineering, for example. Even such occupations are rather difficult to quantify, however.

In principle, official data can be very revealing about occupational categories. The 1972 Classification of Occupations and Directory of Occupational Titles (CODOT) groups occupations into 17 orders, composed of 162 minor groups, in turn composed of 548 units, and around 20,000 specific job titles. The Department of Employment (1972a) presents the CODOT in three volumes; most of the job titles relevant here fall into volume 2. Subsequent supplements (MSC/Employment Services Agency, 1977, MSC, 1980) amend and elaborate on some of these titles.

Two of the minor groups - 33 (office machinery operators) and 34 telecommunications operators and mail distributors) - and two of the unit groups - 044 (ADP planning and programming) and 224 (a set of electrical and electronic engineering jobs) - are particularly relevant to IT employment. Among the key job titles we find in these classes are:

- office equipment operators: 330 supervisors; 331 accounting and calculating machine operators; 332 ADP equipment operators; 333 key-punch operators; 334 document reproducing operators; 335 office machinery operators n.e.s.
- telecommunications operators: 340 supervisors; 341 telephone operators; 342 radio and telegraphy operators. (The job titles of groups 33 and 34 are further differentiated by the use of decimal points, e.g. 342.10 is radio operators, 342.20 teleprinter operators.)
- ADP planning and programming: 044.10 DP manager; 44.20 systems analyst; 44.30 computer programmer; 44.98 trainee; 44.99 other. Additional refinements have been made in revisions of CODOT to these categories: for instance, in systems analysis it is now possible to distinguish between financial systems specialists, stock control specialists, high-level language specialists, etc., and among programmers in addition to high- and low-level language specialists, minicomputer programming specialists have been distinguished (1980 revision). The distinction between programmers and systems analysts has not been accepted in the new standard occupational classification being introduced for the 1990s: see the article in *Employment Gazette*, April 1988 (pp214-221).

- electrical and electronic engineering (these two categories are not distinguished) is 224., with figures after the decimal point giving more information on the specific positions: .00 refers to managers, .98 to trainees, .99 to others n.e.s. Additionally, the first digit after the decimal point refers to job functions as follows: .1 refers to general engineering, .2 to R&D jobs, .3 to design jobs, .4 feasibility studies, .5 applications, .6 liaison, and .7 consultancy and advice. The second digit after the decimal point then refers to job types as follows: .01 general, .03 telecommunication systems, .04 EDP systems, .06 instruments and appliances, .07 components, .09 other. (We have omitted the titles .02 (power generation, etc) and .05 (heavy electrical plant) where only electrical, and not electronic, engineers are specified.) The 1972 CODOT guide notes (p178): "nomenclature varies widely in this area and is not necessarily a useful guide to function".

Even this range of titles, impressively large though it is (at least in the case of more hardware-oriented jobs), is incomplete, since further scrutiny of CODOT uncovers relevant job titles in other locations. Examples are 244.20 and 224.30 (respectively, electronics and radio operators on ships), 259.20 (includes programmers of numerical control devices), and 256.35 (test engineer, including electronic engineering). There are also many job titles in broadcasting and other media industries that relate to the use of communications technology, much of which is heavily based on IT. And it will be apparent that in some instances, especially as we move into higher levels of aggregation, non-IT jobs are being bundled together with IT posts.

Occupational breakdowns of employment are provided in a number of sources, but they are far less readily available, on the whole, than are industrial breakdowns. Firms regularly report on their employment levels, but since they are coded by SIC categories this does not provide direct data on occupational structures. There are, in contrast, relatively few surveys of the workforce that can elicit occupational data. The most comprehensive source is the *Census of Population*, but since this is only decennial the most recent data refer to 1981. (For a convenient guide to the Census, see Dewdney (1985).)

Results of the *Census of Population* are published in a large number of documents, with national occupational disaggregations provided in the volumes *Economic Activity* and *Qualified Manpower*. The former provides data for Great Britain as a whole on a 10% sample of the population: over 1.5 million economically active men, and almost a million economically active women. Occupational data are tabulated by sex, by region of the country, and by industry (100 sectors are distin-

Table 7.1

Census of Population Data on Occupations, GB, 1981

	Men	Women	Code
Total economically active	1,552,671	987,888	-
Economists, statisticians, systems analysts & computer programmers	7,995	1,974	004
Electrical & electronic engineers	6,713	128	027
Office machinery operatives	2,921	11,388	050
Telephone, radio & telegraph operatives	2,144	11,328	051

Note: 10% population sample, from *Census of Population 1981, Economic Activity* (Table 8), prepared by the OPCS and the Registrar General, Scotland.

guished). However, the categories are more aggregated than we might hope for on the basis of the CODOT. Table 7.1 presents the data of most relevance to IT occupations: it will be apparent that the categories include a variety of non-IT roles. Census data may be obtained in electronic form for more detailed analyses, however. Statistics to district level are provided for 162 occupational groups in other published reports; it is possible to obtain data as small area statistics for wards, parishes and enumeration levels, and in principle much Census data can be obtained for computer analysis.

NEDO (1980) estimated the size of the computer workforce at the beginning of the 1980s, suggesting that there were some 60-62,000 professional electrical engineers (including managers) in work related to electronic systems, with a further 90,000 employed in computing-related occupations such as programmers and analysts. This would put the IT core component of the jobs portrayed in Table 7.1 as rather a high one: nine-tenths of the economists, statisticians, systems analysts, etc. category, and a similar proportion of electrical and electronics engineers.

The *New Earnings Survey* is a valuable source of annual data, and thus provides for more recent estimates of IT occupational employment. It draws on a 1% sample of employers involved in Pay-As-You-Earn schemes in Great Britain (a similar survey is carried out in Northern Ireland); the data are thus provided by employers rather than direct from employees (as in the case of the Census of Population.) This will, of course, mean that some classes of worker, e.g. self-employed and freelance programmers, will be omitted. The most recent *New Earnings Survey* (1987) is published in six parts by HMSO; Part D focuses on earnings and hours for different occupations, while Part A gives summary analyses disaggregated in part by occupational group. The occupational classification employed (the List of Key Occupations) is described in Part B, Appendix 2; it includes the following categories: systems analysts and programmers; electronic engineers (as distinguished from electrical engineers - but in the published tables these are aggregated together); electrical/electronic engineers; ADP operators; key punch operators; other office machine operators; telephonists; supervisors of office machine operators; etc.

Part A provides one table which provides wage breakdowns by occupation and sex; data are not always provided at a fully disaggregated level when one gender has few occupants in a particular job. The "male" jobs of systems analyst/programmer and electrical and electronic engineer both received over twice the weekly wage of the more "female" ADP operators. The data also suggest that male ADP operators receive considerably more than their female counterparts: however, the variation in the relatively small male group was regarded as too high for reliability of estimates.

Part D provides data on the sample characteristics, and gives occupation-by-industry breakdowns that enable some estimation of the variations in occupational composition across industries - this is a particularly valuable set of annual statistics. The total sample of full-time male workers in 1987 being paid at adult rates was 85,903. Of these 1,042 were systems analysts and programmers, 1,008 electrical and electronic engineers, and 214 ADP operators. Of the female sample, 470 were in the latter category and 71 key punch operators (for comparison, 138 were other office machine operatives, and 440 telephonists). (To obtain estimates of the total workforce in these groups, multiply the New Earnings Survey data by 100; just as the Census figures from Table 7.1 need to be multiplied by 10.)

Among other relevant official sources, the annual *Labour Force Survey* reports do not provide the occupational details that they could potentially do: if they did they would be valuable, since the 1987 survey, for instance, is based on a fairly large sample of interviews (these are with members of about 60,000 households). Our inspection of data sets from these surveys suggests that several hundred systems analysts and programmers, and over 100 electronics engineers, are picked up in the samples in recent years - insufficient for substantial sectoral analyses, but probably enough for some worthwhile studies - e.g. of training, wages, and job mobility.

Employment Gazette used to publish an annual set of data on occupations in engineering industries (with all professional engineers grouped together, but office machine workers distinguished with their own category); the last such study was Josephs (1982) analysing 1980 data. The *Annual Abstract of Statistics* now provides basic occupational breakdowns (by sex) for engineering industries; it is possible to look at employment in IT-producing industries within the electrical and electronics engineering sector (eight branches of which are distinguished) from this source, but specific IT occupations are subsumed under headings such as "managerial, administrative, technical and clerical". The proportion of the employees of all manufacturing industries falling into this category is also provided in this source, but clearly it includes many non-IT workers, and will exclude not a few IT workers.

One unofficial source which we have already encountered (Chapter 5 Yap (1986)), though relatively small-scale (just over 700 establishments in manufacturing and private services), provides some useful material on IT-related employment. The mail questionnaire elicited data on overall full-time and part-time employment at each establishment, and disaggregated this (in terms of full-time employees) into six job categories and in terms of percentage of the wages bill (into three categories). But it also obtained data on the numbers of personnel in five computer occupations at the site: computer managers; systems analysts; programmers; operators; and other. Analyses of these data are presented in Miles (forthcoming); for now it is worth noting that across sectors we find substantial variations in the structure of computer employment. For instance, while computer operators are the largest occupational group for seven of the eight sectors studied (constituting over 50% of computer employment in six sectors), in banking and financial services they constituted only 21% of computer employment and were outnumbered by "others" (36%). The two sectors with fewest operators, banking and business services, had comparatively large numbers of systems analysts and programmers; and different types of user (varying in terms of scale and sophistication of computer installation) also vary in terms of occupational composition.

Presenting the results of an NCC survey, Buckroyd and Cornford (1988) provide estimates not only for the numbers of professional systems staff employed in the UK, but also for computer operatives and for data preparation staff (Table 7.2). These results diverge rather sharply from Yap's data, presenting operatives as being outnumbered by professionals rather than vice versa. This is probably accounted for less by the different years concerned (1984 and 1987) than by different sampling strategies, since Yap had never intended that his study be a basis for estimating total computer employment in various categories, nor did he seek to survey comprehensively all sectors of the UK economy; nevertheless, the variations are rather disturbing. The NCC estimates are certainly more in line with those implied by the New Earnings Survey data discussed earlier. In their forecasts for trends in these categories (reported in Table 7.3 below) the NCC authors anticipate a continuing decline in the share of these relatively less skilled jobs, with an actual decrease in data preparation staff.

Table 7.2

UK IT Skilled Employment by Job Category (1987): NCC Estimates

Job Category	Number Employed
DP management	35,200
Systems analysts	25,200
Analyst programmers	39,000
Programmers	37,000
Systems programmers	14,900
Network staff	6,200
Professional systems staff	157,500
Operations	59,600
Data preparation	49,300
Total employed	266,500

Source: Buckroyd and Cornford (1988)

The focus of most attention and commentary has not been on the employment circumstances and trends of these relatively unskilled workers - many of whom work in "office factory" conditions. Instead, it is the skilled and professional workforce, where skill shortages are apparent, which has received most effort at statistical exploration.

7.1.2 IT Professionals

Despite what has been said above concerning the amount of attention given to IT professional staff, there are surprisingly few comprehensive statistics on employment of IT professionals in the UK, and relatively little effort to define precisely what is meant here. The IT Skills Shortages Committee (1985b) distinguishes between professionals in IT subjects (many of whom may be qualified in another relevant discipline), and professionals in any discipline who use IT in their practice without necessarily being knowledgeable in the fundamentals of IT. The present discussion concerns the former group, but even so there are at least two distinct career routes which lead people into these professional posts. Some professionals have graduated in "heartland" IT subjects such as computing or electronics; others have acquired their proficiency by moving, say, from elementary to more sophisticated programming tasks and then to systems analysis, with their skills being acquired on the job, and many of these may not even have higher education qualifications at all (although some will have been graduates in non-IT subjects). Definitions of IT professionals vary in how inclusive or exclusive they are in terms of professional formation processes.

In Chapters 2 and 5 we have discussed the Census of Production (which only covers Divisions 1-4 in the SIC). In 1986 this Census requested information on professional computer employees; it presents these data disaggregated by SIC code for manufacturing and some other sectors, and is thus a useful guide to the distribution of computer professional staff. The total estimate for these sectors (which notably exclude services - even computer services) amounts to 53,779 professional computer employees.

A number of semi-official and unofficial surveys have attempted to provide more comprehensive, and more detailed, data on IT professionals. These studies attempt to classify the different sorts of job involved here in an adequate way, conceptualising professionals in terms of the work done rather than just in terms of qualifications held.

The classification used in recent studies by the Institute of Manpower Studies (IMS) in their research on IT manpower (Pearson, Connor and

Pole, 1988) is one such attempt. IMS developed an "occupational framework" consisting of two dimensions - activity or function, and skill/knowledge base. There are eight main functional areas: research, design and development; production; test/quality assurance; communication/distribution; marketing/ sales/customer service; finance/accounting; other data processing; and other (as specified). There are also eight occupational groupings, for each of which a number of typical different job titles were included:

- software/systems engineering: systems design engineer, software engineer, systems development engineer
- communications engineering: microwave engineer, telecommunications engineer, network specialist, systems engineer (switching)
- electronics and product engineering: electronics engineer, design engineer, product development engineer, hardware engineer
- research/design specialists: specialists in IT areas such as materials, integrated circuit design, VLSI design,artificial intelligence, knowledge-based systems, CAD systems, opto-electronics
- marketing/technical sales:sales engineers and others with IT skills whose main responsibility is in marketing/selling of IT equipment/ systems
- customer service: field service engineer, customer support engineer
- computing: programmers, analyst/programmers, systems analyst, DP managers
- other professional: as specified by firms
- technicians with IT skills: as specified by firms.
  (Connor and Pearson, 1986a p3)

In addition to this, in line with the different applications that IT is put to across the economy, IMS listed such occupations as software/systems engineering, communications engineering, electronic and product engineering, research/design specialists, marketing/technical sales, computing and other for electronics providers and industrial user companies; and programmers, analyst/programmers, systems analysts, software/ systems engineers, electronics engineers and other for IT service providers and service user companies.

Connor and Pearson (1986a) review several data sources, and in their own study combined data from the 1985 IMS survey of 357 organisations with official data to estimate the population of UK IT professionals at around 200,000 , of whom approximately 70,000 were in electronics-related occupations and about 130,000 in computing occupations. This study also cites data from the 1981 Census of Population (note that since this is based on the respondents' own definition of their occupation, it is likely to veer toward the "inclusive" definition of professionals) so as to suggest a total of 40,000 (about 1,000 of which were women) employed as electronics engineers and 89,000 (of which 17,000 were women) employed as systems analysts and computer programmers at the beginning of the 1980s. (Compare with Table 7.1; again these estimates are large proportions of the more aggregated categories.) But even though "inclusive", this total of 129,000 is likely to be an underestimate, since certain other IT professionals - e.g. some managers, some communications staff - do not fall into the two categories.

Subsequently IMS has revised its estimates, based on a new survey of 143 organisations and on a growth rate of between 5 and 10% per annum; for 1987 they estimate the total number of IT professionals at 230,000 (Pearson, Connor and Pole, 1988).

The IMS survey, as the listing above indicates, sets out to cover all IT professionals; most other surveys have been limited to occupations in computing and sometimes communications. These other surveys in the UK have, however, considerably more detailed occupational breakdowns for computing occupations. For example, the NCC's report on salaries and staff issues in computing (Cornford and Gott, 1987) lists 24 job categories ranging from Head of Management Services down to operator level. These are arranged in four groupings which can best be described as: management; support/communications services; analysis/programming; and operations. The NCC surveyed some 640 computer user organisations employing around 11,000 IT staff (including data preparation staff and operators). The NCC extrapolated from these findings to produce estimates of the current size of the UK IT population (Buckroyd and Cornford, 1988). Their estimates (for a reduced set of occupations) are reproduced in Table 7.2; note that these refer to computing staff rather than to all IT professionals, and thus, for example, do not include all the electronics engineers covered in the official data.

This NCC survey also asked respondents about future employment expectations. The replies allowed for projections of IT professional and other staff levels in 1989 and 1992 (Table 7.3). These forecasts suggest that the UK needs to find over 30% more professional systems staff by 1992 - a remarkable increase. (Note also the forecast decrease in data preparation staff.)

Another recent survey was carried out by Computer Economics Limited (1987) for the Information Technology Skills Agency (ITSA). Based on questionnaire returns from 475 computer installations, the report examined employment of people in middle management, development, technical support, communications and operations support groups. More than 20,800 people worked in these categories in the 475

Table 7.3

NCC Forecasts of UK IT Employment in 1989 and 1992

Job Category (% change from 1987 in parentheses)	**Number Employed** **1989**		**1992**	
DP management	37,000	(5.1)	38,200	(8.5)
Systems analysts	32,100	(27.4)	35,100	(39.3)
Analyst programmers	54,000	(38.5)	60,100	(54.1)
Programmers	41,800	(13.0)	43,500	(17.6)
Systems programmers	18,100	(21.5)	20,200	(35.6)
Network staff	9,500	(53.2)	11,500	(85.5)
Professional systems staff	192,500	(22.2)	208,600	(32.4)
Operations	62,100	(4.2)	60,800	(2.0)
Data preparation	39,500	(-19.9)	33,800	(-31.4)
Total employed	293,900	(10.3)	303,300	(13.8)

Source: Buckroyd and Cornford (1988)

establishments surveyed; in this case there was no attempt to gross up the estimates to produce a national estimate of IT employees. The ITSA study provides a list of occupations in computing even more detailed than that of the NCC study, arranging them within six functional groupings: management; systems analysis; programming; analyst programming; technical support; communications; and operations support. Of considerable interest in view of the different routes into IT professional work discussed above, there was an effort to assess the "average experience" of workers in different occupations, based on the number of months spent in the current function plus time spent in related functions (with earlier employers if appropriate). The results of this analysis (together with the average ages of the workers) are provided for a large number of job titles, but are then only related to salaries; however, the approach might well be worth further elaboration.

Table 7.4

Employment of Professional IT Staff by Organisations in Different Sectors (Percentages)

Number of Professional IT staff Sectors	Sector Electronics Providers	IT Industrial Services		Service Users	All Users
1-5	19	7	53	22	27
6-10	9	9	12	9	10
11-20	9	17	9	13	11
21-50	24	29	6	23	20
51-100	7	24	5	18	12
Over 100	32	14	15	16	21
Number of organisations	119	42	85	111	357
Approx. number of professional IT staff employed by sample	14,300	4,500	2,800	5,200	27,000
Average number* in each organisation	120.1	106.7	31.2	46.5	58.9

* postal survey excluding the major electronics groups

Source: Table 2.5 in Connor and Pearson (1986a)

7.1.3 Organisation of IT Professional Work and Skill Requirements

The pattern of IT employment varies across different sectors of the economy, reflecting the different applications to which IT is being put; a number of studies address this. The IMS distinguished between four main groups of users in its 1986 study of IT employment (Connor and Pearson, 1986a): providers of electronics products and systems, providers of IT services, industrial users of IT, and service sector users of IT. A questionnaire survey of 944 employing organisations resulted in 482 usable replies; 375 employed professional or technician IT staff, with 107 employing no IT staff at all and 125 employing no professional IT staff. The 357 organisations with professional IT staff employed a total of 27,000 IT professionals (Table 7.4).

This table shows that nearly a third of the electronics provider companies employed more than 100 IT professionals - and the IMS report notes that over 1,000 IT professionals might be based at a single location in the major electronics companies. In the IT service provider sector, one in eight firms employed more than 100 IT professionals. The concentration of IT professionals was much smaller in the user firms - 74% of industrial user organisations and 48% of service users employed 20 or fewer IT professionals (53% of industrial users employed fewer than six IT professionals). Fifteen per cent of industrial users and 16% of service users employed more than 100 IT professionals.

Differences in the occupational structure of IT staff were apparent across sectors in this study. In the electronics providers and industrial users, occupations were more oriented towards the following electronics and engineering occupational groupings: software/systems engineering; communications engineering; electronic and product engineering; research/design specialists; marketing/technical sales; computing; other. In the two service sectors (IT service providers and service users) the occupational groupings were more oriented towards software skills: programmers; analyst/programmers; software/systems engineers; electronics engineers; other. Employment in the various sectors in these occupational groupings is summarised in Table 7.5.

Computing occupations dominate IT professional employment in the IT service providers (94%) and service users (82%). Industrial users also have a high proportion of their IT staff (46%) in computing occupations. Twenty per cent of IT professionals in industrial users were software/systems engineers. The proportion of electronics engineers is small in IT industrial providers and service users (2% in both cases). Not surprisingly, electronics providers were the heaviest employers of electronics engineers and software/systems engineers (25% and 28% of employment), followed by industrial users (11% and 20%).

The larger organisations across all sectors tended to employ higher numbers of IT staff - more than half the organisations with more than 1,000 employees in total employed more than 50 IT professionals.

Table 7.5

Proportions of Professional IT Staff in Different Occupational Groups (Percentages)

Occupational Electronics Grouping	**Providers**	**Industrial Users**
Software/systems engineering	28	20
Communications engineering	6	6
Electronics and product engineering	25	11
Research/design specialists	9	5
Marketing/technical sales	9	3
Customer service	11	9
Computing	11	46

Occupational Grouping	**IT Service Providers**	**Service Users**
Programmers	45	39
Analyst/programmers	24	21
Systems analysts	25	22
Software/systems engineers	4	16
Electronics engineers	2	2

Source: Figures 3.3, 3.4, 3.5 in Connor and Pearson (1986a)

About one-third of medium-size (101-1,000 employees) organisations employed more than 50 IT professionals. About one in eight small organisations employed more than 50 IT professionals.

IMS has recently conducted a further study, updating the information discussed above. The samples are not strictly comparable, and in 1987 (Pearson, Connor and Pole, 1988) IMS used a much simpler classification of occupations: electronics engineers; software engineers; computing/DP staff; and others. Using this categorisation IMS found that computing/DP jobs still dominated employment in the service sectors - 82% of IT professionals in service providers and 76% of IT professionals in service users were employed in computing/DP occupations. They were also the major category of IT professional employment in industrial users (61%). In the electronics providers, nearly 70% of IT professional jobs were in electronics engineering (32%) and software engineering (37%) occupations.

The skills needed by IT professionals vary depending on which job they are doing and where they are working. The 1985 IMS survey addressed how the skills needed to develop and apply IT reflected the sector in which the technology was being put to use. The skills most needed by electronics providers were design and development skills for microelectronics, software or systems. As shown in Table 7.5, the most important occupational groups were software/systems engineers and electronics and product engineers. IMS noted an increasing requirement for a mix of hardware and software skills in the electronics providers - electronics development/design engineers were increasingly expected to have programming and systems design expertise. In the IT service providers, in contrast, the emphasis was on software skills and the largest groups were programmers, systems analysts and analyst/programmers. The employment of software/systems engineers was small in comparison, although there have been moves to invest in software engineering techniques in these firms. Since the organisations in this sector often work for a wide variety of different end-user sectors, different applications expertise is needed depending on the end sector. In recent years, there has been a vast expansion of work for these organisations in the financial sector and so corresponding expertise has become necessary.

In the user sectors DP/computing skills are those most in demand. About two-thirds of industrial user organisations employed staff in this occupational category mainly for commercial and administrative systems work. Less than 40% of industrial users employed software/systems engineers. More recently, there has been a decline in in-house programming in certain organisations as they move to buy software packages. This has led to a shift towards systems analysis skills (Pearson, Connor and Pole, 1988, p18).

In its 1987 survey (Buckroyd and Cornford, 1988), the NCC noted a number of distinct trends in technology which were likely to have implications for the skills of DP/IT staff. In particular the authors noted the growing use of fourth-generation computer languages and relational data-base techniques. These were thought to be the major driving force behind a deskilling of pure programming work - 4GLs automatically generate code which can speed up the process considerably and may not require high-level programming skills. The NCC also noted the growing needs for analysis skills - pointing to the rise of the programmer/analyst role as a "systems development all-rounder" with both business/analytical skills and some programming expertise - and for communications and networking skills. People with the latter skills are now being regarded as specialists in much the same way as systems programmers have been regarded as specialists in the past - the important expertise is the technical knowledge required to design and implement communications networks. As, during the 1980s, the technology has become more sophisticated and the networks more complex, several quite separate and definable roles have emerged to take the place of the single networking person of the 1970s.

Northcott (1988) provides data on a number of professional IT occupations in his surveys of UK manufacturing. He notes a rapid increase in the number of engineers with IT expertise in the factories surveyed, estimating that the numbers of such engineers had risen from 1.6 to 4 per user plant in UK manufacturing. However, it is interesting to note that when, in order to achieve consistency with the use of the term "engineer" in France and Germany, for purposes of comparative analysis, a tighter, less "inclusive" definition was used - engineers with degrees in engineering and/or membership of an engineering institution - this number is more than halved. Variations among establishments of different sizes are pronounced (a very few large plants employ 2% of the professional IT engineers) as are regional and industrial variations. Over half of the professional engineers are employed in the electrical, electronic and instrument engineering industry; vehicles is also engineer-intensive, while some other sectors employ remarkably few. Northcott suggests that these variations in part reflect recruitment problems, in part the very different skill requirements of different types of application and different orientations to IT innovation.

7.1.4 IT Labour Markets

Many studies have focused on the issue of skill shortages in IT professions. Tarsh (1984), for example, reports on research carried out in the Employment Market Research Unit of the Department of Employment. Data are presented on graduate unemployment and job destinations, and on a survey of a small number of employers' perceptions of graduate shortages. Skill shortages for graduates, it was concluded, are rather highly concentrated (on electronics and for people with industrial experience), rather than erupting widely as higher education fails to adjust to the demands of new technology.

On the other hand, Northcott (1988) reports half of the IT user factories in his manufacturing sample as mentioning lack of people with microelectronics expertise as a very important problem. His study presents data on perceived shortages by manufacturing sector and by region of the country, and also by the type of innovation (product or process) involved. On a small sample of establishments ranging across several sectors, Senker et al. (1985) document similar widespread complaints of shortages of software engineers. And Connor and Pearson (1986a) report that, in a large sample of employers, half had recruitment problems, most expected IT skill requirements to grow but were unable to specify by how much, and high salaries and the use of subcontracting were common strategies for gaining access to skills. The press release for a £180 report by Judd and Virgo (1988) - which we have not yet inspected - claims it to be a comprehensive compilation of UK statistical sources on current and forecast skill requirements in the UK.

Government concern about skill shortages at technician as well as graduate levels led to its forming of an IT Skills Shortages Committee (the Butcher Committee), whose reports (1984, 1985a, 1985b) provide useful documentation of graduate and technician labour market developments, and technological developments that may create new needs.

Another initiative in this area has been the formation, under the aegis of the Confederation of British Industry's (CBI's) Education Foundation, of ITSA. We have already referred to the survey carried out for ITSA by Computer Economics Limited (1987), based on a survey of 475 computer installations. While containing a considerable amount of information about overall staffing trends and salary levels, the special focus of this study is on recruitment, retention and training problems.

An annual survey conducted jointly by the CBI and the Manpower Services Commission addresses skill shortages in manufacturing industry in general. The 1987 survey (CBI, 1987) received replies from 1,225 firms, about half of the target sample, and reports management perceptions of skill shortages of all types and their implications for output. Data are disaggregated by branch of manufacturing, and on a national and regional basis. Computer and management services are generally one of the six most frequently mentioned categories of skill shortage. Data are also provided on the perceived reasons for the shortages, and strategies for coping with them.

The general shortages of IT professionals have meant that it is a suppliers' market to some extent. Staff shortages have led to a situation where poaching of trained staff has become prevalent. Employers seek to attract and retain their IT staff by such means as changing grading structures and salary progression systems and alterations in the review procedures. Recruiting and retaining highly skilled staff has been a problem in many sectors, and this is reflected in a proliferation of studies of salary levels for different IT professions in various sectors of the economy and regions of the country, with firms such as Computer Economics, Income Data Services, and Reward Regional Surveys being prominent here - but the NCC (in its annual *Salary Survey)* and other bodies also produce reports on wages. Computer Economics publishes a biannual *Computer Staff Salary Survey* based on a sample of over 600 organisations, providing data on salaries and earnings for over 50 different job functions, with disaggregations by ages, sex, region, etc. Data are also provided on turnover rates and other related topics. Reward Regional Surveys produces a large number of reports, including the biannual *Software and Electronics Specialists Survey*, *Software Engineers*, and *Computer Salaries and Benefits* (in collaboration with the NCC).

Such surveys are frequently reported in the computer and DP trade press (see Chapter 2), where there is almost obsessive interest in news of pay differentials and trends. To take just one example, *Computer News* of November 19 1987 contained a lengthy discussion of salary prospects for freelance programmers, comparing different regions, sectors, and skills requirements. The computer press - especially *Computer Weekly*, which as well as undertaking surveys of establishments, has also published a number of studies based on content analysis of the advertisements it has carried for different types of job - on occasion commissions its own surveys of pay and recruitment issues.

7.2 Education and Training

The Census of Population provides statistics on professional qualifications; for 1981, for example, some 48,000 people are recorded as having degree level qualifications in electrical or electronic engineering. Connor and Pearson (1986a) point out that we are unsure of what proportion of these are practising engineers; and while they also report that one-third of the total recorded electrical and electronic engineers (that is, about 26,000 - this figure is surprisingly lower than the former, perhaps reflecting the recruitment of technically qualified staff into general management?) are qualified to degree level in science and technology subjects, exactly what these qualifications are is also uncertain.

A general review of training statistics is provided in *Employment Gazette* March 1988 (pp 130-142); this provides a useful guide to sources of information, but has little specific to say about IT training or training in IT-producing industries.

Table 7.6 First Degree Graduates in the UK

	UNIVERSITIES			POLYTECHNICS	
Subject	**80/81**	**85/86***	**86/87***	**80/81**	**85/86**
Mathematics	2,097	2,484	2,500	}	563
Computer				573	
science	922	1,388	1,492	}	810
Physics	1,993	2,311	2,277	107	163
Electrical/ electronic engineering	1,755	1,913	2,116	595	897

* Institute of Manpower Studies estimates

Note: for universities, home students only; polytechnic data excludes overseas graduates returning home on completing their course.

Source: University Grants Commission figures and Polytechnic First Destination Statistics drawn from Table 5.1 in Pearson, Connor and Pole (1988)

7.2.1 Higher Education

R&D in higher educational establishments has already been treated in Chapter 3.

UK universities and polytechnics offer no IT first degrees as such, but there are a number of first degrees which contain many elements relevant to the ''heartland'' of IT (see Chapter 4): computer science, mathematics, physics and electrical/electronic engineering are thus often considered IT subjects (e.g. by the IT Skills Shortage Committee). Data on graduate degrees and on the job destinations of new graduates can be put together from a number of sources: the annual *Statistics of Education* (volumes 3 and 6), the University Grants Committee's *First Destination of University Graduates*, the Council for National Academic Awards' *Annual Report* and the Committee of Directors of Polytechnics' *Polytechnic First Degree and HD Students: Statistical Supplement*. Pearson, Connor and Pole (1988) have put some of these data together, and Table 7.6 displays the number of university and polytechnic first degree graduates in these subjects from 1980 to 1986/87: an increasing trend is apparent. (See also the IT Skills Shortages Committee, 1984, Mason, 1987.)

An additional source of graduate-level skills derives from post-graduates undertaking conversion courses. Such courses are aimed at graduates with first degrees in non-IT disciplines, whether in science, arts or social sciences, and result from a major government initiative in 1982. In 1982/83 fewer than 200 studentships were awarded by SERC which is responsible for managing the initiative. This was expanded to about 800 studentships in 1983/84 and slightly more in subsequent years. The total number of IT conversion students is also boosted by some employer-sponsored students and by some support from the Manpower Services Commission. Table 7.7 shows the number of conversion courses in 1984/85 by different (main) IT subject areas, although most courses cover more than one subject area.

In addition to the conversion courses, a number of specialist postgraduate IT advanced courses, approved by the SERC, are aimed at people with first degrees in related IT subjects. In 1983/84 there were 30 such courses, all but one at universities. In broad categories, 6 of these 30 were computing courses, 13 were microelectronics courses and the remaining 11 were on other subjects (Connor and Pearson, 1986b, p10).

It is arguable that the definition of IT courses used in the discussion above is far too narrow. Innovative courses are being offered by various institutions that attempt to provide skills in IT applications of various

Table 7.7

IT Conversion Courses 1984/85

	Number of Courses		
Main IT Subject Area	**University**	**Polytechnic**	**All**
Computer science/systems	18	12	30
Microelectronics	8	2	10
Special applications	3	3	6
IKBS/MMI/AI	2	-	2
Control	2	-	2
Instrumentation	1	-	-
Communication	1	-	1
All subjects	**35**	**17**	**52**

Source: Connor and Pearson (1986a, p146)

sorts (e.g. video technologies), or in policy and social research issues around IT. (Examples include the new postgraduate courses established at CURDS and SPRU as part of the PICT initiative; and at graduate level, the North East London Polytechnic has just launched a BSc on "New Technology", with options on media and communication, manufacturing, education, and research, information and social policy. Courses which can form part of wider degrees - such as the Open University's new second level course, "An Introduction to IT: social and technological issues", should also be considered.) A similar qualification must be lodged in connection with the data available for further and higher education.

7.2.2 *Further Education*

Training and education in computing skills takes place below degree level via a wide range of college- and industry-based courses. These may be full- or part-time, short- or medium-term. Some of these courses lead to formal qualifications being awarded - examples are those run by the City and Guilds London Institute (CGLI) and the Business and Technician Education Council (BTEC). Mason (1987) has prepared a valuable report for the Engineering Industries Training Board on computing qualifications, and this presents data on further education alongside higher education and school level courses. Currently it is probably the most convenient single source of statistics on IT educational qualifications.

The CGLI offers computing-related qualifications in courses including Applications Programming (jointly certificated with the NCC), Computer Programming and Information Processing, Data Processing for Computer Users (aimed at management staff who work with computer departments), and in 1986 launched a course on IT (modules at four different levels - from introductory to advanced - covering programming and software; electronics and hardware; computer operations and applications). The number of people registered on the first three courses rose throughout the late 1970s and early 1980s. But considerably fewer people pass the exams, and the number of people with formal computing qualifications from further education represents only a small proportion of the total IT workforce.

At technician level, BTEC is responsible for qualifications in computing. (In Scotland a different body, the Scottish Vocational Education Council, (SCOTVEC) administers the courses.) Table 7.8 displays some data on the activities of these bodies in computer-related fields. A major expansion in training is clearly indicated, but pass rates for some of these courses are, in Mason's words, "low and variable".

Considerable innovation is under way in the IT courses offered in the further education sphere, which again makes tracking of trends rather difficult. New courses have been created by BTEC which focus on IT (including applications, implementation, system development and maintenance), understood as including electronics and communications in addition to computing. Short training courses also proliferate.

Table 7.8

Further Education in IT Subjects

BTEC Registrations and Awards in Computer Studies

		1980/81	1984/85
National Certificate			
	Registrations	361	1,828
	Awards	776*	678
National Diploma			
	Registrations	1,234	2,611
	Awards	49	1,310
Higher National Certificate			
	Registrations	349	1,062
	Awards	-	513
Higher National Diploma			
	Registrations	783	2,751
	Awards	-	1,133

SCOTVEC Advanced Level Awards, 1985/86

Course	Qualification	
	HNC	HND
Computer studies	59	120
Computer data processing	104	199

* This anomalously large figure, not repeated in subsequent years, apparently reflects the inclusion of awards to students previously registered under an earlier scheme.

Source: Tables A5, 3.2 in Mason (1987), based on BTEC Annual Reports and other sources

7.2.3 Secondary Education

Computer studies has become a very popular subject at 'O' level and CSE and at 'A' level during the 1980s as shown by Table 7.9 below. This is based on data assembled by Mason (1987) from a variety of sources including DES, Welsh Office, and CSE Examination Board statistics. The reporting of examination statistics is currently being revised with the introduction of the new GCSE examinations to replace 'O' levels and CSEs.

Mason provides several valuable tables and numerous incidental statistics in his discussion. He notes, for example, the continuing domination of boys in secondary level computing examinations, even through the rapid expansion of this subject. And he reports on surveys carried out by the DES which suggest that teacher training in the use of microcomputers is itself extremely limited, with over three-quarters of secondary school computer science teachers in England in 1984 having themselves no tertiary qualification in the subject. Although, as we have argued, IT is a pervasive technology with implications for and applications in most disciplines and areas of life, computing is habitually treated by schools as the responsibility of mathematics departments. (See Chapter 6 for more discussion of IT in education.)

Table 7.9

Computer Studies Entries at 'O' level, CSE and 'A' level, England and Wales

	1978	1982	1985
ENTRIES			
'O' level	9,088	36,606	68,462
CSE	14,757	30,217	60,398
'A' level	1,986	5,399	9,868
PASSES			
'A' level	1,290	3,618	6,946

Source: Tables 2.1, 2.2 in Mason (1987)

7.2.4 Retraining and Recruitment

From the IMS, Rajan (1985b, 1987) describes the results of a survey of strategies for acquiring skills needed for new technologies in technician-level occupations in 900 firms in the manufacturing and distributive sectors. (These are the 59% response rate from a sample of 1,650 manufacturing and 100 distributive firms approached in a national postal survey; they provide a reasonable range of branches and employment sizes.) Technical change in the last five years was reported by over 80% of the respondents, and one-quarter of these considered that this involved a large impact on their skill requirements. In both sectors, retraining was by far the most common method used, with recruitment of permanent staff a poor second, and very little use of permanent contract staff, temporary staff, or secondments from affiliated firms. Recruitment is most evident in batch production jobs, where Rajan sees new technology as creating demand for multiple skills. Rajan is sceptical of the quality of much on-the-job retraining, on the basis of the case study research accompanying this survey, and argues that this has limited the use of IT and the upgrading of work skills that might be involved.

Northcott's (1988) surveys of manufacturing establishments also investigate the training strategies adopted, which make interesting reading in the light of the prevalent complaints among his respondents concerning skill shortages. Half the user establishments had sent no engineers on special training courses in the last two years, two-fifths did not anticipate so doing in the next two. Recruitment rather than retraining seemed an important means of gaining skills, though the larger plants and those which are more advanced and intensive in their use of IT use training more extensively. Northcott also presents data on the training of non-engineers and the reasons for not using training, which suggests that only a minority attribute this to unsuitability of courses or difficulty in selecting appropriate courses.

A set of studies of technological change and training needs and practices in the north-west of the UK has been prepared by the Centre for Educational Development and Training, Manchester Polytechnic. These studies include interviews with a small set of firms in five sectors (both manufacturing and services), and a mail survey of 331 mainly small firms: see Bagenal (1986a,b), Dorsman (1986), Griffith (1986), Shaw (1986).

As noted in the labour market discussion above, the computer press has devoted much coverage to pay and recruitment issues. An instance of a survey organised by one magazine is reported in *Computer Weekly* (September 4 1986, p32; September 11 1986, pp34-35). This study assesses costs of recruitment, reasons for using contract staff, turnover rates and related issues, and demonstrates the reluctance of employers to train DP staff (other than data entry operators). There is a strong tendency to search for experienced staff rather than to train inexperienced staff. In line with this analysis, Penney (1986) uses NCC data to argue that shortages of skills are a result of a failure to exploit the pool of talent available; for more NCC material on sources and qualifications of recruits see Buckroyd and Cornford (1988), Cornford and Gott (1987).

7.3 Industrial Relations

The magazine *Labour Research* and its associated newsletter *Bargaining Report* provide considerable volumes of descriptive statistics on a range of industrial relations issues. In the mid-1980s this included much documentation of new technology agreements. Another useful source of material is the journal *Industrial Relations Research Review*, while the *Industrial Relations Journal* carries more academic research. Income Data Services' reports carry data not only on pay and conditions, but also on unionisation and bargaining practices. Studies of attitudes to IT (including worker attitudes) are discussed in Chapter 9 below.

The series of studies from the PSI, discussed in Chapter 5, contain a great deal of material on industrial relations issues; indeed, this is the focus of the study by Daniel (1987). This uses the 1984 WIRS of over 2,000 establishments, covering all sectors of the UK economy (but not sites with fewer than 25 employees), and included data from shop stewards as well as management respondents. Technical change in terms of the use of microelectronics on the shop floor, and of computers and word processors in offices, was contrasted to "conventional" technical change and to organisational change.

Rather high levels of technical change were found, and these were generally accepted by the workforces; there was no evidence suggesting that trade unions inhibited the rate of change. (Indeed, shop stewards and union officials tended to be particularly supportive of new technology.) Manual workers supported the introduction of IT in three-quarters of cases, according to management respondents, and strongly resisted it in only 2% of cases; office workers tended to be even more strongly supportive. In contrast, organisational change was much less popular.

The Daniel study presents many tables outlining the data obtained in this survey, contrasting different types of change, and different types of organisation. In addition to the attention given to the role of industrial relations in influencing technological change, and the reactions of workers to such change, it covers a number of related issues. These include the quality and organisation of work, loss of jobs, increases in earnings, and the involvement of personnel managers and trade unions in decision-making about technological change. In line with several other studies to be discussed later, Daniel finds a relatively low level of union involvement in managing technical change - even in sites where unions are recognised, only around 50% of shop stewards were consulted at *any* stage of the introduction of IT affecting manual workers. Where there was no union recognition, a similar proportion of cases involved no consultation (or even discussion with individual workers) about the innovation. Consultations were more prevalent when office workers were involved, however, and Daniels suggests that this is an indicator of the British class system in operation.

Northcott's study (1988) is less centrally concerned with industrial relations, though he too argues that worker resistance to IT is a relatively insignificant factor (despite a few well-known areas of conflict) (see also Northcott, 1985). Only some 8% of establishments surveyed saw opposition from unions or shopfloor workers to be a very important problem - as compared to 7% so regarding opposition from senior management, 51% citing skill shortages, and over 20% citing each of a range of other (mostly financial and technical) problems.

New technology agreements formed an important part of British trade unions' strategy for coping with the introduction of IT. Williams and Steward (1985) present a survey of some 240 such agreements adopted in the period 1977-83 - this is believed to constitute the majority of such agreements, and to be a broadly representative sample. A wide range of analyses are presented - on the year of adoption (1980 seems to have been the peak), the unions involved (white collar unions are responsible for most agreements), the industries involved (engineering - especially "high tech" firms - and public services dominate), the type of labour involved (again overwhelmingly white-collar), and the main provisions of the agreements (treatment of employment, quality of work, and control of jobs), etc. The researchers conclude that both the adoption and content of new technology agreements have been limited compared to trade union objectives; unions tend to be involved at relatively late stages in the introduction of new technology, and the agreements tend to be defensive and reactive in character. While fairly tight standards are often achieved over, say, health and safety, there is little progress (from the worker viewpoint) in terms of job design and reductions in working time.

A detailed review of trade unions' policies concerning new technologies is provided by Dodgson and Martin (1987). (For an earlier review, paying more attention to the attitudes and responses of specific unions, see Webster and Robbins (1982).) Dodgson and Martin present two interesting sets of data. The first is CBI Pay Databank information on settlements achieved in UK manufacturing over 1980-84. Settlements are cross-tabulated according to, on the one hand, whether or not they included the introduction of new technology (the great majority did), and, on the other, what dimensions of work organisation they involved (e.g. removal of restrictive practices, reduction in numbers employed).

The second data set addresses trade unions' research efforts on new technology. It covers the numbers of researchers employed by unions (fewer than 150, mostly concentrated in the large unions), and the numbers of these researchers in major unions responsible for monitoring new technology (some 16 out of 118 researchers), and it provides estimates based on a telephone survey of whether the researchers responsible for monitoring new technology issues are able to devote more than half their time to this topic (only a small minority are). The researchers suggest that this lack of research effort is partly responsible for unions tending to be reactive with respect to new technology, and for their policies having at best limited success.

A large-scale study by Batstone and Gourlay (1986) draws on a survey of over 1,000 shop stewards. (They were mainly from large organisations - over a third have over 500 employed at their establishment - and from a wide, but not comprehensive, set of industries within which some manufacturing and some services were included. The sampling strategy was designed to complement, in terms of sectors and unions studied, in-depth parallel case-study analyses.) Data are presented on the course of technological change and the involvement of unions in this process, and on the "effects" of the change on job content and rewards and on union organisation itself. Very detailed information (typically disaggregated by economic sectors) is provided on these topics.

For example, studies of the process of technological change include tables on areas of negotiation over technical change; areas of disagreement between unions and managements; the role of unions' own proposals concerning new technology; the threat and use of sanctions; and the prevalence, coverage and perceived usefulness of new technology agreements. The study concludes that the "effects" of new technology are in large part a product of management and union strategies. The main consequence for union organisation has been less a weakening of union structures - indeed, stronger union organisations tended to be strengthened, weaker ones weakened - than an increased awareness on the part of unions of the need to understand the broad context of management policies.

NEDO (1983a), by contrast, presents a small study of 46 plants in the electronics industry, considering how the introduction of IT is handled in this "heartland" sector. This is accompanied by a study of the new technology agreements in the industry. Data are provided on the extent of employee involvement and union consultation at different stages in the process of technological change, on the topics covered by consultative procedures, and related issues. An effort is made to assess the utility to the firms surveyed of consultative arrangements - while management and unions report different benefits, the responses of both groups tend to be positive. Nevertheless, it is apparent that consultation is much more prevalent at later stages of technological innovation (implementation) than at earlier stages (planning, choice of equipment). For a comparative study of consultation practices in different Western European countries, see EFILWC (1985).

7.4 Work and Employment Consequences of IT

When the "microelectronics revolution" first began to be announced in the late 1970s, one of the chief topics of debate was the likely consequences of IT for employment levels. In the context of a world economic recession, the threat of high and long-term displacement of jobs by the new technologies appeared an ominous prospect to many, and at this time there were many speculative attempts to estimate the scale of the threat. The great majority of these studies are now recognised to have been substantially flawed, displaying such errors as failing to take into account the uneven rates of diffusion of new technologies (just because a job can be done by a robot does not mean that it will be so accomplished in the near future), the upstream and downstream implications of innovation (demand may be increased for cheapened products, and new jobs may be created in supply, maintenance, etc.), and the scope for the creation of new products and associated new areas of demand and employment.

There have been a number of studies which review this literature and provide their own accounts of potential consequences of IT for employment in different sectors. To cite merely a few of the better studies which provide statistical documentation, Braun and Senker (1982) and especially Sleigh et al. (1979) represent early examples of such an effort; Cooper and Clark (1982) and Freeman, Clark and Soete (1982) relate such work to the economics literature; Leach and Wagstaff (1986) present a strong case for major declines in current forms of employment (complete with projections of employment trends); and Driver (1987) provides international comparisons and argues for industrial restructuring.

The PSI survey studies of Daniel and Northcott address the employment effects of IT. Both of these are limited in one important way, in that they concern only job losses and gains at the individual workplaces surveyed. Whether changes in employment requirements are occasioned elsewhere in companies, or whether, for instance, the fact that one establishment has innovated and preserved jobs but that its improved performance has led to a loss of trade and jobs at a non-innovative establishment, are questions that are not readily handled with this sort of empirical approach.

Daniel (1987) reports that the introduction of IT in his sample of workplaces had much less "impact" upon numbers employed than on the structure of employment; and that other factors (e.g. changes in demand, cash limits) tended to be given more weight here. He finds that shopfloor IT tended to be associated with a reduction in manual employment - or, more precisely, that increases in manual employment were involved in about one in ten cases, but these were outweighed by often substantial decreases in about one in five cases where IT was introduced. Office IT was associated with an increase in non-manual employment, though again the trend was not dramatic. Daniel shows that the trends are more pronounced in private services than in other sectors. Finally, the consequences for occupational structure seemed to be reinforcing established occupational trends, with a shift toward skilled and office staff.

Northcott (1988) also pays considerable attention to the direction of employment changes in his manufacturing sample. While a majority of factories reported no employment changes as a result of their use of microelectronics, this number has decreased over the surveys from 1981 to 1987 (from 73% to 58%). The proportions reporting employment increases and decreases were roughly similar, but overall there appears to have been a direct decrease of 1% (in the earlier period) and 25% (in the more recent period). He estimates that in the earlier period there was actually a net gain in jobs, but that more recently job loss in manufacturing has been running at around 46,000 per annum in consequence of the use of microelectronics. Data are further presented on changes in different types of job (male and female employment, skilled, unskilled and non-shopfloor jobs), and on regional and sectoral variations.

A set of studies carried out under the rubric of TEMPO (Technological Change and Employment Opportunities) at SPRU in the first half of the

1980s sought to depict employment trends in the main sectors of the UK economy in the light of technological change, and to outline the main consequences of anticipated innovation. Five volumes of detailed studies, each containing a wealth of data - unfortunately already rapidly dating - have been published. These cover the following sectors: consumer goods (Guy, 1984), basic process industries (Clark, 1985), electronics and communications (Soete, 1985b - and see also Soete and Dosi, 1983), vehicles and engineering (Freeman, 1985), and commercial services (Smith, 1985). Projected volumes on non-market services and construction and transport have unfortunately not materialised, although some draft chapters are known to have been prepared. Results of the research programme are synthesised in Freeman and Soete (1987).

As well as the sector studies and a general overview of the relations between technological change and employment that draws attention to the phenomena of "long waves" (Freeman, Clark and Soete, 1982) and changing "techno-economic paradigms" (Freeman and Soete, 1987), the TEMPO studies also engaged in some economic modelling. This line of work involved efforts to take account of different vintages of capital stock within simulation models, using this to derive scenarios for employment in various sectors. (See Clark (1980).) Some of this work was undertaken in conjunction with the Institute for Employment Research at the University of Warwick, and it is worth noting that the latter group have also presented some efforts to incorporate employment effects of microelectronics within UK economic models (Whitley and Wilson, 1983, 1987). Such an approach is able to take into account some of the indirect employment implications of technological change, although it typically involves making rather heroic assumptions as to the productivity gains to be achieved with IT. In the earlier study, the modelling suggests that the direct displacement of labour is largely compensated for by indirect effects, and while some job loss is probable, improved performance may further offset this - while failure to innovate would probably be disastrous. These results are amplified in the later study, where it is argued that rapid diffusion of IT in manufacturing might actually lead to employment increases, though, without service product innovation, rapid process innovation in services might lead to substantial job loss by 1995. (See Attenborough (1984) for a discussion of modelling approaches, in the context of an analysis of implications of microelectronics for manufacturing employment.)

Beyond studies of the quantitative "effects" of technological change upon employment, there has been much discussion of the ways in which working patterns and skill requirements are developing in the context of technological change. Here IT is at best admitted to be only one of a number of factors which are leading to a restructuring of working patterns towards what some commentators label "neoFordism". Discussions of these issues, and UK case-study research, can be found in such journals as *Industrial Relations Journal* (the Autumn 1985 special issue (vol 16 no 3) of this journal is particularly interesting, with overviews of studies of IT applications of various types in various sectors), *Work, Employment and Society*, and especially *New Technology, Work and Employment*. There are relatively few efforts at statistical analysis of these issues, but a number of studies in recent years are beginning to contribute to our picture of changing skill levels and working arrangements. For a comprehensive review of early case study research on this topic, see Brady (1984).

One of these we have already encountered: Rajan's (1985b) study of training and recruitment in a sample of manufacturing and distribution firms. We have already discussed the finding that retraining was a major source of new skills; of the 80% of the sample reporting technical change since 1980, about three-quarters claimed that this involved no or little change in skill requirements. In manufacturing this appeared to reflect fairly close matches between existing skill availability in internal labour markets and skill requirements, given limited technical change, some deskilling of work, and management lack of awareness of changing skill needs. In distribution, this reflected limited technical change at single-site firms, together with deskilling of work in multiple chain stores.

In the one-quarter of firms with technical change that reported large consequences for skill requirements, Rajan found two types of "loading" of jobs were common. In distribution, "horizontal loading" was most evident - this involves workers acquiring multiple skills to perform a series of independent functions. In manufacturing, this was also accompanied by "vertical loading", where multiple skills are needed to perform a cycle of related functions. While new technology was one of the factors leading to such job restructuring, efforts to reduce job demarcation lines in the economic recession also played a prominent role.

Rajan (1985a) extends the scope of this study by relating its results to an earlier (Rajan, 1984) study of four service sectors - insurance, banking, building societies and retail trades. The studies suggest a complex pattern in which some deskilling - loss of job-specific skills - is taking place alongside job enlargement and enrichment. Rajan goes on to provide a review of a number of other British studies of IT and work organisation. And Rajan and Pearson (1986) provide an even more ambitious overview, spanning the whole economy and providing forecasts as well as trend analysis, drawing on questionnaire surveys of almost 3,000 employers and interviews in several hundred firms (not omitting small firms).

The Rajan and Pearson (1986) study describes employment trends and their perceived causes, as experienced to 1985 and as forecast to 1990, for a 10-sector disaggregation of the economy, with a separate analysis for small firms. The chapter on public services - potentially the most important influence on quantitative trends - is weak in comparison with the other sectors, however. (The error margin on the forecast of employment trends here, plus or minus 100,000 jobs, is rather larger than the forecast trend of 60,000 jobs lost!) The study draws attention to a number of themes which have already been noted: the role of IT in service activities, the trend toward contracting-out of work, the development of various kinds of "flexibility", and expansion in technical and professional jobs (including multi-skilled craft workers). Similar themes are echoed in Daniel (1987).

A smaller-scale study, based on in-depth interviews, was carried out by Cross (1985). This also focuses on the creation of multi-skilled jobs, in this case looking at engineering maintenance craft workers in UK process manufacturing firms. Interviews were conducted on 67 sites operated by 51 companies, and depicted, as a common development, the creation of new core mechanical, fabricating, and electrical/instrument jobs. In relatively few instances these are combined in multiskill multirole engineering craft jobs, and in a few cases production and maintenance jobs have also been combined. Cross argues that these are indicative trends to which both companies and training institutions are slow to react. Despite the small sample, the study contains much interesting data on changes in craft organisation, craft training requirements, and problems experienced in craft maintenance and repair.

The Batstone and Gourlay (1986) study of shop stewards also included an analysis of changing work organisation. Considerable change in demarcation systems was noted, especially in sectors like food and drink, chemicals, and printing - rather little change here was apparent in Civil Service, finance and production and electrical engineering jobs. Overall the respondents indicated that skill levels had more frequently increased than decreased in all sectors covered, though in some sectors (notably printing) there were considerable proportions reporting decreases. Far more mixed pictures - with divergent trends common in many sectors - were apparent where answers to questions concerning worker control of tasks, amount of effort required, and health and safety standards were involved. The study also carries data on the extent of retraining (very variable across sectors, and often extremely limited), and worker attitudes to technical change (levels of opposition are notably low, though "uncertain or neutral" attitudes outweigh favourable ones in several sectors).

ACAS (1988) provides a general survey of the trend toward enhancing labour flexibility in the UK. While IT is not at the centre of this study, it does provide some evidence on the role of technological change as well as documenting the pattern of restructuring of work more generally. Data are derived from 584 visits by Advisory, Conciliatory and Arbitration Service (ACAS) staff to employers, and are biased toward the private sector and toward manufacturing. Attention is paid to different kinds of labour force flexibility: *numerical* (e.g. using part-timers. temporary workers, job sharing, subcontracting, homeworkers, and fixed-term contracts); *functional* (relaxing demarcations); *hours of work* (shift working, flexible shift patterns); and *costs and rewards* (merit pay schemes, integrated pay structures and job evaluation, harmonisation of terms and conditions of employment). The extent of many of these forms of flexibility was quite low, but there had been increases over the past three years in shiftworking, profit sharing, merit pay and payment systems rewarding the acquisition of new skills, and functional flexibility. Manufacturing industries tended to have gone further in introducing flexible practices than service organisations. Blandy (1984) discusses changes in working time in the context of the introduction of IT, though little data are available.

Respondents (usually senior managers) in this study were asked to give reasons for introducing flexibility: some 26% cited technological change as a reason (ranging from a third of respondents in metal goods and electrical engineering and vehicles, to 7% in hotels, distribution and catering). Far more commonly cited were reasons such as increasing productivity (41%) and reducing labour costs (40%). Though such factors might also be associated with technological change, this study reinforces the point that the complex restructuring of work and organisational practices that is under way is one in which the use of new technology is itself part of the strategy of change, rather than the cause of change.

7.5 Conclusions

While we confront many familiar problems when addressing the question of data on IT's relation to formal work and employment, this is one area to which rather a lot of effort has been directed, both by official and especially unofficial statisticians. Professional IT employment has been the subject of several useful studies, and we can be hopeful that more detailed cross-sectoral and multivariate analyses may be brought to bear on these data. Non-professional IT work, and the IT components of a wide range of jobs that will typically be classified otherwise, still demand further attention.

Compared to employment, data on training for IT and the various issues of quality of working life and industrial relations have received relatively little statistical analysis (though there has been a great deal of case study research on the latter topics). The diversity (and controversial nature) of the phenomena in question are liable to make development of a comprehensive set of statistics rather difficult, but there is every reason to recommend that researchers attempt to build upon the studies described above.

8 Consumption

This chapter centres on the role of IT in what is generally termed "final consumption". This phrase is actually rather misleading, since a great deal of productive informal economic activity takes place with the use of consumer goods and services. Some commentators have even argued that the estimates of output in the national accounts (e.g. GNP) should be augmented by estimates of informal labour's outputs, such as self-service transport and domestic work. (Miles (1985b) reviews discussions about augmenting or replacing GNP and related indicators.) Futurologists have argued that more production will be shifted into the home by use of new technologies. (See Gershuny (1977) on the "self-service economy", and Gershuny and Miles (1983) for a statistical analysis of shifts between household consumption of goods and services.) Extrapolation of these developments is taken to mean that "prosumption" (Toffler, 1980) would be more appropriate to describe the mix of activities taking place outside of formal employment.

Be that as it may, it is evident that many new goods and services based on IT are being oriented toward what are potentially vast consumer markets (Miles, 1988a). This chapter will review data and data sources which enable us to examine trends in, and features of, consumer demand for, and use of, IT-based and IT-using products.

8.1 Household Expenditure

The most valuable source of data on household expenditure is *The Family Expenditure Survey*, published annually by the OPCS. This is based upon a relatively large sample (c11,000) households, with data produced throughout the year so as to encompass seasonal and other fluctuations. One of the main intents of this survey is to assemble information appropriate for the construction of cost-of-living indicators, by determining the composition of, and trends in the price of, households' "shopping bundles".

At the outset we should note that defining a "household" turns out to be more problematic than might have been expected. Thus the OPCS changed its definition in 1981, so as to include people who share living rooms in the same household, even if their catering arrangements are separate. Todd and Griffiths (1986) report that this resulted in a reduction of over 100,000 households; and while this was less than 1% of the total, it proved to be 17% fewer households in the privately rented furnished housing sector.

The *Family Expenditure Survey* elicits data on the expenditure of all members aged over 16 years of the households sampled. (Thus it may be an inadequate guide to the use of pocket money - some of which may be going on IT-based arcade game machines, for instance!) Completion of the survey is relatively arduous, since it involves keeping a diary of expenditures over a fortnight, and it is believed that there is some under-representation of low-income households. Questions are also asked concerning items of regular expenditure that might not be captured in these daily records.

In the published data, disaggregations are provided by household income level, household composition, tenure of dwelling, and region. Expenditures are classified into a number of broad groups, such as transport, clothing and footwear, and services. It will come as no surprise to learn that none of these broad groups are particularly relevant to IT use, and relatively few of the detailed classifications within them are, either. IT components may be entering household activities - the car or television may utilise microelectronics technology, the telephone licence may be supporting users of computer communications - but this will not be visible. The 1986 *Survey*, (published in 1987 and the most recent available at the time of writing) does, however, provide a disaggregation of expenditure on audio-visual goods (purchase or rental) within which information is provided on, *inter alia*, home computers and TV games, video recorders, video cassettes, telephone answering machines, etc.

(OECD (1988) presents comparative data for a small number of countries on trends in household expenditure on ''communications services'' - for the UK this involves only telecommunications - and for a larger number of countries, data provided by BT on telephone bills for companies and households.)

The problem we confront here is how to index IT penetration into everyday life, when the core technology is often embodied in goods (e.g. microwave or conventional ovens) and services (e.g. use of automated teller machines or of teletext on one's TV set) that are unlikely to be singled out for specific treatment in the statistics. This problem is widespread in data on final consumption. We know, for example, that many musical instruments are electronics-based, or that contemporary gramophones use ICs, but often it will be necessary to use judgement as to how far expenditure on, or possession of, goods and services involves traditional or IT-based systems. In some cases - home computers, CD players - we may be completely confident that (if we can obtain data on these items) we are dealing with IC-using equipment; in other cases there is less certainty (although the microwave oven is generally viewed as having only emerged when microelectronic timing and control was available, there are non-microelectronic models around); and in many more cases conventional items of domestic equipment are gradually being transformed by the introduction of new technology into them, but the process is far from complete.

One possibility which we have yet to explore would be to analyse household expenditure data in conjunction with input-output statistics (as discussed in Chapter 5). In principle we should be able to develop indicators estimating (1) the volume of IT "heartland" products being consumed *en route* to different elements of final consumption and (2) the volume of IT "heartland" products embodied in final consumer goods and services (other than imports, unfortunately).

8.2 Consumer Goods and Services

8.2.1 Official Statistics

The *Family Expenditure Survey* again offers some data on the possession of various classes of consumer goods, with the same sorts of disaggregation as for consumer expenditure. Televisions, telephones and (since 1985) video recorders and home computers are among the items listed. According to this source, in 1986 the average household possession of these items was, respectively, 97.1, 80.9, 36.3 and 15.1%. (This latter figure, as far as can be judged, makes the UK one of the most, if not the most, computer-intensive countries in the world.)

The *General Household Survey* is another annual survey carried out by the OPCS, with a sample size of c12,500, which contains information on consumer durables and leisure activities as well as on other topics. As with the *Family Expenditure Survey*, the published report provides disaggregation by household type for ownership or availability of durables, but it also classifies data on social activities in terms of individual characteristics. Also as with the *Family Expenditure Survey*, raw data can be re-analysed to allow for more elaborate disaggregations than provided in the published report.

The *1985 General Household Survey* (published in 1987) includes, among the set of consumer durables considered, TV (the number of sets per household is not presented, but a distinction is drawn between access to a colour set, and to monochrome only), telephone, video recorder, and home computer. (The 1985 figures for each of these latter two items - respectively 43% and 19% - are slightly above those from the 1986

Family Expenditure Survey suggesting either sample biases or - rather implausibly - disposal of both of these items over a short period.)

8.2.2 Unofficial Statistics

To the best of our knowledge, there have been no national academic surveys of domestic IT use, although there have been several localised and case-study research projects (see Mansell and Richards, 1986). There has been considerable market research into a number of consumer IT products, however, reflecting the volatility and competitiveness of these new markets.

As with surveys of business computer usage, these market surveys can take a number of forms. The two main classes of data are those derived from analysis of sales and/or shipments, and those based on consumer surveys. Also as with business use of IT, the bulk of market research data remains rather inaccessible, although some reports are available in specialist libraries, and the trade press often publishes results of such studies. *Screen Digest* in particular makes an effort to cover data on consumer electronics and media. Key Note Publications has produced a number of reports which provide convenient summaries of what is known about markets for such items as home computers and video recorders. Unfortunately, trade press reports are often less than forthcoming about the methods whereby data were produced, and thus it is difficult to assess their validity.

An instance of a rather different type of academic research approach is represented by the work of Batty (1986). This author estimated the regional distribution of home computer ownership on the basis of analysis of the readers' letters published in three popular computing magazines over a period of two years. Marked regional differences were noted, with the South-east generating by far the biggest number of letters - suggesting in turn that home computer owners tend to be more often located in this region. The result was in line with that of an earlier study of software (Batty, 1985). (It should be noted that most magazines are specific to companies or to machine types; Batty's research sampled those with more serious/educational applications.)

8.2.3 Sales Data

Trade associations are a source of sales data on a number of IT-using "brown goods" - these are consumer electronics, which essentially involve information-processing of audio or video data, and where microelectronics is now commonly used in many classes of equipment).

They also provide such data on "white goods" - household electrical appliances, where the situation is more ambiguous, since IT is being incorporated increasingly into controls and displays, but where the information-processing function is less central to their operation than in brown goods. One exception here may be new classes of consumer goods such as home security and alarm systems. These are particularly poorly covered in statistics - as is not uncommon for products that have entered mass consumer markets after previously being mainly restricted to businesses and elite groups. The National Supervisory Council for Intruder Alarms does maintain a register of certified installations, but this excludes do-it-yourself systems and those installed by non-certified contractors.

Several trade associations were noted in Chapter 2, with BREMA covering brown goods (and home computers, which are covered in the *Annual Report*, but not in its regular publications on consumer electronics markets), AMDEA white goods, the BPI music recordings, and the BVA videograms (mainly videotapes: BREMA covers, but does not produce - on account of the few companies involved - data on videodiscs).

BREMA's *Annual Report* (1987) contains several types of data, including research from ORACLE concerning the use of its teletext service; comparisons of trends over 15 years in the relative costs of a consumer electronics item (colour TV) as compared to other items of consumer expenditure (the message is that the TV has got cheaper while other items have inflated dramatically); and comparisons of the purchasing power of working time in various countries (at one extreme, an American worker would only need to work for 55 hours to buy the colour TV, the British equivalent is 69 hours, while at the other extreme the Japanese would need to work for 157 hours). But the main data are presented in the "Economics and Statistics Review" section of the *Report*. Here, in the 1987 edition, are presented trend data on sales of TVs of different types, and of video recorders, camcorders, music centres, and CD players. The text discusses some trade issues - for instance, the increase in exports of both TVs and video cassette recorders (VCRs). BREMA also publishes statistical yearbooks, which cover the historical development of consumer audio and TV/video markets.

Caution needs to be exercised in interpreting suppliers' data - are only members covered? what is the treatment of imports and exports? how are British-based Japanese firms being treated?

Haddon (1988) discusses divergences between different sales-based estimates of market size for consumer goods, via a case study of video recorder data. He notes three main types of indicator that are in use:

- apparent consumption (home production plus imports minus exports - this measure is liable to conflate manufacturers' own stocks with deliveries, and there may be further problems with re-imports and re-exports with such data);
- deliveries to the trade (numbers of items reaching distributors and retailers, which tell us about their stocks but not necessarily about consumer purchases - trade associations may collate such data from their members, and include estimates of non-members' deliveries);
- consumer off-take (numbers of items sold - and, perhaps, rented - to consumers, based on data supplied by panels of retailers. The representativeness of the sample may be difficult to determine.

BREMA recognises that its panel over-represents the major multiple retailer, and makes some effort to weight its data accordingly.

While each indicator has its problems, consumer off-take is evidently the best guide to final consumption of IT-based goods. It is a statistic that is liable to show wide seasonal variations (Christmas sales booms are common for several types of brown and white goods, and thus it is important to beware of generalising from short-run statistics), but the other indicators are even more volatile - especially apparent consumption. Estimates of "installations in use" are sometimes derived from sales data, using assumptions about the rates of replacement and disposal of equipment to arrive at a proxy for the numbers of items currently held by consumers.

In addition to data on volume of sales as discussed above, statistics are often provided on the value of sales. The volume measure is liable to hide variations in sales between devices of different levels of sophistication. This can be very important in such areas as home computers where prices may vary by an order of magnitude, with devices representing extremely different levels of technical sophistication - for example, the RAM offered currently varies between 32 and 1024k, and the first Sinclair computers offered only 1k.

The value measure provides an estimate of expenditure, and when taken in conjunction with the volume measure it can provide some guide as to the average cost of the devices in question, which offers some evidence as to trends in the level of sophistication. Market research firms are often oriented toward providing information on the sales of different manufacturers and of different models, while trade associations are for obvious reasons more likely only to make very crude disaggregations (e.g. between colour and monochrome TVs, teletext and non-teletext TVs, etc.).

The diversity of consumer IT equipment is reflected in the diversity of statistics and sources that is available - and in a diverse quality of data. A rough assessment of the information to hand suggests that it varies considerably by the area covered:

- Brown goods are generally well-documented, especially such items as video recorders and TVs. CD players, home computers, and software are also covered by trade sources.
- White goods statistics generally draw few distinctions that would enable us to treat microelectronics-using systems separately from others. However, data are available on such (mainly IT-using) items as microwave ovens and food processors.
- Automobile equipment: though cars have been a major route for the entry of IT into everyday life (in-car entertainment, mobile communications, electronic braking and fuel injection systems, etc.), there is relatively little statistical information available on this topic: it might well be possible to develop estimates from data on the sales of different car models. Mobile telephones - largely a professional application - have been studied in some detail, as we saw in Chapter 6, although this again reminds us of the difficulty in distinguishing between consumer and business purchases in the case of many goods and services; company car purchases are of course very important in the UK. In-car entertainment systems have been the subject of some market studies.
- Other products: there seem to be very few data on sports equipment and consumer health products, both of which are witnessing IT applications. Data on toys and musical instruments are likewise of very limited use.

For IT-based services, data from suppliers may be a major source of evidence. For instance, patterns of use of consumer-oriented videotex services may be recorded as by-product data by the service suppliers (e.g. numbers of page accesses, levels of use of various service providers). Rather detailed information is provided on the use of Minitel in France, but statistics on Prestel use are far more limited. The main relevant figure released by Prestel concerns the division of its subscriber base between business and residential use: a little under 50% of the c70,000 users are residential.

Sometimes services on Prestel such as Micronet, a computer hobbyists' information, teleservice base and messaging system, and on Compunet, a competitor to Prestel originally established for users of Commodore computers, but now of wider scope, provide a few figures on usage patterns. Electronic mail systems, such as Telecom Gold, do not provide data distinguishing between business and consumer use, though there are known to be some consumer (or at least semi-professional) users. This reflects a general problem with data on residential users of telecommunications services, since some of these are certainly home-based workers who are avoiding paying business connect charges; others (using, say, Prestel or Telecom Gold) will be professional workers who are carrying out some of their office-type work at home, and yet others will be service workers who are using ordinary 'phone connections to transmit data from, say, handheld terminals on which they have been entering details of repairs carried out or visits made, to their employers. BT does release data on residential connections to the telephone network; and, as we have seen, the *Family Expenditure Survey* and *General Household Survey* provide survey data on this topic.

Where it comes to IT-based broadcast services, such as teletext, the supplier can only determine usage patterns through survey research, since even data on the diffusion of teletext equipment (i.e. teletext TV sets) only inform us about capability to use the service, not about actual use levels. The Cable Authority marshals data on cable TV subscriptions; here it is worth noting that as well as actual household penetration, a statistic estimating the number of households that cable services "pass by" is also often cited.

8.2.4 Survey Data

Three broad classes of sample data are produced, reflecting different supplier interests: actual and intended purchases/ rentals, patterns of use of products, and attitudes to products. Where durables are involved, all types of data are produced; for "non-durables" and software (e.g. videotapes) the focus may be on recent purchasers only.

Sample surveys are almost always disaggregated by socioeconomic group (i.e. "social class" of household), although there is considerable variation as to the level of disaggregation involved. Regional breakdowns are also often provided, and for some classes of product, household composition (e.g. whether there are children in particular age ranges). Sample sizes vary considerably across different studies, and are typically much smaller than those of the two official surveys (the *Family Expenditure Survey* and *General Household Survey*); they are thus less likely to be reliable sources of information on subcategories of the population.

Additionally, the survey methods employed are often more rough-and-ready than those of official statisticians; for example quota samples are regularly involved, and so various sample biases are liable to creep in - thus it is as well to treat their data as indicative rather than as precise, and to weigh the results of any one survey in the light of others on similar topics. (Quota surveys aim at achieving specified proportions of given target groups in the population, rather than at surveying specific households (as identified, say, from the electoral register). They may thus be more prone to omit those households which have no members at home in the main hours of work. Sometimes, too, surveys are based not on doorstep interviews but on recruiting respondents in shopping centres or other public places, which again introduces sources of bias.)

Consumer electronics are relatively well covered in sample survey studies. Market surveys have covered a wide variety of products:

- video recorders and both pre-recorded and blank tapes, video cameras and recorders;
- TV sets (including monochrome and colour, multiple TV ownership, remote control, teletext, cable systems);
- CD players and discs;
- among record players, stereo hardware, LP records;
- audio cassette players, "personal stereos", radio cassette recorders, blank and pre-recorded tape;
- radios;
- home computers, software, some peripherals (e.g. printers);
- video games machines and software (often included with home computers);
- calculators (these have not been studied recently);
- telephones, multiple and cordless, telephone sockets;
- in-car cassette and radio systems.

Home computers, perhaps the archetypal consumer IT product, have been much studied in recent years. *Computer Trade Weekly*, which frequently reports such studies, noted on April 25 1988 (with only a little exaggeration) that:

> "(w)here once there was a market bemoaning the lack of market research to tell it things it wouldn't believe, wouldn't want, or knew already, these days you just cannot move for tables detailing the precise geographical split of MSX [a Japanese computer standard] sales in the north west in 1985 or whatever. You just can't open the pages of *CTW* without finding yet more...for the umpteenth time in recent weeks, here is some market research..." (p17)

Thus the issue of *Computer Trade Weekly* for April 11 carried a report of a large-scale Gallup survey (8,733 adults sampled) about the computer industry. Tables are presented concerning the 882 individuals living in computer-owning households and using the machines, with sex, age and class disaggregations provided on such variables as ownership of home computers versus video game consoles (the sex bias is rather less than one might guess); volumes of software purchases; whether or not there are non-games programs (56% of the sample - the text goes on to note that three-quarters of users of the more expensive machines have non-games software; there are also data on users copying and sharing programs); the type of computer owned, and also the type that is in mind among prospective purchasers; source of hardware purchase (by store name and type). The same disaggregations are presented for the whole sample on a question concerning expectations of a computer purchase over the next year.

White goods possession is also heavily documented in its own market studies and trade literature, but suffers the problems noted with sales data in that determining the IT component is extremely difficult. A problem that applies to all types of possession data is determining the appropriate level of analysis:

- is this a possession of the whole household or of one member?
- given this uncertainty, who is the appropriate person from whom to generate data (given that the person who buys the product may not be the owner - many consumer goods are bought as gifts)?
- how are possession questions to be asked (e.g., what is the respondents's interpretation of such questions as "do you have product X?"? is "you" taken to be personal, to refer to the whole household's communal property, or to refer to possessions of any household member?)?

Gender issues are raised in such sample surveys, and this is explicitly recognised by some survey firms. Since patterns of usage of goods and services often vary by gender, an effort may be made to sample the supposedly appropriate population: for white goods, for instance, female respondents are typically sought. These issues are most prominent when data concern usage, rather than just possession, of IT goods and services.

Usage data are sometimes provided in market surveys, typically by asking who uses an item, how much the respondent makes use of it, or whether (and sometimes when or even where) they use it. (Other data sources here, from broadcasting and time budget research, are reviewed in Section 3 below.) Market research firms have covered in particular the use of video recorders (for time-shifting or viewing films), the levels of use of audio products, etc. Haddon (1988) notes a wide variety of usage data recorded in surveys of home computer users - who the main user is in the family, profiles of use across family members, main types of activity engaged in by different family members, software used most often, frequency and amount of use by different users and applications, etc.

Usage information on use of telecommunications and white goods seems to be rather limited, For example, published telephone usage statistics may differentiate between local, national and international calls, and between residential and business users, but not between both at once. Market research firms have been known to present views on different types of consumer which suggest that they have processed at least some data on usage patterns. Gershuny (1982) presents data from a local survey of the gender uses of different items of domestic technology, while Gershuny et al. (1986) provide data on male and female claims to have engaged in various types of domestic work.

We have already encountered one of the most frequent types of subjective data produced in survey research-buying intentions, whose interest to suppliers is unsurprising. Such data are often produced where new products are emerging - e.g. home computers, CD players, video recorders have featured in this way in recent years; and, perhaps reflecting the liberalisation of the market, so have telephones of different types. Other research goes more deeply into attitudinal issues, such as whether respondents feel they have sufficient information to make choices, whether they feel the new product offers superior performance to traditional devices, whether they feel capable of using the product easily.

8.3 Leisure Activities, and the Use of Mass Media and New Media

The *General Household Survey* is a source of some data on social participation and leisure activities (much of which, together with other relevant material, is reported in the annual *Social Trends*). Leisure items do not appear in every *General Household Survey*, and the most recent enquiry - for 1983 - presumably reflecting policy interest in sports and related provisions, mainly concerns out-of-home activities. However, data are provided, disaggregated by gender, age and social class, of mainly home-based activities such as watching TV, listening to the radio, and listening to records or tapes. (Tables are provided with gender by age, and gender by class, breakdowns of leisure activities.) The Henley Centre publishes quite extensively on leisure patterns, using recall measures of participation to give time-use estimates.

Time budgets, derived from asking respondents to record (or recall) their sequence of activities over a period of time, are a good source of information on relatively frequently performed activities - for infrequent activities (such as holidays) other types of enquiry are more appropriate. As they are laborious both for researchers and respondents, time budget studies are relatively rare, although the BBC has carried out a number of such studies and the ESRC funded one in 1983/84 (see Gershuny et al., 1986). While TV viewing and radio listening have long been recorded in such diaries - and the BBC's interest, of course, is in establishing media usage patterns - it is only in recent studies that categories such as "using a home computer" and "watching videos" have been added, and we are not aware of substantive published information based on such data. It is also likely that some types of home computer use are lost within categories such as "writing", while recorded use may not distinguish between work-related applications, hobbies, and games.

The broadcasting companies engage in a large volume of research concerning patterns of media use, only a proportion of which enters the public domain. The BBC jointly owns, with the Independent Television Companies' Association, a limited company, the Broadcasters' Audience Research Board (BARB). BARB monitors TV audiences, and both the BBC and the Independent Broadcasting Authority (IBA) have their own research organisations which provide it with data. BARB obtains an ongoing survey of c3,000 households whose viewing patterns are monitored by a meter in the TV. It also commissions, annually, an Establishment Survey: a sample of c20,000 households serve as a source of data on TVs and related equipment (e.g. video recorders), and apparently information is also requested on viewing habits.

The BBC's Broadcasting Research Department engages in a number of survey activities. Its "Daily Life" studies (one carried out in 1983/84 and published as *Daily Life in the 1980s* (time use data) and *Information for Broadcasters* (media access and leisure activities), one due for 1988/89) involve a large sample (c12,000 in 1983/84) and include time budget surveys, together with questions about their ownership of consumer electronics, their media preferences, and their patterns of audio-visual media use. (Rather than ask respondents to keep a diary, as earlier BBC time budgets did, these ask them, with prompts, to recall their activities in the previous day.) The BBC also runs a weekly survey of two panels of some 3,000 respondents who supply data on their reactions to programmes which they have viewed, in one case, or listened to, in the other.

The BBC's *Annual Review of BBC Broadcasting Research Findings* (previously the word "Audience" was used instead of "Broadcasting") is a useful source of information on BBC projects. How far it deals with IT issues is very variable, but the issue no 8 (1981/82), for instance, carried several relevant pieces. As well as more general studies - patterns of TV viewing in the UK population, characteristics of "small hour" radio audiences, effects of a TV documentary on knowledge of the topic covered - two papers directly focus on IT issues. One describes the market research used in the preparation of "The Computer Programme"; one surveys awareness of teletext and videotex, providing age, class and sex breakdowns of recognition of names such as Prestel, Intelsat, Ceefax, etc. The issue also provides a discussion of the research philosophy being pursued by the BBC in general. In 1987/88 the BBC was known to have studies of teletext use, of teletext subtitle use, of the use of car radios, and a large range of other topics under way.

The IBA is known to conduct a similarly wide range (although apparently a smaller volume) of research, some of which is available in the form of reports in the IBA library. Cable TV companies have been undertaking a few studies of their subscribers' media use, some of which are reported on in the publications of the Cable Authority.

The relevance of much of this broadcasting research to IT use is debatable. Certainly IT components are used in the production and delivery of broadcast media, and there has been a general shift from electronic to microelectronic technology over recent decades. With this has come new capacities for TVs and other equipment, such as remote control and teletext, and more recently facilities such as freeze-frame and multiframe viewing. Data on overall use of TV are readily available, but use of these new facilities is more obscure. (The IBA has released data on teletext usage levels, which contrast with the wide diffusion of teletext equipment - it is only used intensively by a small proportion of viewers. It is thus conceptually far from easy to develop appropriate measures of the IT content of household time use (as opposed to the rather easier notion of the IT-intensity of household expenditure). Just as the cheapening cost of microelectronics may lead to paradoxical decreases in apparent IT expenditure as the volume of IT equipment used increases, so might any labour-saving associated with new IT goods result in an apparent decrease in the IT-intensity of domestic labour time. (More realistically, rather than decreases, we might forecast smaller increases than would be expected from physical measures.)

8.4 Conclusions

While there is a great deal of information on some topics in the consumer use of IT products, this is very uneven. Few data are subject to adequate scrutiny, many only enter the public domain (if at all) in heavily processed form, and there has been remarkably little effort devoted to assessing the possibilities for assembling time-series and comparative data. It would, perhaps, be worth investing resources into reworking existing data as well as into commissioning new studies: for instance, it might well be possible to estimate the income and price elasticities of IT-based products from such sources, which would throw some light on to arguments about consumer demand in "information society".

Reflecting the concerns of market researchers - with creating data that enable assessment of market shares and market potentials - there is very little information which goes beyond the charting of diffusion of IT products to examining how they are used and with what consequences. The implications of IT for everyday life are being tackled in a few academic studies, but lack the sort of large-scale analysis that is common for possession studies. Yet it is at least arguable that interpretation of possession and even usage data is radically incomplete without more detailed analysis - for instance, of whether a TV that is turned on is actually being watched, of what other activities are being undertaken at the same time, of whether household members are sharing their experiences or wrapped up in their private worlds.

9 Social Implications

Earlier chapters have touched upon some of the implications of IT for organisations, employment and leisure activities. However, the scope for changing social practices around this technological revolution is wide indeed, since the new technologies can be used in virtually any activities with an information-processing component - which means virtually any activities, period! This is reflected in the "information society" literature by speculative discussion on "electronic democracy" and similar concepts, but these are not as yet the subject of statistical analysis. The PICT network is carrying out research which will, it is hoped, shed light on the interrelations between technological development and social inequalities (as structured by gender, region etc.), and on the cultural dimensions of new technologies.

The present chapter will, then, restrict itself to reviewing data on the very few of the broad range of social topics on which we have been able to locate existing data sources. The topics which we will consider include social attitudes, computer crime, and privacy and surveillance.

9.1 Social Attitudes

Attitude surveys and opinion polls are widely used as guides to likely social responses to everything from the naming of new soft drinks to the profile of political leaders - despite scepticism from many social scientists about the usefulness of brief and superficial interviews as guides to future behaviour. This scepticism is particularly pronounced when respondents are asked to describe their views of, or their likely actions in respect of, some new technology of which they have had little experience. Nevertheless, studies of attitudes toward IT have proliferated over recent years, and they do cast a surprising light on certain familiar assumptions about, for example, national differences in receptiveness to new technology. Unfortunately, in this area as in others, there is considerably more research carried out than is made generally available; many studies are carried out for interested commercial actors who require the data for their own activities and who do not want competitors to share it - indeed, who often do not want the world at large to know that they have commissioned the studies. (Chapter 8 has considered market-related surveys.)

In the early 1980s, in the wake of political concerns that resistance to IT might be in part responsible for economic problems - these were expressed by the British participants in the Versailles conference of Heads of Government in 1982 - the ESRC and DTI commissioned a study of public attitudes to new technology. The research was largely undertaken by the Technical Change Centre and its reports bring together much of the publicly available survey results. Notably, they suggest that expressed attitudes to new technology in Britain as elicited in surveys are relatively positive, and seem to have little relation to institutional behaviours (Williams, 1986a,b). The main outputs of the study that are of relevance here are Williams and Mills (1986) who present a compilation of studies from different countries concerning new technologies (it is not always clear in these studies which technologies respondents are referring to), and Hartley et al. (1986) who provide a set of studies which combines theoretical analysis of the dynamics of consumer diffusion of new technologies with small-scale studies of household use of IT and more general accounts of international experiences.

Some national surveys have involved large batteries of questions about attitudes to IT. Thus the Technical Change Centre asked respondents to state which of a range of technological terms they knew the meaning of (78% claimed to know what a computer program was; 70% what computer software was; 63% what a data bank was, and 37% a data base; 67% a word processor, 59% a microprocessor; and 43% IT!). In the same survey, respondents were asked which applications of new technology they favoured. Not surprisingly, "computers in the office for rapid communication" and "computers to help children learn" were overwhelmingly favoured, while "telephone tapping by the government for national security" and "keeping information on everyone in a computer" were rejected; perhaps more surprisingly, "computers in the home for banking and shopping" met with a mixed response but one that was on balance approving, while "computers to replace routine visits to doctors, lawyers, etc." also had a mixed response, but this was generally disapproving (Williams, 1986a, Williams and Bryan-Brown, 1985; the survey is fully reported in MORI, 1985).

Williams (1986b) reports on some trends over the period 1981-85, yielded by asking the same questions in surveys in these two years. Over this period there was an increase in the proportion of people reporting impacts of technology on their jobs in the last five years (as Chapter 5 would lead us to expect), and also some tendency to consider these impacts as being more profound (Table 9.1). Overwhelmingly respondents considered technological change to have improved their jobs (though the apparent trend here is a potential cause for concern), and belief in the economic necessity of innovation remains at high levels.

Table 9.1

Trends in Attitudes to IT in Britain in the 1980s

	Percentages	
	1981	**1985**
Impact of Technology on your job:		
a great deal	14	20
fair amount	16	22
just a little	23	26
none at all	34	28
no opinion	13	4
On Balance, were changes for:		
better	82	73
worse	11	17
other	2	6
no opinion	5	4
"New Technology is essential for Britain's prosperity"		
strongly agree	36	44
tend to agree	46	40
tend to disagree	4	5
strongly disagree	1	2
no opinion	13	9

Source: Tables 3, 4 in Williams (1986b)

Table 9.2

Comparative Data on Attitudes to IT (1985)

	Percentages							
	Fr	**Ger**	**GB**	**It**	**Nor**	**Sp**	**US**	**Jap**
1 Experience with IT	26	11	28	7	21	12	37	14
2 Interest in using IT	37	23	22	29	29	41	32	41
3 Willingness to retrain	60	37	58	46	57	53	65	28
Information Processing Systems								
4 Worsen Unemployment	47	53	63	48	45	63	43	47
5 Help Create Jobs	23	12	22	19	25	13	50	24
6 Reduce Tedious Tasks	65	38	79	63	74	75	77	39
7 Help Solve Problems	44	27	52	42	46	64	63	47
8 Threaten Privacy	71	51	75	37	56	69	68	50
National Priority								
9 Modernise	38	18	43	21	24	40	35	14
10 Protect Jobs	46	67	46	60	57	54	60	63

Source: Various tables in Vine (1985)

Notes on the questions:
1 "I have already used an information processing system such as a computer or word processor"
2 "I have never used one but it would interest me"
3 Percentages responding "absolutely" or "probably" to statement "Some think that in order to keep their jobs in a world of rapidly expanding modern technology, such as the use of information processing systems, people should undergo special training. Would you personally be prepared to undergo such training?"
4 and 5 Respondents asked to state which opinion comes closer to their view
6 to 8 Data represent percentages agreeing with statements, respectively: "In the workplace information processing systems will cut down on the more tedious tasks", "these systems will help people like me solve everyday problems", "it will be increasingly possible to use computer data banks to infringe upon personal privacy".
9 and 10 Respondents asked to state which opinion comes closer to their view: "it is essential that we modernise the outdated sectors of the economy as quickly as possible even if this will make unemployment worse", "it is more important to preserve jobs even if this means slowing down the modernisation of industry".

Cross-national surveys are usually less detailed than the Technical Change Centre studies, but in some respects are more interesting in that they allow a test of stereotypes of cultural variations in enthusiasm for technical change. Of course, these studies have to be treated with some caution, since national differences in response bias (answering in a way thought to please or impress the interviewer), and linguistic differences which may give translations of the same questions different emphases, can also be at play. Vine (1985) reports a study carried out for the Atlantic Institute which involved surveys in six European countries, Japan and the USA. Workforce attitudes are compared, and examples of the international variations are provided in Table 9.2.

These results show that, despite fears about the labour displacement consequences of IT, there are generally quite positive attitudes toward working with IT and undergoing retraining where necessary. Surprisingly, Germany and Japan are exceptions to this rule, which reinforces the point that attitude measures may be of limited usefulness in predicting national rates of innovation; and that it is not a matter of those with more experience of IT being more negative is suggested by the US data - high experience, high positive responses. (The low levels of experience in Japan may reflect the slow diffusion of office IT in many sectors of that country's economy.) One feature of these results that might increase our caution about relying upon them is that in Vine's survey rather a higher proportion of British respondents admit to feeling that data banks are a threat to privacy than in the Technical Change Centre studies claim to know what a data bank is! Among other results of this and related surveys we can note that younger respondents tend to express more positive attitudes than their elders, suggesting that the acceptability of IT is liable to continue to grow.

Some studies have addressed the attitudes of specific groups in the population - for example PA Technology/MORI (1984) present comparative data on the attitudes of senior executives (from "manufacturing, electronics, telecommunications and process computers") to new technology. It is almost inevitable with a study of this sort that the samples chosen in each country will be rather small (c100 in each of five countries), and exactly how comparable they are is arguable. Nevertheless, given the arguments made by Williams (1986b) that management attitudes may well restrict technical change in the UK, it is interesting that in this survey the British managers were least likely to claim that new technology had made a great deal of impact on their products and processes, but they were among the most confident about the technological supremacy of their products (though not their processes) and the least dissatisfied with their companies' use of R&D. While we may have reservations about attaching too much significance to the precise numerical variations revealed in such studies as this, they do constitute one of the few available approaches to quantifying national differences in corporate strategies.

Another specific group that has been surveyed is youth, whom the large-scale surveys have generally found to be more welcoming of IT than their elders. Furnham (1987) describes a study of young people's attitudes to IT among 500 young people aged 12 to 19 in Britain, however, which revealed a number of reservations about IT - two-thirds thought it would increase unemployment, although nearly three-quarters felt that computers improve the quality of life. Ninety per cent of the sample claimed to have used computers, and as many as 43% had computers at home.

9.2 Computer Crime and Security

Various forms of computer crime exist. Computers may be used as instruments in fraud, for instance in appropriating money by unauthorised EFT transfers. Such activities have received considerable attention. But the integrity of computer systems may be tampered with for reasons other than financial gain - although blackmail may motivate system-threatening behaviour. "Logic bombs" which lead to the corruption of computer files have sometimes been left in systems by disgruntled employees - or by programmers who fear redundancy, and trigger such "bombs" to go off if they are taken off the personnel register. "Viruses" which are transmitted from machine to machine, sometimes on computer-communication networks and sometimes on floppy discs, may also corrupt systems, or simply jam up communications networks with junk mail. And "hackers" often seem to enjoy the challenge of broaching the security safeguards intended to protect computer systems, whether or not they make use of the data obtained.

One thing that most computer crimes have in common is the difficulty in quantifying their incidence. *First,* like all forms of crime, many may pass undetected - indeed, given the intangible nature of computer-based transactions, this may be more so in this instance. *Second*, again perhaps amplifying the situation for other crimes, victims may not wish them to be reported - in this case, so as not to generate concern about the security of their computer systems, for example. On the other hand, there are interests in the hardware and software supply sectors who will wish to stress the potential dangers of computer crime by exaggerating those cases that are reported. *Third*, IT-related crimes are liable to pose courts a problem and to be classified under all sorts of traditional offence titles. Thus "hackers" have been charged with the theft of electricity and with connecting illicit devices to a network, as well as with the more apposite charges concerning tampering with correspondence, obscenity, and causing financial loss to system operators.

Cornwall (1988, p25) presents a sceptical view of computer crime statistics - this essentially meaning statistics on computer fraud:

> "The generally accepted statistic for the incidence of computer crime is around £400 million per year. Its authority derives from its being frequently quoted. A rich publicity reward awaits the 'expert' who announces that this is a huge underestimate. A much less attractive prize is in store for the sceptic who says, on the contrary, there is hardly any computer crime at all...The fact is no one knows, or even has the basis of knowing. Few items in the criminal code mention computers at all...the insurance industry doesn't collect any 'computer crime' figures either - what it knows about is claims under Fidelity or Banker's Blanket Bond....by altering the definition of computer crime you can make it as large or as small a problem as you wish."

But there have been some efforts to estimate the scale of the problem. Evans (1986 p9) reports a study sponsored by the Home Office, the Police Federation and Arthur Young, based on data from senior executives of 56 companies, which, while casting serious doubt on claims that computer fraud is costing UK industry hundreds of millions of pounds per annum, does suggest that a serious problem is felt to be emerging. It finds that:

> "concern about the possibility of computer fraud was identified by nearly half of those interviewed...when asked to give specific examples of fraud within their companies only 3% [one wonders how 3% is obtained from a sample of 56!] were able to accuse computing staff...most admitted that their own company had not experienced any incidents of computer crime....an earlier report - carried out last year by the Audit Commission - found that of the 67 firms surveyed, computer fraud losses amounted to only £1.12 million...the commission's findings failed to placate the industry's general alarm about the risks of computer embezzlement. Last year the UK's four leading banks put aside £85 million as surety against computer crime."

The Audit Commission report cited above is the "Computer Fraud Survey", reported in the *Audit Commission Review* of March 1985. This outlines incidences of frauds reported by economic sector, and by type of fraud; the amounts of money involved are related to the types of fraud, the method by which the fraud was discovered, and the occupational role of the perpetrator (interestingly, clerks and supervisors are dominant here, rather than the archetypal hackers, programmers). Some comparisons with a 1981 survey are offered. The response rate to the survey was 55%, and it is hard to know whether victims of fraud are over-represented (keen to share experiences) or under-represented (seeking to avoid potential publicity) in the study. In any case, 92% of 943 respondents claimed not to have suffered computer fraud in the past five years.

In this study, data are presented along several dimensions. The sector of the organisation involved is given - most frauds were reported from local government, but as in many other surveys this is a sector with a high response rate, and the average incidence of fraud is similar to that of the whole sample. A sector where fraud seems to be reported more than usually is utilities, with 9 of 45 responses indicating fraud. Perhaps more valid comparisons can be made between types of fraud, methods of discovery, and the posts held by perpetrators. Table 9.3 reproduces some key statistics.

As indicated, we are aware of no adequate statistical sources that deal with the full range of computer crime in the UK, although the publicity given to a number of cases of "hacking" at the time that this is being written suggests that this may soon be rectified. The *Computer Fraud and Security Bulletin* (published by Elsevier Science Publishers) does, however, carry statistics from BIS consultants' annual *Computer Crime Casebook*. Although there must be very real doubts concerning the quality of these data, they do depict trends in types of crime (for example, the February 1987 issue analyses trends from the 1960s to 1986, with system penetration by hackers apparently becoming a more common problem).

Security is the other side of the coin; but computer security issues extend to the protection of systems against natural catastrophes and fires as well as against physical or electronic intrusion. With the increasing dependence of critical decisions and information flows on computer systems, their ability to evade, or recover from, damage is obviously important. Even in financial terms, the losses that may be associated with a computer system being "down" for a few hours may well exceed the typical amounts stolen in computer frauds. (Large (1987) reports the author of BIS Applied System's *Computer Disaster Casebook* as estimating that computer disasters are costing the UK some £300 million per annum - at least 10 times more than computer fraud.) This gives rise to back-up systems of many kinds, as well as physical and software protection. These issues are covered quite frequently in the computer trade press, as well as in specialised sources like the *Computer Fraud*

Table 9.3

Features of Computer Fraud, 1984

	Number of cases	Size of fraud (£)
Type of Fraud		
Input	58	901,001
Output	2	230,185
Resources	17	2,301
Method of Discovery		
Internal control	40	624,149
Internal audit	9	197,200
Other	23	312,057
Not disclosed	5	81
Post of Perpetrator		
Clerk	27	326,013
Supervisor	29	775,278
Programmer	8	452
Customer	3	7,300
Other	3	21,800
Not known	7	2,644
Outcome of Frauds		
(1) Downgraded/redeployed	2	
(2) Termination	13	
(3) Prosecution	16	
(4) (2)+(3)	20	
Other	15	
Not disclosed	11	

Source: *Audit Commission Review,* March 1985

and Security Bulletin (whose January 1987 issue summarises a study of computer risks by the consultancy Hogg Robinson).

9.3 Privacy and Surveillance

Concern about computer systems holding sensitive (and/or inaccurate) data about individuals mounted in the 1970s, and in 1984 the Data Protection Act established the Office of the Data Protection Registrar, with whom details of some such data bases have to be registered. There are many types of data base that need not register: those not including material on individuals, certain types of membership and mailing lists and of accounts and payroll data, non-automated records (e.g. a manual file card system, even if this is used in conjunction with a computerised system), and national security systems. ("The Registrar does, it seems, have the duty to ensure that the security services comply with the Data Protection Principles; but since he has no power to issue enforcement notices, and no powers of entry and inspection, it is difficult to see how he is going to carry out this duty." (Cornwall and Staunton, 1985, p96).) Nevertheless, estimates as to the number of organisations that should be registered run from 80,000 (the government's 1984 estimate) to 250/300,000 (the Registrar in 1986 and 1987) to as many as one million (Garrett, 1986).

The Registrar's *Annual Report* carries information on registrations under the Act, on complaints received and checks made on organisations that were believed to be failing to comply with the Act - and, presumably, on prosecutions. In the Third Report of the Data Protection Registrar (1987) the Registrar reports that about 115,000 organisations have registered, and suggests that this is around half the number that should have.

This report carries appendices containing substantial data. Among the statistics included is an analysis of the purposes registered by data users - the three leading purposes are personnel/employee administration, customer/client administration, and purchase/supplier administration, but many other uses are also listed. Information is provided on over 7,000 checks carried out for non-registered data users; of this sample of likely holders of personal data, only 49% had registered - but 19% claimed not to process personal data. A telephone survey of registered users, and of a sample of small firms, is also provided; this contains some data on the computer applications they pursue, as well as their reasons for registration/ non-registration. A further appendix details a study of public attitudes to data protection: questions assess the perceived importance of the topic, types of information felt to be sensitive, how far different organisations are trusted to hold data and to what extent data should be open to inspection, and attitudes to and knowledge of various aspects of the Data Protection Act.

A number of journalists and civil libertarians have displayed a keen interest in the use of IT to process personal data. While their reports are scattered across the computer trade press, political weeklies and journals of campaigning groups, Campbell and Connor (1986) have pulled together a large volume of information concerning both government and private data bases in the UK. Table 2 of this book - four pages long! - lists major data users and provides information on the number of records held and the number of terminals able to access them. Even a private population register (CCN, whose data are used for junk mailshots) is reported as having data on 43 million people living in 18 million households. Chapters are devoted to the main data bases in the UK, from which one learns, for instance, that 11 million people and 19 million vehicles are checked per annum on the Police National Computer.

9.4 Conclusions

This chapter has dealt with a heterogeneous set of topics, each of which is beset by data problems, but, nevertheless, where it is possible to cite some relevant statistics. There are many other social implications of IT for which as yet we have uncovered no useful data - including such important issues as health and safety at work, cultural images of IT (although we did come upon one researcher who is subjecting cartoons about computers to a content analysis!), and legal issues like intellectual property and product liability. As the "IT revolution" unfolds, however, we may expect data to be developed in these and other areas.

10 Conclusions

10.1 Data for What?

The preceding chapters demonstrate that a very wide range of data are available on different aspects of IT use and the information economy in the UK. We have tried to render this proliferation of material somewhat less bewildering, and to point out some of its possible applications and, equally, its limitations. We have pointed to various areas where data are particularly weak or effectively unavailable. The next section of this chapter will summarise our main conclusions as to what improvements may be made in data production.

But there is a prior question - what is the point of putting resources into data production, documentation, and dissemination? While we were preparing the present study, eager interest in seeing the final report was expressed by many of those with whom we consulted. There was considerable confusion about, and concern with, IT-relevant statistics, then. The quotations reproduced in the Introduction constitute more evidence of such interest. But interest is one thing - what about interest*s*, the reasons why these types of data are sought? Perhaps everyone would like to see better statistics, but the data involved are different - perhaps even contradictory (requiring divergent definitions, or the suppression of some material). Are potential users really concerned about the same data?

There are, without doubt, many divergent interests associated with the use and potential use of the different types of data discussed in this study. For some actors, highly specific data will be of key interest, and such data will often be at best only background material for others. It is in general unlikely that such data will be worthy of the expenditure of public resources, and they will often be produced by private market surveys. We have not, for instance, paid much attention to a class of statistic that evokes great attention from many IT suppliers - the breakdown of markets between the competing suppliers. In such cases, the interests involved can usually afford to bear the costs of data production - and are disinclined to release much of the data into the public domain.

Many other data are of more common interest, however. Given the growing centrality of IT-related activities in social and economic affairs, this will increasingly apply to many IT-related statistics. As IT (hardware, software and services) continues to become a more strategic area for national economies, as its use becomes strategically vital for more sectors of the economy, and as markets and occupations are reshaped in the light of new IT products and processes, IT-related statistics will be sought by decision-makers, commentators, social movements, and concerned citizens seeking to understand the changes with which they are confronted.

The demand for such statistics is already being felt, and all the signs are that it will grow. The vitality of the market research and consultancy industries is evidence for the strength of this demand from industrial interests. But by their nature these agencies are likely to work with strictly delimited sets of data - even when their data are of high quality, as is the case for some survey organisations, the range of issues they address reflects marketing concerns to a large extent. At a price, they may be motivated to broaden their spheres of activity, and current discussions in the UK about "privatising" large swathes of official statistics production suggest that similar commercial considerations may become more dominant in determining the availability of data in the future.

One obvious worry here concerns the quality of data in a privatised regime. Less obviously, but of particular relevance to mapping and measuring the information economy, there may be few incentives for developing innovative data. The "market" for "information economy" statistics is hardly an established one at present. While broad, the interests represented are very varied, and to some extent have yet to articulate their specific needs. The demand is for more data, but specifications of what form these data should take are more muted. Any change in the system of producing official statistics needs to be engineered, at the least, so as to avoid both deterioration in data quality and a lack of vision in exploring new areas.

It can be argued that it should be a duty of official agencies to seek to develop improved data along the lines examined in this study, as a means of promoting greater enlightenment - and thus more informed debate and policymaking - about the socioeconomic transition through which we are living. A similar argument was successfully carried through in the 1960s and 1970s by the social indicators movement, which criticised the inadequacies of data on the social outcomes of economic change and social policies, and led to the augmentation of national statistics and a variety of new publications (Miles, 1985b). In the present instance we are addressing a major set of changes in industrial society, and not simply the over-emphasis of economic issues in official statistics.

Improvements in statistical systems so as to capture better the nature of the current socioeconomic transition are in the broad public interest. If we cannot track the development of this transition, then policies and even broad strategies are likely to be seriously misinformed, and thus to go awry. This point is made by the House of Commons Trade and Industry Committee (1988, volume 1), whose specific recommendations concerning IT statistics we shall outline later. Taking an even broader view, we can follow Fred Block, who in common with other commentators argues that:

> "The irony is that post-industrial development undermines the established economic categories, leading to the statistical illusion of a productivity crisis, and ultimately to the imposition of economic policies that operate to slow economic development. Escaping from this conundrum requires a fundamental rethinking of economic categories and economic theory." (Block, 1985, p97)

In this quotation Block seems to portray the rethinking of economic (we might use a broader category such as "socioeconomic" or "political-economic") data and theory as going hand-in-hand. This is a highly reasonable position. While it might appear that what we really need to do is to achieve a new theory (note the repeated calls for "a new Keynes") and then derive our statistical categories from this, life is rarely so simple.

Of course, any statistical concepts are bound to be theory-laden (cf. Miles, 1985b), and we need to be aware of the baggage of potentially inappropriate theoretical assumptions that data carry with them. But this is often a risk that is far better to take - in an informed way - than taking the alternative risk of waiting for the new theory to arrive. In many cases researchers need to make the best that they can of existing data, or at least of those data that seem most adequate (or whose weaknesses are most easily "factored out") in terms of the incomplete elements of new theory that they have been able to assemble.

Often we cannot afford to wait for theoretical precision: decisions need to be made, whether or not there is sufficient theory to guide them (and it is doubtful that theory is very often sufficient in real-world policymaking). Theoretical precision is indeed rather rare in social sciences, where most of our concepts are "fuzzy" (and often contested) ones. Theory development can itself be enhanced by new data - as is evident enough in the physical sciences, where new instruments (e.g. telescopes for astronomy) have often enabled observations that stimulate advances in understanding. This is not to support the empiricist view that knowledge flows from data, so that simply accumulating observations allows us to understand things. Rather, data and theory are dialectically related, each capable of being used to examine critically the other. Thus, statistics are produced by using conceptual tools to transform some ''raw material'' (verbal reports, sense data, etc.); but they can be used themselves to expose inadequacies in the theoretical apparatus which informs some of these tools.

Thus a wider use of existing data, and an improvement of statistics, can be important as steps toward understanding the ''information economy'' better. They can be important at the level of description - where statistics can help determine the scale and pace of particular trends, for example. (Often agreement about the empirical reality of a trend conceals considerable disagreement about how substantial it is.) And they can be important at the level of developing models and theories for understanding and forecasting the course of events and their underlying dynamics. NEDO (1986) shows that informed opinion in the UK supports several views of the emerging ''information economy'', with problematic trends as common as benign ones; and notes that commentators who may happily agree concerning the direction of evolution of a trend over the coming years may be unaware that they differ dramatically in their evaluation of the scale of the trend.

As such, these improvements in ''information economy'' statistics should contribute to the design of policy (and other) interventions which can help social actors realise the positive potential of the growing range and intensity of IT applications, as well as minimise the problems that may well be (and are certainly widely perceived to be) associated with current developments. They can provide private individuals, social movements, firms and public organisations with social intelligence which will enable them to make better decisions. While this does not rule out the scope for both commercial and charitable activity, facilitating these steps is thus clearly a pressing candidate for public funds.

10.2 Data Production

We cannot hope to identify feasible improvements in data production for each of the topics covered in this study - at least not in any great detail. Specific proposals, concerning particular classes of statistics, will typically require detailed studies of their own. The most that we can hope to achieve in this chapter is a brief guide to the main areas where new or improved data might be hoped for. We recognise that improvements in official statistics are frequently costly, so that the proposals made here will be competing with other claims upon (and against) public expenditure. The preceding section has argued that at least some investments here should be well worth while, and, indeed, vitally necessary. Before turning to specific areas of statistics, let us consider some more general points that arise in this context.

10.2.1 Data and Data Sources

In the long term, there can be little doubt that large areas of official statistical systems will have to be restructured so as to reflect changes in economic life and social organisation associated with the development, diffusion and application of IT. However, this restructuring cannot be accomplished in a vacuum: it will involve experiments and incremental changes, it will require careful attention to the experiences of other countries, and coordination with international changes in accounting systems. With the integration of the UK into Europe, and the globalisation of economic activities, this latter point will loom even larger than it currently does. Official statisticians already invest considerable effort in establishing the requirements of the users of established classes of data, and similar consideration of the needs of current (and potential) users of IT-related data will also be required.

Several issues arise here. First, how far should the experimental work in statistical development be carried out by official statisticians, how far by academic and other researchers? Indeed, how far should some classes of data concern official statisticians? Data on IT diffusion - such as the PSI survey and WIRS reviewed in Chapter 5 - have been largely collected by academics (we should also mention the numerous market research studies in this vein), and official statisticians may well argue that these fall outside the main scope of economic and industrial statistical exercises. They are frequently laborious to generate, and impose an extra burden on respondents and statisticians alike; furthermore, there is rarely a strong argument for such data requiring comprehensive censuses rather than sample surveys. Policies as to the balance of efforts between official and other statistics producers could be a useful guide for funding agencies (Research Councils, etc.) in seeking to establish the value of different types of research - for instance, it might be that academics undervalue descriptive research in their current practices.

Second, there is a question as to how to reconcile new experimental measures and studies with the standard statistical framework. In France the term "satellite accounting" has achieved some success as a way of describing a strategy that seems particularly appropriate. Essentially, this involves developing new data systems - for example, more detailed analyses of "information sectors", or filière models (an input-output-like analysis of the interrelated chains of production required to obtain various final products) - in such a way that they can be related to the conventional accounts. They thus supplement these accounts, and provide new ways of classifying the data (and using them to provide insight on specific topics), rather than replacing them.

The House of Commons Trade and Industry Committee (1988, volume 1) made some 52 recommendations on aspects of IT policy, of which a number bear on statistical issues. The most relevant of these are set out below:

> "3. We recommend that the DTI should collect and publish figures for the balance of trade of the larger electronics companies... 4. ...that immediate action is taken by the DTI in conjunction with the supply and user companies to measure more accurately trade in information technology products... 5. ...that the Government should, in collaboration with the European Community and the Organisation for Economic Cooperation and Development, seek a new standard industrial classification covering information technology goods and services... 6. ...that the Government should compile and publish comparative figures and trends in the UK and competing countries for expenditure... by industry in training both in IT skills and in management generally... 10. ... that the DTI proposes to the European Commission the conduct and publication of a regular survey of information technology applications in all countries of the Community... 14. ...that the Government should collect and publish statistics identifying basic research separately within R&D..." (pp xlii-xliii)

Let us now consider specific areas of statistics as treated in the preceding chapters of this study. We shall briefly summarise what the main data requirements in each area would seem to be - recognising, of course, that this is a selection of possible lines of development that reflects our own interests. While we have tried to be open-minded and to represent a range of data users, readers would be advised to consider what conclusions they would draw from each chapter!

10.2.2 Research and Development

There are several improvements in data that could be achieved, as the House of Commons Trade and Industry Committee noted. We can be more specific than that Committee, however. In particular, it would be worth examining the scope for disaggregating some enquiries - in the spheres of both basic and applied research - to obtain data specifically on IT R&D. This would mean clarity in the definition of the relevant terms, for instance, so that software development activities could be included where appropriate. More effort on developing R&D measures appropriate for service sector activities is also desirable, and while the growing IT-intensity of services is liable to mean that some of the differences between services and manufacturing R&D will diminish, the numerous new services associated with IT (e.g. network management, software maintenance) may render conventional measures more problematic.

10.2.3 The IT Heartland

The review of data and data sources in Chapter 4 revealed that there is considerable information on the production of core IT goods - and rather less on IT services and software. While it is clearly difficult to launch statistical enquiries into new and rapidly changing areas, and while questions of commercial confidentiality are posed in telecommunications (where some activities are reigned by duopoly or oligopoly, others are the sites of struggle for uncertain markets), official studies in the USA, and consultancy reports in many countries, demonstrate that it is possible to make progress in these areas. The House of Commons Trade and Industry Committee makes a strong case for better statistics on trade in IT goods and services (data are particularly problematic where services are concerned, and effort here would certainly be desirable).

10.2.4 Diffusion

Here Chapter 5 reported few official statistics that could be brought to bear on the patterns of diffusion of IT, and these document financial expenditures rather than the adoption of particular equipment. Non-official studies have accumulated data on equipment, but have typically been rather limited where it comes to assessing the patterns of use of the equipment - especially where it comes to newer profiles of IT application such as networking. Again we found a remarkable lack of attention to the service sectors of the economy, and to the use of telecommunications services. There are certainly problems in diffusion research (for example, should one study establishments, organisations, or both?), and sample surveys may be more appropriate tools than the comprehensive exercises more commonly featured in official statistics, but the establishment of even the most elementary data on diffusion would be a marked improvement on the current state of affairs. (Greater access to market research data might improve matters here.) It is surprising that the recommendations of the House of Commons Trade and Industry Committee did not deal more specifically with diffusion data, since this clearly exercised the committee in its sessions (see volume 2 of its 1988 report); however, its suggestions for an improved industrial classification would be useful for diffusion analysis, and we know that the UN Statistical Office and the OECD are making some progress in this direction.

The most useful official data we were able to identify in this area were the Census of Production's material on computer expenditure and employment, and the Input-Output Tables' broad picture of sectoral investment in and absorption of IT (hardware). It is to be hoped that the relevant questions will be asked regularly (and extended) in the Census of Production; as for the Input-Output Tables, these would ideally be disaggregated further (especially the services sectors) and both produced more frequently and released more rapidly. (This may sound like wishful thinking, but annual tables are produced by several countries, making various analyses possible that are ruled out for the UK.) Perhaps it would also be possible for more detail on services to be provided for some historical tables; for instance, the distinction between post and telecommunications services drawn in the 1984 Tables could be valuably extended to earlier years.

10.2.5 Major IT Applications

Chapter 6 covered such a range of topics and sources that it was difficult to establish how far the considerable unevenness of the data which we encountered reflected the real situation, how far lack of awareness of sources. Evidently documentation efforts along the lines developed here could well be intensified. As so often, it appears to be service sector activities, and the newer applications of IT, that are poorly addressed in the data we reviewed. As the range of IT applications has expanded, so investigations become rather more difficult; it is often no longer appropriate to ask similar questions about IT use across all sectors. Academics and industry bodies might well be encouraged to redouble their efforts at tracking the evolution of specific IT applications, to pay attention to the achievements of their colleagues in parallel areas, and also to consider how they may develop and diffuse indicators which can better capture new types of application and activity. The House of Commons Trade and Industry Committee's proposal for European Community-wide surveys of applications would be extremely useful for research and policy analysis - whether, given the cost of such an exercise, it is politically feasible is another matter.

10.2.6 Work and Employment

Professional IT employment, and industrial relations issues posed by the introduction of some prominent ITs (e.g. robots, word processors), have received relatively great attention. Data on non-professionals, and on less common ITs, are less well developed. What is also lacking is information on the encounters of the broad labour force with IT, the insertion of new technologies into work processes in general. In some Scandinavian countries, efforts to tackle this latter problem have revolved around an initiative that might well be emulated: the inclusion of questions about the use and experience of IT in the regular Labour Force Surveys. In Chapter 7 we also noted the comparative paucity of data on education and training issues; the policy relevance of such information should hardly need to be underlined, and is evidently recognised by the House of Commons Trade and Industry Committee in its recommendations.

10.2.7 Consumption

Chapter 8 uncovered considerable volumes of market research, a quantity of which is openly published, and some of which is available for re-analysis. Rather few official sources bear on the diffusion of IT to private households, by comparison; and even the market research data seem to concentrate on a small number of fashionable (or profitable) items. With the exception of mass media, attention concerns the possession of equipment (and sometimes software) rather than its use. All of these are topics that might appropriately be addressed by academic research; perhaps this will be forthcoming as a new wave of consumer product innovations demonstrates that final consumption can be just as much a "serious business" as the industrial application of IT.

10.2.8 Social Implications

The social implications of IT are wide-ranging; indeed, are so extensive that it is often difficult to disentangle the role of IT from that of the many other components that enter into concrete circumstances. In Chapter 9 we considered a limited range of topics where some statistics are available; on some of these, such as security and privacy, the growing realisation of the problems that are posed here will hopefully lead to efforts to improve data. Other topics require fresh thinking, and it might be an interesting exercise to invite statisticians and researchers working in *apparently* non-IT areas - health and safety, law enforcement, equal opportunities, social participation, etc. - to consider what, if any, statistics of the information economy might stem from, or contribute to, their work.

10.3 Documentation and Dissemination

Apart from noting various areas where IT-related data need to be improved, this study has identified many useful data sources that are already in existence. Bringing together data from such diverse sources is a task whose scope we have been able to illustrate (while not pretending to perform it here). A single source which combined a wide range of good-quality statistics on IT activities, within a sensible structure of chapters, would be of value to many would-be users of data who are deterred by the numerous documents that would otherwise need to be consulted. It would form a reference book for policymakers, the general public, and industrial actors, if prepared with sufficient care (as to the meaning and limitations of data, as to the clarity of presentation, etc.) and adequately marketed. *Social Trends* is perhaps the best analogy; this collection of social and economic statistics is able to command considerable newspaper coverage and achieve substantial sales every year, and reaches a high standard of graphical and pictorial presentation.

Social Trends, and parallel "social reports" that are produced in other countries, resulted in part from the "social indicators movement" of the 1970s, which argued for improved preparation and publication of social statistics (Miles, 1985b). No comparable movement has as yet emerged around "information economy" indicators, although concern is widely expressed as to the limitations of available data for grappling with emergent sociotechnical phenomena. But it is interesting to note that various attempts have already been made in other countries to document IT-related statistics; we briefly discuss two of these.

In a recent volume of *Data-Sverige* (Statistiska Centralbyran, 1988), the Swedish Statistical Agency presents a collection of data and commentary resembling nothing so much as the CSO's *Social Trends*. The compilation covers a range of topics; by chapter (omitting the introductory chapters summarising the report and outlining the development of IT) these are:

- people and technology (use of computers by different social groups, by regions, by different types of institution and industry)
- diffusion (trends in the use of various types of IT, and main applications, with some international comparisons)
- telecommunications (telephony, data communications, telex, teletex, mobile communications)
- production and trade (the electronics industry, trade in IT products)
- labour market (information work and IT employment)
- education (the use of IT in schools and other education and training institutions)
- R&D (R&D expenditures in industry and higher education)
- work environment (work with automated equipment and with keyboards, and office IT work)
- databases and "integrity" (data protection and personal data, attitudes to use of data)

The notes above only hint at the topics covered in the report. Each chapter contains a summary presenting a few key statistics, and then presents a wealth of data - tables, charts, graphs and maps are all used. Supplementary data are presented in appendices, and the names and telephone numbers of the statisticians responsible for Swedish IT data are provided for reference.

The second study we shall consider is French - *L'Etat d'Informatisation de la France* (Agence de l'Informatique,1986) which is much more of an essay on the development of IT use in France than a compilation of statistics as such. While there is some discussion of, for example, legal issues, and the use of microcomputers and Minitel in the home, the focus is very much on the contribution of IT to French economic development. Most of the data presented (again there are numerous maps, charts and tables) are concerned with the diffusion of IT across sectors and regions. The French report resembles studies prepared for other countries in an effort to depict their current status in terms of IT, although these tend to be even more essay-like. The nearest equivalent we know for the UK, NEDO (1987), is a forecasting study.

While both of these reports are useful, it is our view that official statistical agencies would do better to follow the Swedish model, leaving more interpretative studies to others. The range of topics which we would ideally like covered is provided by the Table of Contents of this study! Additionally, it would be important for such a report to include data on trade and on the military use of IT, both topics which the present study only touches on briefly; and it would be useful to include international comparisons. We can envisage an annual IT report for the UK becoming an accepted part of the statistical scene in coming years.

A documentation exercise such as this need not, of course, be carried out by an official agency. But such bodies have two important advantages: they are perceived as authoritative, and they are in a better position to elicit data from the private sector than many independent actors would be. If the task were to be contracted out to, say, a consultancy or academic institution, then a "letter of recommendation" of some sort might be required - and even then rivalry from competitors might limit the data secured.

The European Commission is currently greatly interested in establishing "observatories" which will serve as resource and documentation centres on various features of socioeconomic change. (Examples include the service sectors, and information markets.) In some cases these would be nationally based, in others Europe-wide. If such initiatives could encompass the topics addressed in this study, and an agreed base of statistics be identified, the scope for international and regional comparisons would obviously be enhanced. The OECD is also displaying interest in pursuing the topics, and may also provide a significant lead in coordinating statistical developments, and stimulating new initiatives (as it did in the social indicators field - even though its own efforts at compiling indicators only achieved modest success in the end). Given the current constraints on new developments at a national level, where statisticians are faced by financial constraints that severely limit their efforts to improve data, such international activities are certainly worth encouraging.

In addition to better documentation of IT-related statistics, it should be noted that improving the dissemination of many types of data would be helpful. We have not paid a great deal of attention to data from consultancy sources in the present study - even though for some topics these are the only sources of data that there are - for two reasons. First, the high cost of these publications (when they are made publicly available, and publicised, in the first place) has kept many of them out of our reach; second, the quality of the data reported is often hard to evaluate given the common evasiveness about methodology. While we cannot propose that large sums of public money be spent on securing consultancy data for public release, at least two measures could be taken to improve the dissemination of at least some such data. We would hope that improved availability of consultancy material would facilitate a higher level of critical discussion about the data they include.

These two measures are simple enough, in principle. First, when consultancy reports are commissioned at public expense for the activities of specific parts of the civil services - and vast sums of money go to obtaining such studies on IT topics every year (probably mostly from the DTI within the UK, although the CEC is also known to commission many IT studies) - these should wherever possible be made accessible to the general public either via deposit in libraries or via commercial release. At present there seems to be little logic in the tendency to maintain confidentiality on such reports, which only really makes sense if issues of commercial confidentiality are raised by the contents (e.g. if sensitive description of specific firms is entailed), or if the consultancy is making material available to civil servants at well below cost on the grounds that the study will be financed by sales to commercial sponsors (this may sometimes be the case, but the excessive cost of many reports suggests that this is an exception rather than the rule).

Second, better documentation of what consultancy studies are available is required. Many studies are deposited with The British Library and can be borrowed from this source (though there are often delays associated with long queues for topical items). The British Library publishes regular guides to the reports and conference proceedings it receives, and overviews of publications and press coverage in a number of areas related to the theme of this study (e.g. a quarterly on science and technology policy). But it would be helpful to have a regular guide to non-official data sources on IT activities - ideally organised so as to map easily on to the sections of the annual IT Report proposed above.

Finally, in general terms it is important that opportunities to access and use data concerning IT issues be increased. Researchers in the field should be encouraged to deposit their data (with full supporting material) in the ESRC Data Archive, for instance. It might be appropriate for the catalogue of the Archive to be revised to make searching for such topics easier than it currently is. (There is a "Science and Technology" heading, but many IT-related topics will feature in, for instance, "Social Issues and Values" and "Industrial Relations"; often researchers will be fairly clear as to which categories they need to search for IT-related questions, but this will not always be the case - for example, WIRS may be used for the analysis of diffusion of IT.)

Other holders of IT-relevant data should also be encouraged to make their material available for re-analysis; several of the major non-official surveys discussed in this study, for instance, are not generally available. The "intellectual property" argument (that social scientists should be able to gain credit for data production efforts by making the most of their statistics) begins to wear thin after the first few publications have appeared - and opposed to this is the argument that other researchers need to examine such data in order to assess the conclusions drawn from them. More substantial is the argument, which we have encountered in at least one case, that there are costs associated with properly documenting and "cleaning up" data, and that they may not have been prepared in a form amenable to commonly used statistical packages. In these cases, grant-providing agencies might consider whether costs of making data bases available could be covered (this will obviously depend on the importance of the data set in question). Such agencies might also more often follow the lead of the ESRC in requesting that data produced with their sponsorship be deposited in the Data Archive.

These proposals have focused on the documentation and dissemination of existing IT-related statistics. While this may seem a minor task as compared to the intellectually demanding one of creating new statistics for the "information economy", it should nevertheless be treated seriously - data preparation and presentation is a skilled task! - and it can contribute to the longer-term task. Advancing our tools is liable to require broader understanding of their capabilities and limitations, and this means more researchers and statisticians grappling with the problems of applying old statistical categories to new tasks. Re-analysis of data, critical examination of concepts and the conclusions that they are used to construct, and efforts to combine data from different sources are all liable to provide insights towards the revision of our statistical systems.

10.4 Data Analysis

It is not our intention to set out a programme for the analysis of IT-related statistics here; indeed, it is important that different approaches to using data are taken, for the testing of, and debate between, a variety of perspectives is required for better analysis of the information economy and the continued improvement of data. The ESRC's PICT programme, which supported the present study, relies on interdisciplinary research from a variety of centres; this model seems appropriate to the multifaceted issues raised by IT, but we would argue that research in this area needs to be expanded, and certainly not restricted to the PICT network. A range of research approaches should be encouraged: not just the disciplinary themes posed by economics, regional science, sociology, and the like, but also new themes and approaches such as are captured by terms such as "technology assessment" (which is currently undergoing something of a revival in much of Western Europe).

Even topics that would seem to have been exhaustively researched are often still far from being settled. This was very much the message of the December 1988 Berlin Conference on the META-Project; this was a major German set of studies into relations between technological change and employment, which one might imagine was a topic that had already been studied sufficiently for one to be reasonably definitive about the conclusions to be drawn (or the factors that would forever prevent such conclusions). The Conference was able to suggest some fairly clear conclusions about recent relations between IT and employment, but equally it posed a whole series of new questions, and demonstrated a range of new data and methods that might be brought to bear on them.

Our own research at SPRU is intended to take up a number of the major themes identified in the present study. Very briefly, there are two major objectives in our current round of work. One is to develop methods for relating different IT-relevant data sets in a common framework - which we are terming an IT Accounting Framework. At present, the heart of this is formed by input-output tables, and we hope to be able to organise other statistics so that they are comparable with the categories that this involves. The second objective is to generate data appropriate to analysis of some of the areas where there are few useful statistics; our current efforts include surveys in the areas of software production and videotex systems, and we plan to research features of the use of new telecommunications services.

In a review of this sort, it is inevitable that there will be types of statistics that we do not consider. To conclude this section, we should mention one particularly interesting direction of research. The studies we refer to below either involve non-territorial data, or have as yet not been applied to the UK. They involve approaches based on the performance of ITs. These studies suggest metrics other than those of price or populations of devices or users, which tend to dominate available statistics.

One of the most ambitious studies focuses on communications systems. Sola Pool et al. (1984) make a brave effort to map and measure communication flows, comparing US and Japanese data for a wide range of media (books, mail, data communications, telex, TV, etc.). They express communications in terms of a metric based on the "word" (converting non-text data flows in terms of the formula one word = 50bits). This represents an interesting attempt to define an IT-relevant metric, a metric which can be used to compare different media; it suggests that similar approaches might be used for other types of IT (e.g. the core memories of computers are also usually expressed in terms of bits, and one measure of computer power is a comparison of this feature).

However, the difficulties that confront efforts to develop measures that are realistic measures of technological performance are demonstrated by the new field of "technometrics". The memory size of a computer, for instance, is not the only performance feature of concern: for some applications we may not be interested so much in the total volume of data that can be stored as in the speed with which data can be retrieved. (Similarly, for communications media, transmission speeds may rank highly alongside volumes of data transmitted - although here bits/second tends to be commonly used.)

These difficulties are illustrated, for instance, in an issue of the journal *Technological Forecasting and Social Change* (May 1985) devoted to this topic, where three papers deal with the problem of how to develop quantitative measures with which heterogeneous technological products can be compared, using computers as an example (Alexander and Mitchell, 1985, Dodson, 1985, and Knight, 1985). Knight, for example, plots changes in computer price and performance over time, and assesses the relation between price and performance at specific points in time; his measures of performance and price were based on ''analysis of many programs on different machines'' to determine the salience of each of a large number of specific features of computers (word length in bits, total number of words in memory, time taken by the CPU to perform one million operations, etc.). Knight concedes that the measure of computer power may, however, be rendered less useful by the proliferation of different computer applications (which may demand different ideal combinations of characteristics). While the method allows for the analysis of computer trajectories in general terms, it is less useful for identifying specific innovations.

''Technometrics'' remains in a fairly experimental stage, but may well provide tools useful for the analysis of IT production, diffusion and applications. Some variety of technometrics may even be applied to the analysis of corporate strategies, as can be demonstrated by one last example. Swann (1987) analyses the characteristics of various microprocessors - in terms of bit size, the level of integration on the chip, and the generation of device. Swann shows that different manufacturers' product designs tend to cluster together (rather than to scatter randomly across the ''space'' of possible innovations). He goes on to examine the product strategies of specific firms in the field, suggesting that product leaders emerge in microprocessors, and that the leader will tend to move into a new part of the design ''space'' when competitors crowd in to the area it already occupies.

This discussion has not been conducted with the intention of advocating technometrics as *the* way forward for IT statistics. It is our opinion that at present the approach is one worthy of exploration, but not sufficiently developed to warrant major reorientation of research efforts. We have outlined it merely as one outstanding example of types of statistics concerning the information economy that have not been considered in the present study.

10.5 Postscript: the Information Economy

Finally, what does this study have to say about the "information economy"? We have not set out to use the data discussed here to test hypotheses about the nature and development of this elusive social formation - this will be the task of other publications - and since this review has been guided by the approach outlined in Chapter 1, it would be surprising if we did indeed have much to add substantively to the topic. (For a general bibliography of "information economy" issues see Whitaker et al. (1988).)

Nevertheless, the study does indirectly tell us several things about the "information economy". Statistics are the products of social organisations, and the slowness of statistical systems to adapt to changing circumstances is indicative of the evolutionary and often sluggish pace of organisational change as opposed to what is sometimes the revolutionary nature of technological change. We have argued that the current wave of IT developments is indeed a technological revolution, and the data reviewed in this study indicate that IT is rapidly finding application within an immense range of social and economic activities.

What the "slow pace of organisational change" means, in this context, is that the rapid diffusion of IT is unlikely to be matched by an equally rapid modification of organisational practices. We also argued earlier that technology does not "cause" human behaviour in any simple way; rather, technological changes modify the range of opportunities that confront people. Organisational change depends upon the active exploration of this range of opportunities: the development of new arrangements and practices which are believed to permit goals to be realised. This exploration is often a protracted and intermittent process; it is influenced by knowledge and skills, by incentives and opportunity costs, by experience and by expectations of future change. The development of IT-relevant statistics (and of social scientific research on IT topics) reflects these factors, and supports our conclusion that the development of the information economy will be a protracted process. The reshaping of social organisation so as to realise IT potentials will require considerably more learning about these potentials - and is bound to involve debate about which of the numerous potentials actually should be realised, and action of various forms to advance specific interests.

Data of the sorts discussed in this study can help advance this process. Better statistics of IT-related activities can provide information about the information economy. Production, diffusion and application of IT itself are the key to the information society. Production, diffusion and, of course, the application of statistics on these activities are the key to understanding it. And without understanding the information economy, the opportunities to shape it - to exercise some choice among the many imaginable "information societies" - will be far more limited than they need be.

List of Abbreviations

ACARD	Advisory Committee for Applied Research and Development
ACAS	Advisory, Conciliatory and Arbitration Service
ACME	Applications of Computers to Mechanical Engineering
ADP	Automated Data Processing
AFRC	Agricultural and Food Research Council
AMDEA	Association of Manufacturers of Domestic Electrical Appliances
ATE	Automated Test Equipment
ATM	Automated Teller Machine
BARB	Broadcaster's Audience Research Board
BEITA	Business Equipment and Information Technology Association
BPI	British Phonographic Industry
BRA	British Robots Association
BREMA	British Radio and Electronic Equipment Manufacturers' Association
BSO	Business Statistics Office
BT	British Telecom
BTEC	Business Technician Education Council
BVA	British Videogram Association
CAD	Computer-Aided Design
CBI	Confederation of British Industry

CCIS	Centre for Communication and Information Studies
CCTA	Central Computer and Telecommunications Agency
CD	Compact Disc
CD-ROM	Compact Disc Read Only Memory
CEC	Commission of the European Communities
CGIL	City and Guilds London Institute
CIM	Computer Integrated Manufacturing
CIPFA	Chartered Institute of Public Finance and Accountancy
CITIIR	Comparative IT Investment Intensity Ratios
CNC	Computerised Numerical Control (Machine Tools)
CODOT	Classification of Occupations and Directory of Occupational Titles
CPE	Customer Premises Equipment
CPU	Central Processing Unit
CRT	Cathode Ray Tube
CSA	Computing Services Agency
CSE	Certificate of Secondary Education
CSO	Central Statistical Office
CURDS	Centre for Urban and Regional Development Studies
DES	Department of Education and Science
DHSS	Department of Health and Social Security
DP	Data Processing
DTI	Department of Trade and Industry

ECIF	Electrical Components Industry Federation
EDC	Economic Development Committee
EDI	Electronic Data Interchange
EDP	Electronic Data Processing
EEA	Electrical Engineering Association
EFT	Electronic Funds Transfer
EFTPOS	Electronic Funds Transfer at Point of Sale
EITB	Engineering Industry Training Board
EPOS	Electronic Point of Sale
ESRC	Economic and Social Research Council
FMS	Flexible Manufacturing Systems
4GL	Fourth-generation Language
GAMBICA	Association of the Instrumentation, Control and Automation Industry in the UK
GDP	Gross Domestic Product
GNP	Gross National Product
GP	General Practitioner
HMSO	Her Majesty's Stationery Office
IBA	Independent Broadcasting Authority
IC	Integrated Circuit
ICCP	Information, Computers & Communications Policy
IEE	Institute of Electrical Engineers
IKBS	Intelligent Knowledge-Based Systems

IMS	Institute of Manpower Studies
ISDN	Integrated Services Digital Network
IT	Information Technology
ITEC	Information Technology Education Centre
ITSA	Information Technology Skills Agency
ITUSA	Information Technology Users' Association
JANET	Joint Academic Network
LA	Local Authority
LAMSAC	Local Authorities Management Services and Computer Committee
LAN	Local Area Network
LASER	London and South Eastern Library Region
LSI	Large Scale Integration
MAFF	Ministry of Agriculture, Fisheries and Food
MAP	Manufacturing Automation Protocol
micro	Microcomputer
mini	Minicomputer
MIS	Management Information Systems
MLH	Minimum List Heading
MOD	Ministry of Defence
MSC	Manpower Services Commission
MSI	Medium Scale Integration
NAO	National Audit Office

NC	Numerically Controlled
NCC	National Computing Centre
NEDO	National Economic Development Office
n.e.s.	Not Elsewhere Specified
OECD	Organization for Economic Cooperation and Development
OPCS	Office of Population, Censuses and Surveys
OSI	Open Systems Interconnection
OTA	Office of Technology Assessment
OTAF	Office of Technology Assessment and Forecast
PABX	Private Automatic Branch Exchange
PBX	Private Branch Exchange
PICT	Programme on Information and Communication Technologies
PREST	Programme of Policy Research on Engineering, Science and Technology
PSI	Policy Studies Institute
PSTN	Public Switched Telephone Network
PTT	Postal, Telephone and Telegraphy Operator
QSE	Qualified Scientist or Engineer
QSI	Quality of Service Indicator
R&D	Research and Development
SCOTVEC	Scottish Vocational Education Council
SERC	Science and Engineering Research Council

SIC	Standard Industrial Classification
SITC	Standard Industrial Trade Classification
SLSI	Super Large Scale Integration
SOCITM	Society of Information Technology Managers
SPRU	Science Policy Research Unit
SSI	Small Scale Integration
TEMA	Telecommunications Equipment Manufacturing Association
TEMPO	Technological Change and Employment Opportunities
TMA	Telecommunication Managers' Association
TOP	Technical and Office Protocol
TUA	Telecommunications Users' Association
TV	Television
ULSI	Ultra Large Scale Integration
UNCSTD	United Nations Commission on Science and Technology for Development
UNIDO	United Nations Industrial Development Organisation
VADS	Value Added and Data Services
VANS	Value Added Network Services
VDU	Video Display Unit
VLSI	Very Large Scale Integration
WAN	Wide Area Network
WIRS	Workplace Industrial Relations Survey
WP	Word Processor

Bibliography

ACARD, 1986, *Software: A Vital Key to UK Competitiveness* London, HMSO

ACAS, 1988, *Labour Flexibility in Britain: The 1987 ACAS Survey* London, Advisory, Conciliation and Arbitration Service

Agence de l'Informatique,1986, *L'Etat d'Informatisation de la France* Paris, Economica

A J Alexander & B M Mitchell, 1985, ''Measuring Technological Change of Heterogeneous Products'' *Technological Forecasting and Social Change* vol 27 no 2/3 pp161-196

J A Alic, 1988, ''R&D in the Services'' mimeo, paper prepared for the Symposium on Technological Advance and the Service Industries, AAAS, Boston, February; Washington DC, Office of Technology Assessment

A Amin & J B Goddard (eds), 1986, *Technological Change, Industrial Restructuring and Regional Development* London, Allen & Unwin

C Angell, 1987, *Information, New Technology and Manpower* London, The British Library (Library and Information Research Report 52)

P Anstey, 1985, ''Computing Advisory Services: a review'' *University Computing* vol 7 pp8-13

C Antonelli, 1986, ''The International Diffusion of New Information Technologies'' *Research Policy* vol 15 pp139-147

Aptus Marketing Services Ltd, 1987, *Focus on Market Surveys* London, Aptus Marketing Services Ltd

F Arcangeli, G Dosi & M Moggi, 1987, ''Patterns of Diffusion of Electronics Technologies'' mimeo, presented at conference ''Programmable Automation and New Work Modes'', Paris, April 1987; Venice, DAEST

E Arnold, 1984, *Computer-Aided Design in Europe* University of Sussex (Sussex European Papers no 14)

E Arnold & P Senker, 1982, *Designing the Future* Watford, Electrical Industries Training Board (Occasional Paper no 9)

N G Attenborough, 1984, *Employment and Technical Change: The Case of Microelectronic-based Production Technologies in UK Manufacturing Industry* London, Department of Trade and Industry (Government Economic Service Working Paper no 74)

Audit Commission, 1986, *Computing in Local Government: An Audit Survey* The Audit Commission for Local Authorities in England and Wales

M Bagenal, 1986a, *The Hotel and Catering Industry: New Technology and Training* Manchester, Centre for Educational Development and Training, Manchester Polytechnic

M Bagenal, 1986b, *The Road Transport, Distribution and Warehousing Industry: New Technology and Training* Manchester, Centre for Educational Development and Training, Manchester Polytechnic

R Barras, 1984, *Growth and Technical Change in the UK Service Sector* London, Technical Change Centre

R Barras & J Swann, 1983, *The Adoption and Impact of Information Technology in the UK Insurance Industry* London, Technical Change Centre

R Barras & J Swann, 1984, *The Adoption and Impact of Information Technology in the UK Accountancy Profession* London, Technical Change Centre

R Barras & J Swann, 1985, *The Adoption and Impact of Information Technology in UK Local Government* London, Technical Change Centre

D Barrett, 1986, "Cobol sees Resurgence" *Computer Weekly* January 30 p18

J Barton, 1987, "Don't Miss the Fax Train" *Lines of Communication* vol 1 no 9 (November) p39

E Batstone & S Gourlay, 1986, *Unions, Unemployment and Innovation* Oxford, Basil Blackwell

M Batty, 1985, *The Spatial Impact of Computer Culture* Cardiff, UWIST Department of Town Planning (Papers in Planning Research no 91)

M Batty, 1986, *Home Computers and Regional Development* Cardiff, UWIST Department of Town Planning (Papers in Planning Research no 97)

C Berman, 1987, ''Hardware that Sparkles in the Bargain Basement'' *Computing* June 11, pp28-29

J Bessant, 1984, ''Flexible Manufacturing Systems - An Overview'' mimeo, Brighton, Innovation Research Group, Brighton Polytechnic

J Bessant, 1986, *UK Experience with Computer-Aided Design - An Overview* report to the ILO, Brighton, Innovation Research Group, Brighton Polytechnic

J Bessant & B Haywood, 1986a, ''Experiences with FMS in the UK'' *International Journal of Operations and Production Management* vol 6 no 5 pp44-56

J Bessant & B Haywood, 1986b, ''FMS in Britain: Good and Bad News'' *The FMS Magazine* January

A Blandy, 1984, ''New Technology and Flexible Patterns of Working Time'' *Employment Gazette* October, pp439-444

F Block, 1985, ''Postindustrial Development and the Obsolescence of Economic Categories'' *Politics and Society* vol 14 no 1 pp71-104

D Boddy, 1987, ''New Technology Survey: Financial Services'' mimeo, Centre for Technical and Organisational Change, Glasgow Business School, University of Glasgow

T Brady, 1984, *New Technology and Skills in British Industry* Sheffield, Manpower Services Commission

T Brady, 1986, ''New Information Technology and Social Change in Europe: Computerisation of Public Administration in the UK'', mimeo, report to EPOS group, CEC; Falmer, Brighton, SPRU

T Brady & S Liff, 1983, *Monitoring New Technology and Employment* Sheffield, Manpower Services Commission

E Braun & S Macdonald, 1982 (2nd ed), *Revolution in Miniature* Cambridge, Cambridge University Press

E Braun & P Senker, 1982, *New Technology and Employment* London, Manpower Services Commission

BREMA, 1988, *Annual Report, 1987* London, British Radio & Electronic Equipment Manufacturers' Association

British Telecom, 1985, *Efficiency at Work: The BT Radiopaging Report on Efficiency at Work in the UK* (brochure) London, British Telecom

D Buchanan, 1987, "New Technology Survey: Chemicals and Allied Industries" mimeo, Glasgow, University of Glasgow Business School

B Buckroyd and D Cornford, 1988, *The IT Skills Crisis: The Way Ahead* Manchester, National Computer Centre

P F Burton, 1987, *Microcomputer Applications in Academic Libraries II* London, The British Library (Library and Information Research Report 60)

Business Computing and Communications, 1987, "Publish and be Damned" *Business Computing and Communication* June pp26-30

N K Buxton & D I MacKay, 1977, *British Employment Statistics: A Guide to Sources and Methods* Oxford, Basil Blackwell

D Campbell, 1987, "The Databank Dossier" *New Statesman* April 24 pp8-10

D Campbell & S Connor, 1986, *On The Record: Surveillance, Computers and Privacy* London, Michael Joseph

Canadian Radio, Television and Telecommunications Commission, 1985, *Decision: British Columbia Telephone Company - Standards for Quality of Service Indicators* Ottawa, Canadian Radio, Television and Telecommunications Commission

B Carsberg, 1987, "From the Director General of Telecommunications" *Oftel News* issue 8, September

CBI, 1987, *CBI/MSC Special Survey: Skill Shortages* London, Confederation of British Industry

CCTA, 1984, *Strategic Study of Government Administrative Telecommunications* London, HMSO

Central Statistical Office, various years, *Guide to Official Statistics* London, HMSO

C Chang & D Hitchcock, 1987, *The VANS Handbook* Pinner, Middlesex, Online Publications

CIPFA, 1986, *Computer Audit: The State of the Art in the Public Sector* London, Chartered Institute of Public Finance and Accountancy

J A Clark, 1980, ''A Model of Technological Change and Employment'' *Technological Forecasting and Social Change* vol 16 no 1 pp47-66

J A Clark (ed), 1985, *Technological Trends and Employment: 1 Basic Process Industries* Aldershot, Gower

Computer Economics Limited, 1987, *Changes in the Employment of IT Staff* (report to the IT Skills Agency, London) Kingston-upon-Thames, Computer Economics Limited

Computer Product News, 1985, *Computers and Professionals in Europe* Brussels, Pan-European Publishing Company

H Connor & R Pearson, 1986a, *Information Technology Manpower into the 1990's* Falmer, Brighton, Institute of Manpower Studies (IMS Report no 117)

H Connor & R Pearson, 1986b, *Labour Market for IT Postgraduates* Falmer, Brighton, Institute of Manpower Studies (IMS Report no 118)

C Cooper & J Clark, 1982, *Employment, Economics & Technology* Brighton, Wheatsheaf

Coopers & Lybrand, Department of Trade and Industry, 1987, *Computer Services Industry 1986-1996:A Decade of Opportunity* London, Coopers & Lybrand Associates Ltd

D Cornford & K Gott, 1987 (eds), *Salaries and Staff Issues in Computing - 1988* Manchester, National Computing Centre

H Cornwall, 1988, *The New Hacker's Handbook* London, Century

R Cornwall & M Staunton, 1985, *Data Protection: Putting the Record Straight* London, National Council for Civil Liberties

J Cottee, 1987, ''Finding the Data for IT Strategies'' *Computer Weekly* February 19 p 20

M Cross, 1985, *Towards the Flexible Craftsman* London, Technical Change Centre

W W Daniel, 1987, *Workplace Industrial Relations and Technical Change* London, Frances Pinter

R Davies, n.d. ?1986, *Teleshopping in the Food Trades: Current Status and Future Potentials* Oxford, Templeton College (Institute of Retail Management Research Papers B3)

Department of Commerce (USA), 1984, *A Competitive Assessment of the US Data Processing Services Industry* Washington DC, US Government Printing Office

Department of Commerce (USA), 1988, *US Industrial Outlook 1988* Washington DC, US Government Printing Office

Department of Employment, 1965, *Computers in Offices* London, HMSO (Manpower Studies no 4)

Department of Employment, 1972a, *Classification of Occupations and Directory of Occupational Titles* (3 volumes) London, HMSO

Department of Employment, 1972b, *Computers in Offices 1972*, London, HMSO (Manpower Studies no 12)

Department of Trade and Industry, 1987, *The Economic Effects of Value-added and Data Services* London, HMSO

J C Dewdney, 1985, *The UK Census of Population 1981* Norwich, Geo Books (Concepts and Techniques in Modern Geography no 43)

DHSS, 1975, *Profile of NHS Computing* London, DHSS

DHSS, 1984, *Evaluation of the Micros for GPs Scheme - Interim Report* London, DHSS

DHSS, 1985, *Evaluation of the Micros for GPs Scheme - Final Report* London, HMSO

DHSS, 1986, *Micros in Practice* London, HMSO

M Dodgson, 1987, "Small Firms' Investment in, and Use of, CNC Machine Tools" in Wobbe (ed) (1987)

M Dodgson & R Martin, 1987, "Trade Union Policies on New Technology: Facing the Challenge of the 1980s" *New Technology, Work and Employment* vol 2 no 1 pp9-18

E N Dodson, 1985, "Measurement of State of the Art and Technological Advance" *Technological Forecasting and Social Change* vol 27 no 2/3 pp129-146

T Dodsworth, 1988, "DTI May Alter Method for Figures on Computing" *Financial Times* October 31

M Dorsman, 1986, *The Plastics Processing Industry: New Technology and Training* Manchester, Centre for Educational Development and Training, Manchester Polytechnic

C Driver, 1987, *Towards Full Employment: A Policy Appraisal* London, Routledge & Kegan Paul

H East, 1987, "Use and Revenue Data for the UK Online Information Market" mimeo, paper presented at 44th FID Conference, Helsinki; London, CCIS, Polytechnic of Central London

H East & V Forrest, 1988, "Statistics of Online Expenditure" mimeo, London, CCIS, Polytechnic of Central London

Economic Commission for Europe, various years, *Annual Review of Engineering Industries and Automation* New York, United Nations

Economic Commission for Europe, 1985, *Production and Use of Industrial Robots* New York, United Nations

Economic Commission for Europe, 1986, *Recent Trends in Flexible Manufacturing* New York, United Nations

Economic Commission for Europe, 1987, *The Telecommunication Industry: Growth and Structural Change* New York, United Nations

Economist Informatics, n.d. ?1985, *Availability, Cost and Use of Telecommunications in the Northern Region* a report for the North of England County Councils' Association by Economist Informatics (London) and Centre for Urban and Regional Development Studies (University of Newcastle)

C Edquist & S Jacobsson, 1988, *Flexible Automation* Oxford, Basil Blackwell

EFILWC, 1985, *The Role of the Parties Concerned in the Introduction of New Technology - Consolidated Report* Dublin, European Foundation for the Improvement of Living and Working Conditions

A J Eggington, "SERC and Industry" *Annual Report 1986-7* Swindon, Science and Engineering Research Council

EITB, 1986, *Sector Profile: Trends in Manpower and Training in the Office Machinery and Electronic Data Processing Equipment Industry since 1978* Stockport, EITB Publications (RM85 04)

Engineering Computers, various issues, *Computers in Manufacturing* Horton Kirby, Dent, Findlay Publications

ESPRIT, 1987, *ESPRIT The First Phase: Progress and Results* Luxembourg, Commission of the European Communities

D Evans, 1986, "Report Exposes IT Fraud 'Myth'" *Computing* March 20 p9

J Evans, J Hartley, J Simnett, M Gibbons & S Metcalfe, 1983, *The Development of Cable Networks in the UK* London, Technical Change Centre

D Eyeions, 1986, "Skills Gap Yawns Even Wider" *Computer Weekly* June 26, pp45-46

D Feeny, 1987, *Creating and Sustaining Competitive Advantage from IT* Oxford, Templeton College, Oxford Centre for Management Studies (Research & Discussion Papers 87/2)

D Finkelstein, 1988, "PSTN Data Connections Increase" *Network* March pp73-77

M J Fitter, J R Garber, G A Herzmark, D Robinson & R V H Jones, 1986, *A Prescription for Change* London, HMSO

T Forester (ed), 1980, *The Microelectronics Revolution* Oxford, Basil Blackwell

T Forester (ed), 1985, *The Information Technology Revolution* Oxford, Basil Blackwell

T Forester, 1988, *High-Tech Society* Cambridge, MIT Press

C Freeman (ed), 1985, *Technological Trends and Employment: 4 Engineering & Vehicles* Aldershot, Gower

C Freeman & C Perez, 1986, "The Diffusion of Technological Innovations and Changes of Techno-economic Paradigm" mimeo, paper presented at IFIAS Venice conference ; Falmer, Brighton, SPRU

C Freeman, J A Clark & L Soete, 1982, *Unemployment and Technical Innovation* London, Frances Pinter

C Freeman & L Soete (eds), 1987, *Technical Change and Full Employment* Oxford, Basil Blackwell

A Furnham, 1987, "Growing Up With Computers" *New Scientist* March 26 pp66-67

R D Galliers, 1987, "Information Systems Planning in the United Kingdom and Australia" in P I Zorkoczy (ed) *Oxford Surveys in Information Technology vol 4* Oxford, Oxford University Press

A Garrett, 1986, "Privacy Act gets tied up in Red Tape" *Computing* May 1 p14

General Technology Systems, 1986, *International Study of Government Support Programmes for the IT Industries* Brentford, General Technology Systems (available also from the Alvey Directorate)

J Gershuny, 1977, *After Industrial Society: The Emerging Selfservice Economy* London, Macmillan

J Gershuny, 1982, chapter in S Wallman and associates, *Living in South London*, London, Gower Press/LSE

J Gershuny & I Miles, 1983, *The New Service Economy* London, Frances Pinter

J Gershuny, I Miles, S Jones, C Mullins, G Thomas & S Wyatt, 1986, "Preliminary Analyses of the 1983-4 ESRC Time Budget Survey" *Quarterly Journal of Social Affairs* vol 2 no 1 pp13-39

J Goddard, 1988, "Mapping and Measuring the Geography of the Information Economy" mimeo, paper presented at Royal Institute of International Affairs, March 30; Newcastle, CURDS

J Goddard, A Thwaites & D Gibbs, 1986, "The Regional Dimension to Technological Change in Great Britain" in Amin & Goddard (eds) (1986)

J Griffith, 1986, *The Engineering Industry: New Technology and Training* Manchester, Centre for Educational Development and Training, Manchester Polytechnic

P C Grindley, 1988, *The UK Software Industry* London, Centre for Business Strategy, London Business School

K Guy (ed), 1984, *Technological Trends and Employment: 1 Basic Consumer Goods* Aldershot, Gower

K Guy, 1985, "Communications" in Soete (ed) (1985b)

K Guy, 1987, "The Use and Development of Expert Systems in the UK" *Alvey News* April pp20-21

L Haddon, 1988, "The Use of Domestic Information and Communications Technologies: A Guide to Statistical Sources" unpublished paper, SPRU

M Hamed, P Patel & M Robson, n.d., "The US Patent Data Base (OTAF): Guide for Users at the Science Policy Research Unit" mimeo, Falmer, Brighton, SPRU

J Hartley, J S Metcalfe, J Evans, J Simnett, L Georghiou, & M Gibbons, 1985, *Public Acceptance of New Technologies: New Communications Technology & the Consumer* (2 vols) Manchester, PREST, University of Manchester

J Hartley, A Noonan & S Metcalfe, 1986, *New Electronic Information Services: An Overview of the UK Database Industry in an International Context* London, Technical Change Centre

B W Haywood, 1987, "Organisational Aspects of FMS in the United Kingdom" in Wobbe (ed) (1987)

B Hochstrasser, 1987, *Does Information Technology Slow You Down?* London, Imperial College, Kobler Institute for the Management of Information Technology

P J Holligan, 1986, *Access to Academic Networks* London, Taylor Graham

House of Commons Trade and Industry Committee, 1988, *Information Technology: First Report* (2 volumes) London, HMSO

House of Lords, 1986a, Select Committee on Science and Technology *Civil Research and Development volume 2 Oral Evidence* London, HMSO

House of Lords, 1986b, Select Committee on Science and Technology *Civil Research and Development volume 3 Written Evidence* London, HMSO

B Hubbard, 1986, ''Communications Survey - no 1'' in C B B Grindley (ed) *Information Technology Review* London, Price Waterhouse

ICL, 1987, *Retailing Today* London, Paragon Communications

ICL, 1988, *Local Government in Britain: An ICL Report on the Impact of Information Technology* London, Paragon Communications

Income Data Services, 1988, *Computer Staff Pay* London, Income Data Services (IDS Study 404)

International Telecommunication Union, annual, *Yearbook of Common Carrier Telecommunication Statistics* Geneva, ITU

J Irvine, 1987, *Update and Analysis of the National Science Foundation Science Literature Indicators Data-Base* report to the Cabinet Office Assessment Office, DTI, mimeo, Falmer, Brighton, SPRU

J Irvine, B Martin, T Peacock & R Turner, 1985, ''Charting the Decline in British Science'' *Nature* vol 316 August 15 pp587-590

J Irvine & I Miles, 1982, "The Dominant Way of Life in Britain'' in I Miles & J Irvine (eds) *The Poverty of Progress* Oxford, Pergamon

IT Skills Shortages Committee, 1984, First Report *The Human Factor-The Supply Side Problem* London, Department of Trade and Industry

IT Skills Shortages Committee, 1985a, Second Report *Changing Technology - Changing Skills* London, Department of Trade and Industry

IT Skills Shortages Committee, 1985b, Final Report, *Signposts for the Future* London, Department of Trade and Industry

N Jagger, 1989, *Prestel's Alter Egos,* Falmer, Brighton, SPRU (CICT Working Paper)

M Jahoda, K Guy & B Evans, 1988, *The Market Place for Expert Systems* report to the ILO, Geneva, mimeo, Falmer, Brighton, SPRU

D A Josephs, 1982, "Occupations in British Engineering Industries" *Employment Gazette* October, pp421-430

S Judd & P Virgo, 1988, *The State of the UK IT Skills and Training Market* London, IT Strategy Services

R E Kahn, 1985, "The Quest: a New Generation in Computing" in E A Torrero (ed) *Next Generation Computers* New York, IEEE Press

H Kania, 1984, *Prestel for People* London, Council for Educational Technology

K E Knight, 1985, "A Functional and Structural Measurement of Technology" *Technological Forecasting and Social Change* vol 27 no 2/3 pp107-128

K Kobayashi, 1986, *Computers and Communications: A Vision of C&C* Chichester & Boston, MIT Press

D F Lancaster, 1988, *The Response to and Effects of Microcomputers in the Education Sector: The Introduction of an Innovation in Local Authority Secondary Schools* PhD dissertation, Birmingham, University of Aston

P Large, 1987, "Disasters Far Outstrip Cost of Computer Fraud" *The Guardian* May 5

G Lawson, 1985, *Sector Profile: Office Machinery and EDP Equipment* Watford, Engineering Industry Training Board

D Leach and H Wagstaff, 1986, *Future Employment and Technological Change* London, Kogan Page

M Lee, 1986, "Slow Response to Formal Methods" *Computing* April 24 p30

C Lewis, 1984 (2nd ed), *Managing with Micros* Oxford, Basil Blackwell

Library and Information Technology Centre, 1987, *State of the Art of the Application of New Information Technologies in Libraries and their Impact on Library Functions in the United Kingdom* London, Library and Information Technology Centre, Polytechnic of Central London

C Macilwain, 1988, "Robots Serve You Right" *The Engineer* vol 266 no 6892 p34

R E Mansell & B J Richards, 1986, *Information and Communication Technologies: Social Science Research and Training vol 2 National Directory* London, Economic and Social Research Council (School Government Publishing Company)

J Marti & A Zeilinger, 1982, *Micros and Money* London, Policy Studies Institute

B R Martin, 1987, "The Structure and Funding of UK Research" *Electronics and Power* (January) pp31-36

B R Martin & J Irvine with N Minchin, 1986, *An International Comparison of Government Funding of Academic and Academically Related Research* Falmer, Brighton, SPRU (ABRC Science Policy Study no 2)

B Martin, J Irvine, F Narin & C Sterritt, 1987, "The Continuing Decline of British Science" *Nature* vol 330 November 12 pp123-126

B Martin, J Irvine & R Turner, 1984, "The Writing on the Wall for British Science" *New Scientist* November 8 pp25-29

G Mason, 1985, "Market Data Inaccurate - Managers" *Computing* October 24, p19

G Mason, 1987, *Trends in Computing Qualifications in Secondary, Further and Higher Education*, Watford, Engineering Industry Training Board

R Mayntz & V Schneider, 1987, "Interactive Telecommunications: the case of videotex in Germany, France and Great Britain" paper presented at Conference on the Development of Large Technical Systems, Cologne, November

J McCalman, 1987a, "New Technology Survey: Electronics" mimeo, Glasgow, University of Glasgow Business School

J McCalman, 1987b, ''New Technology Survey: Mechanical Engineering'' mimeo, Glasgow, University of Glasgow Business School

McKinsey & Company, Inc, (1988), *Performance and Competitive Success: Strengthening Competitiveness in UK Electronics* London, National Economic Development Office (Electronics Industry Sector Group)

A Mehta & S Watts, 1986, ''Retail: Shopping Changes to a Leisure Pastime'' *Computer Weekly* June 26 pp32-37

W H Melody & R E Mansell, 1986, *Information and Communication Technologies: Social Science Research and Training vol 1 An Overview of Research* London, Economic and Social Research Council (School Government Publishing Company)

I Miles, 1985a, ''The New Post Industrial State'' *Futures* vol 17 no 6 pp588-617

I Miles, 1985b, *Social Indicators for Human Development* London, Frances Pinter

I Miles, 1988a, *Home Informatics* London, Pinter Publishers

I Miles, 1988b, *Information Technology and Information Society* London, Economic and Social Research Council (PICT Policy Research Papers no 2)

I Miles, forthcoming, *Patterns of Use of Information Technology: A Secondary Analysis* Falmer, Brighton, SPRU (CICT Working Paper)

I Miles and J Gershuny, 1986, ''The Social Economics of Information Technology'' in M Ferguson (ed) *New Communication Technologies and the Public Interest* London, Sage

I Miles, H Rush, K Turner & J Bessant, 1988, *Information Horizons* Aldershot, Edward Elgar

M Milner, 1988, ''A Booming Mobile Phone Market sets City Buzzing'' *The Guardian* April 30 p11

J Mitchell, 1986, ''Quality of Telephone Service and the Domestic Consumer'' in N Garnham (ed) *CPR '86: Communications Policy Research Conference - Telecommunications: National Policies in an International Context* London, Polytechnic of Central London

J Moggridge, 1987, ''Facsimile Boom Continues'' *Lines of Communication* vol 1 no 9 (November) p31

P Monk, 1987, ''Characteristics of IT Innovation'' *Journal of Information Technology* vol 2 no 4 pp164-170

Monopolies and Mergers Commission, 1986, *British Telecommunications PLC and Mitel Corporation: A Report on the Proposed Merger* London, HMSO

N Moore, 1987, *The Emerging Markets for Librarians and Information Workers* London, The British Library (Library and Information Research Report 56)

MORI, 1985, *Public Attitudes to New Technology* London, Market and Opinion Research International (MORI/2807)

D Mort & L Siddal, 1985, *Sources of Unofficial UK Statistics*, Aldershot, Gower

MSC/Employment Services Agency, 1977, *Classification of Occupations and Directory of Occupational Titles: Supplement* London, HMSO

MSC, 1980, *Classification of Occupations and Directory of Occupational Titles: Supplement* London, HMSO

U Muldur & O Pastr (eds), 1987, *Europe and the Future of Financial Services* Lafferty Publications

F Narin & D Olivastro, 1987, ''Identifying Areas of Strength and Excellence in UK Technology'' paper prepared by CHI Research, New Jersey for Longer Term Studies Group, Research and Technology Policy Division, DTI

National Audit Office, 1987a, *Computer Security in Government Departments* London, National Audit Office

National Audit Office, 1987b, *Inland Revenue: Control of Major Developments in Use of Information Technology* London, National Audit Office

National Audit Office, 1987c, *The Role of the National Audit Office* London, National Audit Office

National Computing Centre, 1986, *Information Technology Trends* Manchester, National Computing Centre

National Interactive Video Centre, 1987, *The IV Box* London, National Interactive Video Centre

NEDO, 1980, *Computer Manpower in the 1980s*, London, National Economic Development Office

NEDO, 1982a, *Policy for the UK Electronics Industry*, London, National Economic Development Office, Electronics Economic Development Committee

NEDO, 1982b, *Policy for the UK Information Technology Industry* London, National Economic Development Office, Electronics Economic Development Committee, IT Sector Working Party

NEDO, 1983a, *The Introduction of New Technology* London, National Economic Development Office, Electronics Economic Development Committee, Employment and Technology Task Force

NEDO, 1983b, *Policy for the UK Information Technology Industry: A Summary* London, National Economic Development Office, Electronics Economic Development Committee, IT Sector Working Party

NEDO, 1984, *Crisis Facing UK Information Technology* London, National Economic Development Office, IT Economic Development Committee

NEDO, 1985, *IT Futures* London, National Economic Development Office, IT Economic Development Committee

NEDO, 1986, *IT Futures Surveyed* London, National Economic Development Office, IT Economic Development Committee

NEDO, 1987, *IT Futures: IT Can Work* London, National Economic Development Office, IT Economic Development Committee

NEDO Advanced Manufacturing Systems Group, 1984, *Flexible Machining Systems* London, National Economic Development Office

J Northcott, 1985, ''Acceptance at Place of Work'' mimeo, London, Policy Studies Institute (presented at Conference ''Public Acceptance of New Technologies'', CESTA, Paris, October 1985 and at workshop on ''Public Acceptance of New Technologies: Research Directions'' at SPRU, Falmer, November 1986)

J Northcott, 1986, *Microelectronics in Industry: Promise and Performance* London, Policy Studies Institute

J Northcott, P Rogers, W Knetsch & B de Lestapis, 1985, *Microelectronics in Industry: An International Comparison* London, Policy Studies Institute

J Northcott with C Brown, I Christie, M Sweeney & A Walling, 1986, *Robots in British Industry* London, Policy Studies Institute

J Northcott with A Walling, 1988, *The Impact of Microelectronics: Diffusion, Benefits and Problems in British Industry* London, Policy Studies Institute

R C O'Brien & M Channing, 1986, "The Global Structure of the Electronic Information Services Industry" in P I Zorkoczy (ed) *Oxford Surveys in Information Technology vol 3* Oxford, Oxford University Press

OECD, 1981, *Information Activities, Electronics and Telecommunications Technologies vol 1* Paris, OECD (ICCP series)

OECD, 1986a, *OECD Science and Technology Indicators, no 2 R&D, Invention and Competitiveness* Paris, OECD

OECD, 1986b, *Trends in the Information Economy* Paris, OECD (ICCP series)

OECD, 1987, *Information Technology and Economic Prospects* Paris, OECD (ICCP series)

OECD, 1988, *The Telecommunications Industry: The Challenges of Structural Change* Paris, OECD (ICCP series)

Office of Technology Assessment, 1985, *Information Technology Research and Development: Critical Trends and Issues* New York, Pergamon Press

Office of Technology Assessment, 1988, *Technology and the American Economic Transition* Washington, DC, US Government Printing Office

H Omdal, 1987, "A Response Strategy for Non-Cash Cross-Border Payment Systems" in RMDP (1987)

PA Technology/MORI, 1984, *Senior Executives' Attitudes towards Development and Use of New Technology in their Companies in Britain, USA, West Germany, Belgium and Australia* London, Market and Opinion Research International

H Pain-Lewins, 1988, "A Study of the Use of Micro-Based Networks in British Schools" *Journal of Information Technology* vol 3 no 2 pp79-84

T Parker & M Idunduin, 1988, "Managing Information Systems in 1987: The Top Issues for IS Managers in the UK" *Journal of Information Technology* vol 3 no 1 pp34-40

P Patel & L Soete, 1987, "Technological Trends and Employment in the UK Manufacturing Sectors" in Freeman and Soete (eds) (1987)

K Pavitt, 1986, "'Chips' and 'Trajectories': How does the Semiconductor Influence the Sources and Direction of Technological Change" in R MacLeod (ed) *Technology and the Human Prospect* London, Frances Pinter

K Pavitt, 1987a, *The Size and Structure of British Technology Activities: What We Do and Do Not Know* Falmer, Brighton, SPRU (DRC Paper no 52)

K Pavitt, 1987b, *Uses and Abuses of Patent Statistics* Falmer, Brighton, SPRU (DRC Paper no 41)

K Pavitt, M Robson & J Townsend, 1988, *Technological Accumulation, Diversification and Organisation in UK Companies, 1945-83, Management Science* (forthcoming)

R Pearson, H Connor, & C Pole, 1988, *The IT Manpower Monitor* Falmer, Brighton, Institute of Manpower Studies

Peat Marwick McLintock, 1987, *Building on IT* London, Peat Marwick McLintock

G Penney, 1986, "The Skills Shortages Myth" *Business Computing and Communications* September pp26-33

C Perez, 1983, "Structural Change and the Assimilation of New Technologies in the Economic and Social Systems" *Futures* October pp357-375

C Perez, 1985, "Microelectronics, Long Waves and World Development" *World Development* vol 13 no 3 (March)

A A Perlowski, 1976, "The 'Smart' Machine Revolution" *Business Week* reprinted in Forester (ed) (1980)

P Petit, 1986, *Slow Growth and the Service Economy* London, Frances Pinter

I de Sola Pool, H Inose, N Takasaki, & R Hurwitz, 1984, *Communication Flows: A Census in the US and Japan* Tokyo, University of Tokyo Press

M Porat, 1977, *The Information Economy* Washington DC, US Department of Commerce, Office of Technology

D Potts, 1985, "Double or Nothing - But Users Can't Lose" *Engineering Computers* November pp26-28

D Potts, 1987, "It's Time to Take the First Step" *Engineering Computers* June/July p17

PREST/SPRU, 1987, *Evaluation of the Alvey programme: interim report* London, HMSO

D J Pullinger, 1985, *BLEND-4: user-system interaction* London, The British Library (Library and Information Research Report 45)

D J Pullinger, 1987, *BLEND-8: cost appraisal* London, The British Library (Library and Information Research Report 53)

A Rajan, 1984, *New Technology and Employment in Insurance, Banking and Building Societies* Aldershot, Gower

A Rajan, 1985a, "The Social Impact of Information Technology" in P I Zorkoczy (ed) *Oxford Surveys in Information Technology volume 2* Oxford, Oxford University Press

A Rajan, 1985b, *Training and Recruitment Effects of Technical Change* Aldershot, Gower

A Rajan, 1987, "New Technology and Training: missed opportunities" *New Technology, Work and Employment* vol 2 no 1 pp61-65

A Rajan with J Fryatt, 1988, *Create or Abdicate: the City's Human Resource Crisis for the 90s* London, Witherby & Co

A Rajan & R Pearson, 1986, *UK Occupation and Employment Trends to 1990* London, Butterworth

J Rendeiro, 1985, "Instrumentation" in Soete (ed) (1985b)

Report of the Review Committee on Banking Services Law, 1989, London, HMSO

RMDP, 1987, *EPOS 87 with EFTPOS 87* Brighton, RMDP (Retail Management Development Programme)

S S Roach, 1987, "America's Technology Dilemma: A Profile of the Information Economy" Special Economic Study, New York, Morgan Stanley & Co

M Robson, J Townsend & K Pavitt, 1988, "Sectoral Patterns of Production and Use of Innovations in the UK: 1945-83" *Research Policy* vol 17 pp1-14

R Sarsons, 1988, "The VANS Race" *Network* January pp62-65

A Sayer & K Morgan, 1986, "The Electronics Industry and Regional Development in Britain" in Amin & Goddard (eds) (1986)

J Schofield, 1988, "Microfile" *The Guardian* September 8 p25

E Sciberras & B Payne, 1986, *Technical Change and International Competitiveness 2: Telecommunications Industry* London, Technical Change Centre

P Senker (ed), 1985, *Planning for Microelectronics in the Workplace* Aldershot, Gower

P Senker, 1986, *Towards the Automatic Factory?* Bedford, IFS (Berlin, Springer-Verlag)

P Senker, M Beesley & M Vandevelde, 1985, *Software Engineering: The Role of the Technician* Brighton, Brighton College of Technology/SPRU

A Shaw, 1986, *The Chemical Manufacturing Industry: New Technology and Training* Manchester, Centre for Educational Development and Training, Manchester Polytechnic

A Sheldon (ed), 1982, *Prestel in the Library Context* London, The British Library (Library and Information Research Report 6)

P Simmonds & P Senker, 1988, "Skills and Training Implications of CADCAM" mimeo, Falmer, Brighton, SPRU

R Simpson, 1987, "BACS: the way to EFT" in RMDP (1987)

G Sippings & H Ramsden, 1987 *The Use of Information Technology by Information Services* London, Aslib (Information Resources Centre)

J Sleigh, B Boatwright, P Irwin & R Stanyon, 1979, *The Manpower Implications of Micro-Electronic Technology* London, HMSO (Department of Employment)

A Smith, (ed), 1985, *Technological Trends and Employment: 5 Commercial Service Industries* Aldershot, Gower

L Soete, 1985a, "Electronics" in Soete (ed) (1985b)

L Soete, (ed), 1985b, *Technological Trends and Employment: 3 Electronics and Communications* Aldershot, Gower

L Soete, 1987, "The Newly Emerging Information Technology Sector" in Freeman & Soete (eds) (1987)

L Soete & G Dosi, 1983, *Technology and Employment in the Electronics Industry* London, Frances Pinter

A Sorge, G Hartmann, M Warner & I Nicholas, 1983, *Microelectronics and Manpower in Manufacturing* Aldershot, Gower

I de Sola Pool, H Inose, N Tabasaki & R Hurwitz, 1984, *Communication Flows: A Census in the US and Japan* Amsterdam, North Holland

Statistiska Centralbyran, 1988, *Data om Informationsteknologin i Sverige* Stockholm, Statistiska Centralbyran

J Steffens, 1983, *The Electronic Office Progress and Problems*, London, Policy Studies Institute

M A Stone & A H Clarkson, 1987, "MIS and the Strategic Development of Financial Institutions" mimeo, Edinburgh, Department of Business Organisation, Herriot-Watt University

D Streatfield & S Jones, 1987, *From Here to Technology: Use of Computers in Administration & Management by Local Education Authorities* London, Peat Marwick McLintock/National Foundation for Educational Research

J Swann, 1986, *The Employment Effects of Microelectronics in the UK Service Sector* London, Technical Change Centre

P Swann, 1987, ''A Decade of Microprocessor Innovation: An Economist's Perspective'' *Microprocessors and Microsystems* vol 11 no 1 pp49-59

W Tagg & R Templeton, 1983, *Computer Software: Supplying it and Finding it* London, The British Library (Library and Information Research Report 10)

M Tarbuck & E Arnold, 1985, ''Office Automation and Service Sectors'' in Senker (ed) (1985)

J Tarsh, 1984, ''Graduate Shortages in Science and Engineering'' *Employment Gazette* August, pp354-361

TCC (Technical Change Centre), 1983, *Information Demand and Supply in British Industry 1977-1983* London, The British Library (Library and Information Research Report 23)

C Thomas, 1987, ''Growing Steadily'' *Lines of Communication* vol 1 no 6 July/August p16

D Thomas, 1986, ''Who Gets What: Patterns of Use Begin to Change'' *Financial Times* December 10 p14

G Thomas & I Miles, 1988, *The Emergence of New Interactive Services* mimeo, report to the Leverhulme Trust, Falmer, Brighton, SPRU

J Tidd, 1988a, ''A Survey of Robotic Assembly in the UK'' mimeo, Falmer, Brighton, SPRU

J Tidd, 1988b, ''Flexible Manufacturing with Industrial Robots: The UK Experience and Some Policy Implications'' mimeo, Falmer, Brighton, SPRU

L Tilley, 1988, ''City Firms take on Outside Help as On-Site Projects run up Costs'' *Computer News* August 11 (no 226) p1

J Todd & D Griffiths, 1986, *Changing the Definition of a Household* London, HMSO (OPCS Social Survey Division)

A Toffler, 1980, *The Third Wave*, London, Pan

J Townsend, F Henwood, G Thomas, K Pavitt & S Wyatt, 1981, *Science and Technology Indicators for the UK* Falmer, Brighton, SPRU, (Occasional Paper no 16)

P W Turnbull & F Hug, 1984, *The Telecommunications Industry: Technology, Supply and Market Structures* Department of Management Sciences, University of Manchester Institute of Science and Technology

Vanguard, 1988, "VADS in View" *Vanguard* vol 1 no 1 pp6-7

R D Vine, 1985, *The Impact of Technological Change in the Industrial Democracies: Public Attitudes toward Information Technology* Paris, Atlantic Institute for International Affairs

W Walker, 1987, "The Allocation of Resources to Military Electronics in the UK; A Review of Published Government Statistics" mimeo, Falmer, Brighton, SPRU

W Walker, 1988, *UK Defence Electronics: A Review of Government Statistics* London, Economic and Social Research Council (PICT Policy Research Papers no 4)

S Wall & P Nicholson, 1986, *Posts and Telecommunications* Oxford, Pergamon Press

V Walsh, J Moulton-Abbott & P Senker, 1980, *New Technology, The Post Office and the Union of Post Office Workers* London, Union of Communication Workers

G Walsham & C S Yap, 1986, *Information Technology and Your Business* Cambridge, Cambridge University Engineering Department, Management Studies Group, Information Engineering Division

F Webster & K Robbins, 1982, "New Technology: A Survey of Trade Union Response in Britain" *Industrial Relations Journal* vol 13 no 1 pp7-26

M Whitaker, 1986, *Results of a Survey into the Use of IT in the Hotel and Catering Industry* Brighton, Innovation Research Group, Brighton Polytechnic

M Whitaker, I Miles, H Rush & J Bessant, 1988, *A Bibliography of Information Technology* Aldershot, Edward Elgar

M White, 1988, "VADS - A Market Forecast" *Vanguard* vol 1 no 1 pp44-45

J D Whitley & R A Wilson, 1983, "Quantifying the Employment Effects of Micro-Electronics" *Futures* vol 14 no 6 pp486-495

J D Whitley & R A Wilson, 1987, "Quantifying the Impact of Information Technology on Employment using a Macroeconomic Model of the United Kingdom" in OECD (1987)

B R Williams, 1986a, *Attitudes to New Technologies and Economic Growth* London, Technical Change Centre (TCCR-86-012)

B R Williams, 1986b, *Do British Attitudes to New Technology Retard Economic Growth?* London, Imperial College (Papers in Science, Technology and Public Policy no 11 jointly published by Imperial College, SPRU and TCC)

B R Williams & J A Bryan-Brown, 1985, *Comparative National Assessment of Public Assessment of New Technologies* London, Technical Change Centre (TCCL-85-003)

R Williams & S Mills, 1986, *Public Acceptance of New Technologies: An International Review* London, Croom Helm

R Williams & F Steward, 1985, "Technology Agreements in Great Britain: A Survey 1977-83" *Industrial Relations Journal* vol 16 no 3 pp58-73

W Wobbe (ed), 1987, *Flexible Manufacturing in Europe - State of the Art of Approaches and Diffusion Patterns* Brussels, CEC FAST Programme (Internal Paper no 155)

Working Party on Computer Facilities for Teaching in Universities, 1983, *Report of a Working Party on Computer Facilities for Teaching in Universities*, London, Computer Board for Universities and Research Councils

C S Yap, 1986, *Information Technology in Organisations in the Service Sector* dissertation submitted to the University of Cambridge for the degree of Doctor of Philosophy, Downing College, Cambridge

C S Yap & G Walsham, 1986, "A Survey of Information Technology in the UK Service Sector" *Information and Management* vol 10 pp267-274

P A Yates-Mercer, 1985, *Private Viewdata in the UK* Aldershot, Gower

R Yeates, 1982, *Prestel in the Public Library* London, The British Library (Library and Information Research Report 2)

Other Reports

Library and Information Research (LIR) Reports may be purchased from The British Library Publications Sales Unit, Boston Spa, Wetherby, West Yorkshire LS23 7BQ, UK. Details of some other LIR Reports are given below.

LIR Report 70. Brittain, Michael (ed). *Curriculum development in information science to meet the needs of the information industries in the 1990s.* 1989. pp 230. ISBN 0 7123 3170 0.

The study reported was mounted to capture the views of a wide spectrum of informed opinion about the nature of the emerging market for graduates in library and information science, the skills and knowledge required in this market, and the courses that universities and polytechnics should provide. Over 100 professionals in a wide range of institutions were visited, and nine of these contributed papers on their own specialism and its implications for education and training. Suggestions and implications are summarised in the editor's concluding chapter.

LIR Report 71. Ennals, Richard and Gardin, Jean-Claude (eds). *Interpretation in the humanities: perspectives from artificial intelligence.* 1990. pp 379. ISBN 0 7123 3186 7.

This Anglo-French edited collection of papers considers issues of interpretation in the humanities, applying perspectives from artificial intelligence (AI). AI is presented as essentially humanising and dependent on non-numerical concepts of representation and interpretation. The book considers first epistemological and methodological issues, then experience from the knowledge domains of archaeology, history, literature and law, before subjecting AI perspectives to the scrutiny of the supporting disciplines of linguistics, logic, computer science and philosophy. An editorial epilogue considers future developments in the field. Papers appear in either English or French, with abstracts in the other language. An index assists in pursuing cross-references.

LIR Report 72. Edmonds, Diana and Miller, Jane, *Public library services for children and young people.* 1990. pp 163. ISBN 0 7123 3195 6.

This report covers two surveys carried out for the Office of Arts and Libraries. The first was a statistical survey of English public library services to children and young people. This covered the years 1982/3 to 1986/7, with data supplied by all 108 public library authorities. Details are given of the structure and staffing of services, the funds available, the level of spending, and performance measures used. The second survey was a review of patterns of services in six library authorities: two London boroughs (Croydon and Islington), two metropolitan districts (Bradford and Liverpool), and two county councils (Dorset and Nottinghamshire). This revealed considerable differences between authorities and also included the views of a number of children's librarians.

LIR Report 73. Brindley, Lynne J (ed). *The Electronic Campus: an information strategy. Proceedings of a conference held on 28-30 October 1988 at Banbury.* 1989. pp 156. ISBN 0 7123 3187 5.

This conference was held in response to the evidence that technology is drawing together the retrieval, storage and communication of information of all kinds, whether this is undertaken by libraries, researchers and educators, or managers and administrators. Senior policy- and decision-makers, academics and librarians were invited to Banbury to share their experiences and visions in this field, and to prepare to take a lead in developments and planning at institutional level. The conference proved both timely and successful, and these edited *Proceedings* present the main papers together with summaries of the subsequent discussion.

LIR Report 74. Clarke, J E. *Public Information in Rural Areas: Technology Experiment (PIRATE) - Phase II.* 1989. pp 235. ISBN 0 7123 3200 6.

PIRATE was a study of applications of microcomputer technology designed to increase access to community information in rural areas. The project created and managed information services at selected locations in Devon. These practical applications provided feedback that guided the project in developing its methods of gathering, managing and disseminating community information. A feature of PIRATE's computer support of community information was its association with rural advice and information centres established in branch libraries. Each centre housed several organisations, which shared the premises and equipment. Phase I of PIRATE was described in LIR Report 64. During Phase II, the PIRATE system expanded into six locations, three rural and three urban. Its computers and other hardware were phased out and replaced with newer, more up-to-date equipment. Although PIRATE confined its studies to selected areas of Devon, its research aimed at developing a community information system that could have wider geographical application.

LIR Report 75. Lester, Ray and Waters, Judith. *Environmental scanning and business strategy.* 1989. pp 156. ISBN 0 7123 3203 0.

This report arises from a short exploratory study on environmental scanning and business strategy carried out during 1986. The project worker for the study was Judith Waters and the experimental results and conclusions of this study are summarised in Part A of this report. The conclusions, together with a review of literature specifically concerned with environmental scanning, raised a number of broader issues, and the results of that literature survey appear as Part B of the report, by Ray Lester. Appendix A gives some details of six large UK corporations studied during the experimental project. Appendix B is a detailed analysis of 15 papers concerned with environmental scanning, published during the 10 years prior to the start of the project. Appendix C is a bibliography.